Tennis

Tennis

2nd Edition

by Patrick McEnroe with Jon Levey

A Wiley Brand

Tennis For Dummies®, 2nd Edition

Published by: **John Wiley & Sons, Inc.,** 111 River Street, Hoboken, NJ 07030-5774, www.wiley.com

For general information on our other products and services, please contact our Customer Care Department within the U.S. at 877-762-2974, outside the U.S. at 317-572-3993, or fax 317-572-4002. For technical support, please visit https://hub.wiley.com/community/support/dummies.

Wiley publishes in a variety of print and electronic formats and by print-on-demand. Some material included with standard print versions of this book may not be included in e-books or in print-on-demand. If this book refers to media that is not included in the version you purchased, you may download this material at http://booksupport.wiley.com. For more information about Wiley products, visit www.wiley.com.

Library of Congress Control Number: 2025930730

ISBN 978-1-394-25466-8 (pbk); ISBN 978-1-394-25468-2 (ebk); ISBN 978-1-394-25467-5 (ebk)

Printed and bound by CPI Group (UK) Ltd, Croydon, CR0 4YY

C9781394254668_150325

The manufacturer's authorized representative according to the EU General Product Safety Regulation is Wiley-VCH GmbH, Boschstr. 12, 69469 Weinheim, Germany, e-mail: Product_Safety@wiley.com.

Contents at a Glance

Table of Contents

Introduction

was about 3 years old when I first picked up a tennis racquet. More than 55 years later, I still haven't let go. This incredible game had an amazing impact on me from the first day: I fell for it hook, line, and sinker. Or better yet game, set, and match.

Before I could ride a two-wheeler, I was hitting tennis balls against a wall, playing make-believe matches with Rod Laver and Ken Rosewall, who were two of tennis's greatest stars at the time. I rode my tricycle to get to the tennis club.

Realizing my childhood dreams, I eventually worked my way up and played in the big leagues of tennis. Even after all these years in the sport, I still want to get out and hit some balls every day. Or almost every day — I'm approaching 60 after all.

You may wonder what keeps me interested in this sport, so interested that I've spent my life with it. More than anything, the thrill of hitting the perfect stroke, of having that day when it all just "clicks," has kept the sport interesting and challenging for me every day I've played it.

I hope that tennis has the same effect on you. No matter where you stand on the tennis ladder in terms of ability and skill, there are always new challenges and new mysteries to solve. That's why tennis is in my blood. With the help of this book, I hope it will get into yours, too.

About This Book

In tennis, everything is in motion, most of the time. The ball. Your opponent. You. Your state of confidence. Your grasp on a match. The already challenging job of developing a consistent stroke is made more difficult by the fact that you have to use that stroke while on the run, out of position, slipping, sliding, changing direction, and even falling or diving. The only thing you won't have to do is hit that stroke with your eyes closed.

With everything happening so quickly on the court, you need a book like *Tennis For Dummies* to put the action in slow motion. In fact one of my favorite teaching techniques with players of all levels and ages is to help them learn how to slow down the swing. I think this really helps players understand how to control their racquet and, thus, better control their shots. How else can you grasp the fundamentals of the game? After you read this book and master the basics of your strokes, feel free to close your eyes and swing away.

Whatever your level of play, you'll find what you need and want to know in this book. For the beginner, I cover the basics of the sport, showing you step-by-step how to play the fundamental shots. For the club player looking for a way to beat that opponent who always has your number, I include some secrets to help you be a more winning player.

If you're a big fan of the pro game, I give you the skinny on the professional tennis tours. I tell you what to look for if you attend a real live pro event and how to maximize that ticket price. If you're stuck at home, I tell you what to look for when you watch on a screen. It's all here.

I grew up in a house full of left-handed people, so I know I'm going to get ribbed for this: I show you everything in this book from the perspective of a right-handed player. If you're a lefty, please just substitute the word *left* for *right* in the appropriate spots in the text.

Finally, within this book, you may note that some web addresses break across two lines of text. If you're reading this book in print and you want to visit one of these web pages, simply key in the web address exactly as it's noted in the text, pretending as though the line break doesn't exist. If you're reading this as an e-book, you've got it easy — just click the web address to be taken directly to the web page.

Foolish Assumptions

You probably picked up this book for one of the following reasons:

>> **You're an absolute beginner and you want a straightforward and fun guide to learn everything you need to know about tennis.** We all have to start somewhere, and you've picked a great resource.

>> **You've dabbled in tennis in the past and now you want to get back in the game, but you need a refresher.** Not only will this book help you brush up on all your strokes, but you'll learn about all the changes in the sport since you last played.

>> **You're a coach or avid player and you want to add to your tennis book collection.** Even if you already have a solid foundation in the game, there's bound to be useful nuggets in this update to increase your knowledge and understanding of the sport.

Icons Used in This Book

Throughout the book, I use icons in the margin to grab your attention. Here's a guide to what the icons mean:

MAC SAYS

This icon marks the stories and insights I've picked up during my years in tennis.

TIP

The Tip icon makes your life as a player or a spectator easier and more rewarding.

REMEMBER

This stuff is so important that I may repeat it a few times. I hope you wake up at night chanting this stuff.

WARNING

Watch out for the information next to this icon — if you don't, you could end up hurting yourself or really flubbing up your shot.

TECHNICAL STUFF

When I get into the weeds on a subject, I mark it with the Technical Stuff icon. You can skip anything marked with this icon if you're short on time.

Beyond the Book

In addition to the information in this book, you get access to even more help and information online at Dummies.com. Check out this book's Cheat Sheet for a diagram of the singles court, tips on how to play a tiebreaker, and essential tennis terms to know. Just go to www.dummies.com and type **Tennis For Dummies Cheat Sheet** in the Search box.

Where to Go from Here

You don't have to read this book from cover to cover, taking care not to miss a single syllable. Of course, I will be very flattered if you do. But if you want to get in and out of the book quickly, you can pick it up, turn to any section that interests you, and start reading (kind of like skipping the meal and going straight to dessert). The great thing about this book is that you can pick it up anytime. You can read it and find out what you want to know about your game, even if you're 20 miles from the nearest tennis court.

If you're a complete beginner, I do advise you, however, to stop by Part 1, which covers some really fundamental concepts regarding the game. If you're looking for help with particular shots, you should probably start in Part 2.

No matter where you start reading, keep your tennis racquet handy as you read — that way, you can play-test my advice as you go along. Think of this book as your guide to developing a lifelong passion for a great sport.

1

Getting Started with Tennis

IN THIS PART . . .

I start you out nice and easy in this part of the book, giving you a firm foundation for exploring the rest of the game. You can read about the basic goals of the game, the structure of the court, all the equipment you need to make it happen, plus all the rules and manners you need to know to play the game like a pro.

Chapter **1**

What Is Tennis?

S o, you want to play tennis. Well, you've made a great choice! And I don't say that just because I made the same choice when I was about 3 years old. Tennis can catch and hold you for life, so be warned! If you pick up a racquet to play tennis, you may never want to put it down.

In this chapter, I touch briefly on all the aspects of tennis that make it such a wonderful game (in case you need a little more convincing). I also tell you the fundamental principles behind the game.

Tennis: The Sport for a Lifetime

Many years ago, the United States Tennis Association (USTA) ran an ad campaign promoting tennis as "The Sport for a Lifetime." This slogan wasn't just a catchy phrase thought up by some advertising genius — tennis really is a game that you can enjoy long-term, both as a player and as a spectator.

MAC SAYS

I sat down and made up a quick list to show you why I believe that tennis can be the sport of a lifetime, for almost everyone:

» **You can play tennis, even competitively, at any age.** If time and work haven't killed your inner weekend warrior, you can compete in organized tennis tournaments and league matches at virtually any age, at almost any skill level.

» **You don't need to find 17 other people to play a game.** Unlike a sport such as baseball or softball, you need only one other person to play tennis (and if just want some practice, you can play by yourself, hitting against a wall). Of course, if you do have 17 other people who want to play tennis with you, then great — you can get a great tournament going. But you may need a few more balls!

» **You don't need a whole bank full of money to play tennis.** Tennis often gets labeled as an elitest sport. This truly rankles me because it doesn't have to be. Sure, for professionals and top amateurs, tennis can be very costly, but at the recreational level, it's a much different proposition. If you want, you can spend all day at the public courts without spending a nickel on anything other than some sunblock.

Because tennis can be a cheap game to get into, people from all kinds of backgrounds can get interested in (and get really good at) the game. Tennis isn't just a game for people who can afford to pay $100 a pop for lessons. In fact, some of the greatest players in history, such as Andre Agassi and the Williams sisters, had pretty humble beginnings.

» **Tennis brings people together.** No, I'm not getting all sentimental on you — in tennis, people of different ages and genders can match up well as partners. For example, you can find yourself in a spirited mixed-doubles game along with your spouse, your grandson, and your daughter-in-law. The only thing you may have to worry about is initiating a family feud.

» **Playing tennis well gives you a sense of accomplishment.** Tennis is a skill-intensive sport. Like playing a musical instrument or learning a new language, playing tennis requires dedication to keep improving — which is what makes it so awesome. When you're good at it, it's very satisfying.

» **Tennis is a great way to keep fit.** Tennis has a high fitness rating, and you can dial in the degree of workout you want.

Getting the Point: Singles, Doubles, and Winning at Both

You can play tennis in one of two formats: singles or doubles. Singles involves two players, one on each side of the net, playing against each other. Doubles is just what the name implies — you've got four people on the court with two people playing as a team against another two-person team.

Singles is a more physically demanding game than doubles, for two reasons:

>> You get the intensity of one-on-one competition.

>> You have more court to cover all by yourself.

Regardless of whether you play singles or doubles, your goal is always the same: to win points. A point begins with a serve (see Chapter 11), which puts the ball into play. The player who keeps the ball in play the longest wins the point. How do you keep the ball in play? Read on, Grasshopper.

Racquet, balls, and an opponent

You don't need much to play tennis, but there are a few essentials. First is a racquet. Racquets come in many different varieties, but all share some basic features (see Chapter 3). Finding one that suits you makes the game more fun and easier to learn. But the racquet won't do you any good unless you've got something to hit. That's where having some tennis balls — preferably fresh ones — comes in. They're sold all over, and you'll want to keep plenty around so you're never caught without them. The final thing you need is a worthwhile playing partner of a similar ability level. You could just practice against a wall (see Chapter 15), but you'll never win bragging rights.

Clearing the net

The biggest obstacle that you face on the tennis court is the net that divides the court into two sides — your side and your opponent's side. The first thing you need to do, no matter how goofy you may look doing it, is to make sure that any ball you hit makes it back over the net. If the ball doesn't clear the net, the point is over. You've lost it.

MAC SAYS

When we first started dating, my wife, Melissa, didn't know much about tennis. Once during a close, important match, she called out between points, "Come on, Pat! Just get the ball over the net!" I looked at her like "Gee, thanks, honey!" But there it is — the fundamental truth about tennis.

Officially, the net must be 36 inches tall at the center strap. (See Chapter 2 for all the details on net and court measurements.) But even though 36 inches may not seem very high, I assure you that sometimes that darned net looks as tall as the Great Wall of China.

Keeping the ball inside the lines

Tennis is basically a game of controlled power. Ideally, you hit the ball pretty hard and pretty far, but it must always land inside the lines (or court boundaries) to remain in play. If you hit a ball and it first bounces outside the lines that define the singles or doubles court (see Chapter 2), you've lost the point.

One bounce only, please

Tennis would be a snoozer if all you had to do was clear the net and keep the ball inside the lines. The real degree of difficulty comes from this little kink: The ball can bounce only once on your side before you hit it. Of course, if you're standing at the right place at the right time, you don't have to let the ball bounce at all before you hit it. But more than one bounce, and you've lost the point.

Causing the ball to bounce twice on your opponent's side wins you the point outright, which is called a *winner.* Winners are by far the most satisfying way to win a point. When I played, often my preference was to keep the ball in play until my opponent missed a shot, which is called an *unforced error.* Whether you smack a winner or your opponent makes a mistake, the points count the same. Cherish them for all they're worth!

Scoring basics

The winner of a tennis match is almost always the player who wins more points. You win points when you hit winners or your opponent makes errors (for example, they hit the ball into the net or beyond the lines). You lose points because of your opponent's winners and your errors.

In some cases, the winner of a match may have won just one single, solitary point more than their opponent. For example, when Pete Sampras and Goran Ivanišević met in the semifinals of Wimbledon in 1995, Sampras won with a grand total of 146 points to Ivanišević's 145 points. It's even possible for a player to lose more points than their opponent and still win the match! At other times, the victor may have won dozens more points than the loser. That's the difference between a blowout and a nail-biter.

Chapter **2**

Meet Me on the Court

P eople make tennis courts out of all kinds of materials — only the dimensions of the playing surface stay the same from court to court. In this chapter, I show you around the court and explain all about the various types of courts you may encounter. I also explain how the different court surfaces can impact your game.

Court Dimensions

The tennis court, which you can see in Figure 2-1, is a rectangle measuring 78 feet long and 27 feet wide for singles and 36 feet wide for doubles. The *doubles alleys* (on either side of the singles court) account for the extra width of the doubles court. (See Chapter 5 for more information about playing doubles.)

Net height

The court is divided into two equal halves by the net, which is anchored to the net posts just outside the boundary lines that make up the court. The net is usually made of a soft, mesh material, and it customarily has an adjustment strap in the center; you use the adjustment strap to achieve regulation net height.

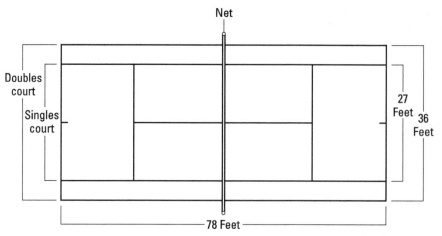

FIGURE 2-1:
The stock-in-trade of singles and doubles players.

© John Wiley & Sons, Inc.

TIP

The net is supposed to be 36 inches high at the center strap and 42 inches high at either side of the court. Unfortunately, nets with center straps at some public courts are about as rare as basketball rims with nets! Not to worry. You don't really need a center strap. Just take a tape measure and check the center height of the net. If it's below 36 inches, raise the net by using the crank on one of the net posts. If it's above 36 inches, turn the crank to lower the net. Don't worry about the height at the sides. When the net is 36 inches high at the center, you'll be fine. All that said, there's no need to get crazy about the net height. As long as it looks reasonably close, play ball.

NO PLAYING IN THE ALLEY

Occasionally, you may see (or even play on) a *dedicated singles court,* a court without doubles alleys. Although most singles games are played on a court also designed for doubles, you can't play doubles on a dedicated singles court, which is why so few of them exist. You may also come across some courts that have *singles sticks* (wooden sticks used to raise the net height to the 42-inch regulation on the singles sidelines on courts with a doubles alley). Singles sticks essentially serve as net posts, but these are for real sticklers and aren't required to play.

Line measurements

The *baselines* define the farthest end of the court on both sides of the net (see Figure 2-2). The baselines are the same regardless of whether you're playing singles or doubles.

Right smack in the middle of the baseline, you see a small hash mark, which divides the court into two equal parts. The center hash mark becomes important when you serve (see Chapter 11).

The lines at the longer sides of the rectangle are called the *sidelines.* The sidelines are the only boundary lines that differ for singles and doubles. The singles sidelines run parallel to and inside of the sidelines created by the *doubles alleys.*

Inside the court you find the *service lines,* which are perpendicular to the sidelines and parallel with the baselines and the net. The service lines are 21 feet from the net, and each service line is divided in half by a centerline. The centerline lines up perfectly with the hash mark that divides the baseline.

The service lines, the centerlines, and the net create four distinct boxes, which are called the *service boxes.* You find two service boxes on either side of the net, each service box measuring 21 feet long and 13½ feet wide.

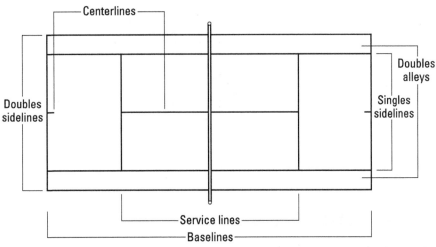

FIGURE 2-2: Getting up close and personal with the court lines.

DON'T HEM ME IN

MAC SAYS

Using different sidelines for singles and doubles may seem confusing, but don't worry — nobody, not even a beginner, has any trouble focusing on the correct sidelines for the game they're playing. It's a snap, I promise you. You may also come across courts with lines for 10 and Under (10U) tennis, which has a shortened area for young juniors, or even lines for pickleball. All these lines may seem to give the court a more chaotic appearance, but none of it gets in the way when you're playing regulation tennis.

On each side of the net, the centerline divides the service boxes into an *ad side* and a *deuce side*, as shown in Figure 2-3. When you serve from the deuce side of the court, your serve needs to clear the net and land inside your opponent's deuce-side service box when you keep score (see Chapter 11 for the details on serving). And when you serve from the ad side, the ball must land inside your opponent's ad-side service box.

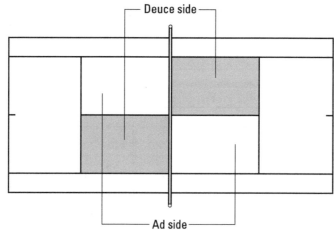

FIGURE 2-3:
The centerline splits the service boxes into two sides — the ad side and the deuce side.

© *John Wiley & Sons, Inc.*

Court Surfaces

Tennis court surfaces come in three main flavors: hard, clay, and grass. Each surface offers its own unique qualities. Surfaces even have different colors, smells, and feels. Most important, each surface treats the ball differently, depending on how soft or hard the surface is and the material from which it's made.

A tennis ball bounces higher off a hard surface than a soft one. If you don't believe me, take a tennis ball out to the sidewalk. Drop the ball from waist height on the pavement, noticing how high the ball bounces. Then do the same on the grass right next to the sidewalk. (You may want to wait until it gets dark to try this little experiment; otherwise, you may get some strange looks from the neighbors.)

The different court surfaces also impact both how high and how fast the ball bounces. A soft, gritty surface like clay "grabs" a ball momentarily as it bounces, and the friction slows it down. This often results in a fairly high bounce. Cement is a hard surface. A ball dropped onto a cement court from above may bounce high, but when it meets the surface with some velocity, at an angle, it skids off and keeps going before it can bounce very high. A ball will always bounce low on grass, but it won't slow down very much even though grass is a soft surface. That's because grass is very slick and slippery. But that shouldn't concern you too much, because tennis is rarely played on grass anymore.

Low bounce, high bounce, hard or soft surface — what's the big deal? Imagine that you're on the strangest tennis court ever built — half of the court is cement, and the other side is clay. A ball machine fires balls to both sides of the court. The machine throws all balls with the same speed and force, and you stand at the baseline. Your task is to start at the centerline and run out to catch the ball after it bounces on the appropriate side of the court. When a ball hits the clay side, it bounces right up and slows down a little, and you don't have to move too fast to get to and catch the ball. When the ball hits the cement side, it skids away with a lower bounce, and you really have to motor to get to the ball and catch it. In other words, court surface can have a major impact on how you play.

TIP

TESTING THE SPEED OF THE COURT

Whenever you play at a court new to you, hit a few balls around at the very start just to get a feel for the surface speed, or ask the other players about the court's surface properties. The speed of the court will affect the timing you use in your strokes, and how quickly you'll need to move to the ball to be on time to make good returns.

When you're used to a court of a certain speed and leave it to play on one that is significantly slower or faster, it may take you up to 20 minutes to adjust your timing and movement to the new surface.

Simply stated, you generally have to move faster to get to the ball on hard surfaces. However, the surer footing compared to a loose surface like clay is why some players find it easier to move on a hard court. This confusing truism leads to some even more confusing tennis terminology (see Table 2-1).

TABLE 2-1   ## Fast versus Slow Courts

Surface	Speed	Explanation
Hard (hard courts, grass courts, most synthetic courts)	Fast	The surface increases ball speeds, so you really have to move it in order to get to the ball when you play on a hard court.
Soft (clay courts, some synthetic courts)	Soft	The surface slows the ball down, so you don't have to move as fast, but you may have to play harder or longer. You also end up running a lot because it's easier for both players to get to the ball in time and return it, which keeps a point going longer.

REMEMBER

Real tennis fanatics refer to how slow or fast a court is as the court's *speed.* If I ever hear you talk like that, I'll know that you've really caught the tennis bug — or, even better, you've read this book.

So, you can see that a court's surface can have a big impact on your game. If you have the opportunity to play on different types of surfaces, you may find that your shots are better on some courts than others. For example, if you like to play aggressively, hitting as hard as you can within the lines, you may find that the speed of a hard court makes your shots that much harder to get to and return. Or if you prefer to play more conservatively or with lots of spin, placing each shot on your opponent's court with consistency and a surgeon's precision, you may find that a soft court enables you to wear an opponent down because of all the energy they have to use to run down one shot after another.

YEAH, BUT WHY WOULD YOU EVER DO THAT?

Roger Federer and Rafael Nadal once played an exhibition match in which half the court was grass (Federer's favorite surface) and the other half was clay (Nadal's favorite surface). Check it out on YouTube. It's wild. Talk about needing to make adjustments on the fly!

PROS HAVE A PREFERENCE WHEN IT COMES TO COURT SURFACES

The four preeminent tournaments in tennis, the *Grand Slam* events — the Australian Open, the French Open, Wimbledon, and the U.S. Open — are played on different types of surfaces (although the Australian Open and the U.S. Open are contested on similar hard courts, with balls bouncing slightly lower and faster in New York). As you see at these tournaments, even top players can be aided or stymied by a court surface.

For example, the great Pete Sampras won three of the four Grand Slam titles at least two times apiece, but he never even reached the final of the French Open. The popular German player Boris Becker never won the French title either; in fact, although Becker won more than 50 pro tournaments in his career, he didn't win a single one of them on clay.

Hard courts: Tried and true

Americans are a practical people who like standardization. That's why we invented fast-food joints that serve an identical burger in New York and Seattle and all points in between. That's why we invented the assembly line. We also invented tennis on hard courts with similar, practical goals.

Hard courts are versatile and virtually maintenance free. Hard courts last and last, through all types of weather. Depending on conditions and usage, it can take many years before it needs resurfacing. The practicality of the surface has made it the most widely used throughout the world. Essentially, the hard court is not the Tesla of tennis courts — it's the Honda Accord.

The majority of hard courts are faster than clay courts but slow enough to give you plenty of time to swing before the ball gets by you.

Builders can also fine-tune hard courts, making them play relatively faster or slower. They modify the court speed by mixing greater or lesser amounts of a granular substance, like sand, into the cement before it's poured. The more grainy the cement, the slower the hard court will play.

Court designers also mix rubber compounds into the cement or use rubber compounds to coat the surfaces of hard courts. Rubber can be used to make a court slower, but it also provides valuable cushioning, which reduces wear and tear on the joints and bones.

Regardless of how much a hard court has been modified with sand or rubber or not, it provides a good surface for developing your game, for the following reasons:

>> **You get a true bounce:** Because the surface of hard courts is smooth, you can expect a reliable bounce, unless the court is covered with litter or cracks. The lines on a hard court are painted on, so you get a true bounce even when you hit the lines. (On clay, surface irregularities can also produce frequent irregularities in the bounce.)

>> **They offer an acceptable speed limit.** Most hard courts built these days are slow enough to let you work on your consistency, but fast enough to reward you with a winner when you hit a good shot near the line. The slower the court, the more chance your opponent has of running down your shots.

>> **They're ready whenever you are:** You can play on a hard court almost any time, even after a torrential rainstorm (provided that a court squeegee — or snow shovel — is available). I kid you not. People often shovel snow from hard courts in order to play. As long as you leave the net up, a hard court is always ready to go.

The disadvantages of hard courts are minor, especially for beginners:

>> **They're tougher on the body.** Most hard courts can be tough on your joints and muscles if you play hard and frequently.

>> **They can run hot.** Hard courts reflect heat and glare, making them less appealing to play on during bright, hot days.

TIP

Keep the following tips in mind to make playing tennis on hard courts more comfortable and beneficial:

>> **Wear tennis shoes with an appropriate amount of cushioning.** Many shoe manufacturers offer shoes designed for use on hard courts, just as they once made light shoes with nubbly bottoms for play on slick grass.

>> **Wear quality socks.** Socks that offer extra cushioning at the heels and around the toes are especially good.

>> **Use the right balls.** The hard, abrasive surface of hard courts calls for the use of extra-duty balls with dense, durable felt covering. You can read more about such balls in Chapter 3.

>> **Avoid sudden starts, stops, and changes of direction until you're well warmed up.** Hard surfaces are less forgiving than soft ones, so take a little more time to work up your full head of playing steam. You can read more about warming up in Chapter 7.

>> **Pay attention to the height of the bounce.** The slower the hard court, the higher the ball bounces. Adjust your swing to the height at which you end up playing most balls.

Synthetic surfaces

One result of the tennis boom of the '70s and '80s was an explosion of new *synthetic surfaces* designed for tennis courts. Better living through modern technology, right?

These new surfaces were developed partly to accommodate the burgeoning pro game that was invading arenas (like Madison Square Garden), which were usually reserved for basketball or hockey. They were also designed for use in the growing industry of indoor tennis.

If you live in a climate with cold winters, the indoor tennis facilities in your neck of the woods probably have synthetic surfaces. They're essentially hard courts. They're built on a solid base — generally asphalt or concrete — and covered with various materials such as rubber, acrylic, and silica. The composition of the top layer dictates the court's playing characteristics. Synthetic courts are often softer and more cushioned than the typical outdoor hard court found in public parks or schools.

Some synthetic courts come in sections that are pieced together and set up for a tennis match in a matter of hours. Because of their quick assembly and dismantling, these surfaces tend to be used in arenas for professional events or exhibitions. They're made either of rubber-based compounds or durable synthetic fibers like the nylons and polyesters that you find in industrial carpeting or indoor-outdoor carpeting. However, it's quite rare to find these types of courts in recreational settings.

Two of the rarer synthetic surfaces are *plastic grids* and *synthetic grass.* The grids are made in interlocking (rather than roll-up) sections that snap together, kind of like the waffle-pattern flooring used in the kitchens of restaurants. Synthetic grass uses fake grass fibers made of plastic with a top dressing of sand to adjust the speed of the court. You may come across these types of courts in tropical resort settings or places looking to set up a functioning, temporary court. Again, not common for the day-to-day player.

TIP

Playing indoors, although it can be costly, gives you as close to perfect conditions as you can get, for the following reasons:

>> **You don't have to contend with the elements.** Factors like sun and wind play no part indoors. These idyllic conditions allow the ball to travel through the air more quickly.

>> **You get good lighting and a non-distracting background.** Indoor courts usually have specially designed lighting systems and solidly colored background curtains, creating ideal playing conditions. The netting that many indoor courts use between courts eliminates time wasted chasing down balls or returning them to players on other courts.

>> **You get a true bounce.** Indoor hard courts are usually very well kept, meaning that you won't find cracks or bumps in the court that could foul up your shot.

To get the most out of playing on synthetic surfaces, make sure that you warm up before you play. This gives you a chance to find out how fast the court surface is, so you don't get an unpleasant surprise when you start play.

Clay: Slow and tricky

The majority of clay courts are found in Europe. Red clay is far and away the most popular in this category. If you've ever watched the French Open at Roland-Garros, you've seen a prime example of red clay courts. (Chapter 20 tells you all about the French Open.) Green clay is much more popular in the United States, particularly in spots like the Northeast, Florida, and the Carolinas.

Clay courts are generally not actually made of clay. They have a solidly packed base of stone or gravel with a layer of smaller and looser pieces on top to help facilitate drainage. On top of the gravel is a third layer, called the *dressing.* This dressing is granular, made from pulverized sandstone or a similar, shale-type stone. The dressing is packed down, but it remains granular and easily dislodged. It's the use of crushed red brick for the dressing that gives red clay courts their distinctive color.

Clay courts need a lot of TLC. They need to be rolled to evenly distribute and pack down the dressing. Otherwise, it may blow away in the wind. Rolling also helps eliminate the irregularities in the surface that could lead to erratic bounces. The dressing has to be topped off now and then, but an overapplication makes the court more suitable for beach volleyball than tennis. During dry, sunny weather, clay courts also need to be watered as often as two or three times a day to keep them in ideal shape. Without sufficient water, clay courts get baked by the sun. The dressing blows away easily in the breeze, and the natural irregularities that develop with use create an abundance of maddening bad bounces.

CLAY REQUIRES RITUAL CLEANSING

When you play on a clay court, it's customary to roll, sweep, and even water the court before your game. It may sound like a chore, but it's a pretty nice ritual, getting the court ready to play. The great Rafael Nadal is frequently spotted sweeping the courts when he has finished a practice session on clay. A court swept free of irregularities or marks (balls hit with any force leave a distinct smudge on a clay court) can make you feel like you're the first person ever to set foot on it. Just remember to sweep the lines, too.

Unlike hard courts, where the lines are painted on, the lines on a clay court are typically made of vinyl tape that is nailed into the porous surface. Even when installed perfectly, they're never completely flush. So your footwork around the lines may call for a little extra caution. Also, balls that hit the lines on a clay court have even more erratic bounces and often speed up after contact. They can skid right by you or jump up above your head.

Clay is a slow court surface, although factors like dryness and a lack of dressing can make clay play significantly faster. But unless the court is truly in dire straits, clay is a slower court surface than even the slowest of hard courts.

The vast majority of public courts in the United States are hard courts, which are great for developing your game. But if you're lucky enough to have access to clay courts, I give them a slight edge over even hard courts for laying the foundations of your game, for the following reasons:

>> **Clay courts are user-friendly.** The inherent softness of clay courts helps protect you from stresses, strains, and injuries. Over the long haul, they're much kinder to your body than hard surfaces.

>> **Clay courts help you keep the ball in play.** Because clay is a slow surface, you can get to more balls and have more opportunities to hit them back than you can on faster court surfaces. In a typical one-hour practice session, you hit more balls on a clay court because you keep more balls in play. Hitting more balls helps keep the game interesting. It also enables you to improve faster.

>> **Clay courts make you consistent.** Clay is the best surface for mastering the consistency of your *groundstrokes* — the forehands and backhands that are the bread and butter of the game (see Chapters 8 and 9). The longer points also teach patience and the value of making your opponent hit one more shot. The most consistent players of all — including Björn Borg, Chris Evert, and Rafael Nadal — grew up on clay courts. (Although Evert is American, she grew up in South Florida, a mecca of clay courts.)

HAR-TRU: CLAY BORN IN THE USA

Red clay courts can be found in the United States, but they're in short supply. The majority of red clay courts are in tennis clubs or resorts.

Americans with feet of clay tend to play on the gray-green Har-Tru court, which is a clay court made from slightly different materials than you find on red clay courts. Har-Tru courts are popular, although never as abundant or accessible as hard courts.

Har-Tru courts are slightly faster than red clay courts, but the difference, especially to beginners, is negligible. The reason Har-Tru is more prevalent than red clay is a practical one: The courts are cheaper and easier to maintain. Har-Tru requires less attention, rolling, and water, and it dries faster when wet. After a heavy downpour, it can take a while to nurse a red clay court back to health.

>> **Clay courts can help you get fit.** A good workout on clay, where you're able to chase down lots of balls and keep them in play longer, is the best way to improve your overall fitness through tennis. You don't waste as much time collecting balls, and you don't have as much downtime, because each point is longer. Clay-court tennis can add muscle and tone your legs, strengthen your lower back, and improve your aerobic capacity. At the end of a brisk 60- to 90-minute workout on clay, your shirt is soaked and your gas tank is empty. (See Chapter 16 for more information on getting fit for tennis.)

>> **Clay courts are cool (temperature-wise) and comfortable.** Clay absorbs rather than reflects heat on hot days, and it doesn't generate any surface glare. Clay courts, especially if they're periodically watered, always feel comfortable on the soles of your feet.

MAC SAYS

So, why, you may wonder, am I so fired up about clay courts when I posted my own best tennis on hard courts? It's easy — I learned the game mostly on clay, as did my brothers, John and Mark. We built our tennis foundations on clay; those foundations proved strong enough to bear any load we put on them.

Playing on a clay court does have a few downsides, however:

>> **The footing can take time to get used to.** Because the top layer of a clay court is loose, it moves under your feet. It's most obvious when you make a sprint to the ball or quick change of direction. You don't have the same built-in traction you get from a hard court, which can cause some slips and stumbles. Maria Sharapova famously said she moved like "a cow on ice" playing on clay.

Like anything in tennis, getting comfortable moving on the surface is a learned skill. Maria got the hang of it — she won two French Open titles — and with time, so will you.

>> **Playing on clay can test your mettle.** A clay court can play slow. If conditions are damp, moist clay — with a heavy, clay-caked ball — plays at a snail's pace. Throw in tricky bounces and longer rallies and your patience and mental stamina will be put to the test. It's a valuable lesson in any player's development, but the tug-of-war of clay-court tennis can be like black licorice — an acquired taste.

>> **The dust from the dressing is messy.** If you're perspiring, this dust cakes on your legs and turns your socks (not to mention the tennis balls) a pale pink (on red clay) or green (on Har-Tru). Discolored, dusty socks may not sound like much of a downside, but it sure is if you're the person who gets to wash the socks.

>> **Clay courts require a fair amount of maintenance.** Playing on a well-kept clay court is a treat; playing on a poorly kept clay court is far from it. *Bald* (sparse top layer), dusty, or overly soft conditions can suck all the fun out of playing on clay. It takes a steady diet of rolling, watering, and sweeping to keep a clay court in tip-top shape. Added chemicals (such as calcium) are often applied to help the courts maintain moisture. At professional tournaments, the courts are constantly watered and swept, even *during* the matches. For these reasons, most public tennis facilities tend to shy away from clay courts.

TIP

If you have the luxury of playing on clay frequently, get the most out of the experience by following these guidelines:

>> **Use regular-duty balls.** Balls manufactured for hard-court play fluff up too much on clay, retaining moisture and fine court grit. That makes them heavier, slower, and prone to travel more slowly through the air. (You can read more about balls in Chapter 3.)

>> **Use shoes with clay-specific outsoles.** If you're going to be playing often on clay, you'd be wise to use a shoe with an outsole designed expressly for the surface. These outsoles generally have a herringbone (zigzag) pattern that provides good traction on clay. (You can read more about shoes in Chapter 3.)

>> **Concentrate.** Because the typical point lasts longer on clay, you need extra consistency and better mental endurance, too.

>> **Don't hold back.** Clay tempts you to just push or bunt the ball back instead of hitting full strokes. It's harder to hit a winner on clay, so this teensy-weensy voice in you asks, "Why bother?" Ignore that voice and observe the preparation and stroking fundamentals detailed in Part 2 of this book.

TIP

SLIP SLIDIN' AWAY

The dressing you find on clay courts gives clay-court tennis its unique characteristics. Because the dressing is granular, it remains loose — so loose that many players slide into shots on clay courts. Sliding saves time and energy when getting to the ball; plus, it looks really cool. At its highest level, sliding is an art form. Pro players even slide now on hard courts. That takes some youthful and strong ankles to pull off without hurting yourself. As my brother John and I like to say when we're commentating at the U.S. Open, "Don't try that at home!"

The secret to effective sliding is in the timing. In baseball, you slide *into* the base, not after it. Same thing in tennis. Slide to the ball as you're about to swing. If you slide *after* you hit the ball, it's too late. If you're moving forward into the court, you always slide *into* the shot with the opposite foot leading the way. If you're a righty, you slide into your forehand with your left foot in front, and into your backhand with your right foot leading the way. If you're a lefty, it's the opposite.

Sliding out wide when moving side-to-side is a bit trickier. You ideally want to slide with the outside leg of whichever direction you're moving. If you're a righty moving to your right to hit a forehand, you'll slide on your right foot. And if you're moving to your left to hit a backhand, you'll slide with your left foot. However, sometimes improvisation is needed in these situations, and you slide on whichever foot helps you get the ball back over the net.

Grass: A rare treat

A good grass court, like the ones at Wimbledon, has a lot more in common with a perfectly manicured putting green than with a sparkling, lovingly weeded lawn. Grass courts even look like a golf green because the grass is packed into the soil so tightly. Although grass courts are softer than hard courts, they're firmer underfoot than an ordinary lawn.

As an everyday playing surface, grass is not ideal. Unlike professional events where the ball bounces more like on a hard court, grass courts found in recreational settings are often much softer and produce much lower bounces. Dead spots and inconsistencies in the surface can cause shots to stay low and skid away from you. The courts at Wimbledon and other professional events are harder and bounce higher and truer. After a few matches, even those courts start to deteriorate around the baseline and can produce some bad bounces. Grass-court tennis requires you to be more instinctive and reactive, which is why it tends to favor the great athletes. This makes learning the game or enjoying extended rallies more difficult.

The time and expense involved in maintaining grass courts all but banish this surface from mainstream play. If you think it's difficult finding a red clay court, grass courts are like spotting Bigfoot. (Can you remember the last time you drove by a municipal park and saw people playing on grass?) In fact, you find grass courts almost exclusively at expensive private clubs (the famous All England Lawn Tennis & Croquet Club at Wimbledon is one such club) or homes. The British respect and maintain their traditions, and they still have a smattering of small clubs with grass courts that they can maintain on modest budgets.

That said, if you ever get an invitation to play on a grass court, take it! Grass-court tennis is really a pleasant experience that differs sharply from playing on hard or clay courts. Grass courts feel spongy underfoot because of the density of the grass. There are some clubs where the members actually play barefoot on them. The court smells great. The color and coolness of the grass is soothing. The novelty of the courts and their playing properties will really help round out your education as a tennis player.

MAC SAYS

AMERICA'S WIMBLEDON

Chances are, you'll never play tennis on an old-fashioned grass court unless you join (or are invited as a guest to) one of the private clubs that still cling to the tradition of using grass courts. But if you're curious about what it's like to play on turf, either for the fun of the experience or just to say that you've done it, I've got the place for you — the Newport Casino, located in the quaint seaside town of Newport, Rhode Island.

The Newport Casino was built in the late 19th century by the wealthy publisher James Gordon Bennett. In 1881, the grass courts of the Casino became the site of the first U.S. Championships, the event that eventually became the U.S. Open. A grass-court tournament is still played every summer at the Casino, ensuring that the Newport Casino is the oldest of the world's active tournament grounds.

The Newport Casino is also the home of the International Tennis Hall of Fame (in 2023, I was named the Hall of Fame's president), making Newport the tennis equivalent of Cooperstown, New York (home of the National Baseball Hall of Fame and Museum). If you're looking to play on grass and learn more about the sport in a wonderful setting, the Hall of Fame brings to life the long, fascinating tradition of tennis. For more information on the Hall of Fame, go to www.tennisfame.com.

But don't expect too much of your game unless you play often on grass. The surface has some characteristics that take a long time to get used to:

>> **The surface is fast and produces very low bounces.** Tennis balls skid more on grass than on any other commonly used surface. Unless a grass court is really hard and sunbaked, the ball tends to squirt away from you like a watermelon seed. It has been said that real jocks do well on grass because you need to be quick and explosive.

>> **You have to stay low all the time.** Because the ball bounces low and fast on grass, you always seem to be playing from a crouch on a grass court. Being agile and limber certainly comes in handy. You can easily pull and injure muscles as you stretch and lunge for balls in spirited games on grass. (See Chapter 7 for more information on warming up.)

>> **There's a greater emphasis on net play.** The surest way to avoid the low and difficult bounces on grass is to hit the ball directly out of the air. That means moving inside the court and attacking the net. The tactic isn't as popular when playing on clay and hard courts, but it's still a smart move on grass. So, it really helps to be comfortable volleying. (Chapter 10 goes into greater detail on the volley).

TIP

If you get the chance to play on grass, pay special attention to two key aspects of tennis fundamentals (you can read more about these fundamentals in Chapter 7):

>> **Keep your knees flexed.** Flexed knees will enable you to get down to the high number of low balls quickly and efficiently.

>> **Get your racquet back as soon as possible and lower than usual.** Grass courts can be so fast that unless you get your racquet into the backswing position immediately, you'll feel rushed or hit the ball too late to make a good shot.

IN THIS CHAPTER

» **Buying and caring for your racquet and strings**

» **Picking out your tennis shoes**

» **Choosing tennis balls**

» **Getting dressed for tennis**

» **Poking into the grab bag of accessories**

Chapter **3**

Getting Geared Up

I n the summer of 1977, just a few months after his 18th birthday, my brother John did a really unexpected and historic thing. He got to the semifinals at the most important tournament in the world, Wimbledon. He got there playing with the wooden Wilson Pro Staff racquet that he liked best (which was not a super-fancy racquet), wearing shoes and clothing that he got in small doses from being on the "free" list, along with other promising juniors, from various manufacturers. Then, because of his astonishing success, every equipment and apparel manufacturer in the free world was all over him, hoping to sign him to endorsement deals. Suddenly, our entire family was awash in all the gear we could use or wear, given to us absolutely free by just about every company that made the stuff.

MAC SAYS

You know what? All that equipment hardly mattered. Tennis is a game that doesn't require a whole lot of gear, accessories, or special clothing to play well. To this day, I'm more comfortable playing in a simple cotton T-shirt with maybe just the little Nike Swoosh logo on the breast than in a fancy tennis shirt made of performance fabrics that retails for $75 or more.

The only two really vital pieces of gear for playing tennis are a good pair of shoes (to protect your feet) and a properly strung, comfortable racquet. Using lively, good-quality tennis balls also helps. Any other equipment you use is a matter of taste and comfort.

That said, I do appreciate that tennis attire can be fashionable. And some players may even believe if they look good, they play good. To each their own. Just make sure you come ready to play with the necessities in tow.

In this chapter, I tell you everything you need to know about all the equipment needed to play tennis.

Even in tennis circles, some of the information in this chapter gets downright nerdy. If you're new to the game, some topics are certainly not required reading. However, you may come back to it as a handy reference as you advance in your tennis career.

The Racquet: Your Trusty Weapon

Yes, you can dust off that racquet that you played with five years ago and give it a glorious return to the court — if it feels good in your hand and it gets your shots where (and how) you want them to go. If you're in the market for a new racquet, however, I want to tell you about the build of a racquet so you know what's up when you set out to select your new tool. Whether you're shopping at a sporting-goods store, a tennis specialty shop, or online, knowing the ins and outs about racquets really helps.

Sizing up the frame

Welcome to Introductory Tennis Racquet Anatomy, where you can find out all the different parts that make up a standard racquet frame, shown in Figure 3-1. In the following sections, I tell you about all the different dimensions of a racquet and how they affect a frame's performance.

MAC SAYS

HANDED-DOWN GLORY

When I was a kid starting out in tennis, I was the Little King of the Hand-Me-Downs, thanks to having two older brothers in tennis, John and Mark. My first racquet was one of John's old wooden ones. In fact, I developed my basic two-handed backhand grip because I couldn't hold John's heavy wood racquet with just one hand. Eventually, my two-handed backhand turned out to be my best shot!

My first tennis shirt was an inheritance from Mark. I didn't think of any of those things as secondhand junk, but as gear that was already, well, nicely broken in.

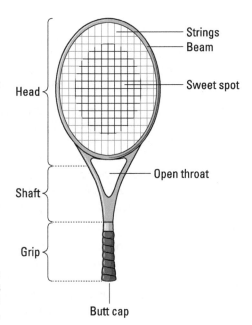

FIGURE 3-1:
The components
of a typical
racquet frame.

Labels in figure: Head, Shaft, Grip, Strings, Beam, Sweet spot, Open throat, Butt cap

Head size

The circular-shaped portion of the racquet is commonly called the *head.* Its measurement is in square inches. The area inside the head where the strings are is referred to as the *hitting surface* or *string bed.* (See the section "Strings: The Overlooked Necessity" in this chapter for more information about the strings.) The hitting surface always contains a *sweet spot* — the area in which the strings create the most power for the least amount of effort. (Chapter 7 tells you more about the importance of the sweet spot when hitting your shots.)

WARNING

The sweet spot is the tennis player's favorite area of the racquet. It's typically found in the center, or just above the center of the string bed. Not only does hitting the sweet spot give shots extra oomph, but it's easier to direct the ball from the sweet spot as well. Contacting the ball outside the sweet spot doesn't feel nearly as good or produce the same results.

The head of a racquet can vary in shape and size. There used to be a greater range between the smallest and largest, but since around 2010 or so, over the past several years, the spread has narrowed. Typically, a racquet's head falls into one of the following categories:

>> **Midsize:** These racquet heads range from 95 to 98 square inches. Most pro players use frames in this category, with a few outliers using models just on either side of it. Skilled recreational players gravitate to these frames as well. Midsize racquets have a smaller hitting surface and sweet spot, making it

more challenging to center the ball and hit it well. When you do, though, there's a higher degree of control over the resulting shot. The smaller face is also easier to manipulate and offers better *ball connection* (the feel of the ball on the strings) at contact. These racquets also tend to be the heaviest.

>> **Mid-plus:** Ranging from 100 to 105 square inches, mid-plus heads have more room on the hitting surface and a bigger sweet spot. This gives them more margin for error than the midsize models. You don't have to center the ball perfectly to hit an effective shot. The larger head size also has more space between strings, which helps create more power and spin. For these reasons, these tweener frames (with performance not quite as refined as the midsize models, but more versatile than the oversize ones) are popular choices for intermediate and developing players.

>> **Oversize:** Beginners and older players appreciate the large hitting surface of oversize frames. At one time, these racquets got so huge, they resembled a snowshoe. (Search the web for the "GAMMA Big Bubba" to see what I mean.) But now they usually measure between 110 and 120 square inches. The expansive sweet spot and wide string spacing mean even more margin for error on off-center hits so newer players can experience success hitting the ball.

The downside of oversize racquets is that their extra help in the power department can make them more difficult to control. Their bulkiness also requires them to be rather lightweight to compensate for added air resistance. (Otherwise, they'd be too cumbersome to swing.) And because they're so light, they also tend to be *stiff* (very little bend at contact) to maintain stability.

Length

The standard length for an adult tennis racquet is 27 inches. It's the size of the overwhelming majority of racquets on store shelves. Junior frames are often shorter, making them lighter and more maneuverable. Extended-length racquets — longer than 27 inches — are available, with 27½ inches being the most common. Longer racquets give you added reach to the ball and more power, especially on the serve (see Chapter 11).

Beam width

The *beam width* is the thickness of the racquet frame. It's measured from the tip of the head down to the throat (refer to Figure 3-1). If you look at a couple racquets from the side (where you can see the *grommets* — the small inserts where strings pass through) you notice that some racquets have wider beams than others. You may also notice that some beams have the same thickness throughout (known as *constant* beams), and other beams are wider or thinner in certain areas (known as *variable* beams).

Wide beams can add power to your shots. They also tend to be firmer and more stable. For these reasons, they can be attractive to new players. One thing you have to watch out for, though: The added power can lead to a lack of control, which can cause you to start bunting the ball rather than taking a smooth, long swing. As players improve, they often gravitate toward thinner beam frames, which favor control more than power.

TIP

Stick with a moderate beam, straight or slightly tapered, until you have enough experience to experiment with more extreme beam configurations. By that time, you'll be able to determine how wider beams affect your strokes and playing style.

Weight

A racquet's weight has a significant influence over its performance. Heavier racquets are preferred by advanced players because they provide greater *stability* (which means they resist twisting) at contact and added power when swung efficiently. The extra mass can also make them more challenging to maneuver. Lighter racquets forfeit some stability, but they're easier to accelerate, which can help create pace and depth on shots.

In recent years, the dividing line between what's considered light and heavy has been drawn at around 10.5 ounces (300 grams). Frames at that weight hit the sweet spot of the popular, midweight tweener category — racquets that combine the user-friendliness of an oversize game improvement model with some of the playability of a smaller advanced player's frame. When the weight climbs to 10.7 ounces (305 grams) and above, the racquet is designed for more accomplished players. On the other hand, as weights decrease, the ability levels migrate from intermediate down to beginners.

TIP

The old adage was that you should use the heaviest racquet possible that you could comfortably swing in order to get the best combination of power and stability. However, racquet materials and technologies have advanced, so racquets don't need as much weight to play at a high level. Even on the pro tours, players are using increasingly lighter racquets. I think it's best to use a racquet that has some heft without feeling heavy in your hand. Usually, this means a frame weighing somewhere between 10 and 11 ounces (unstrung). That's light enough to swing easily and securely, but heavy enough to provide you with good power.

Balance

If you start talking about a racquet's balance, people will know you're serious about your tennis. Simply put, a racquet's *balance* reveals how its weight is distributed throughout the frame. If a standard-length racquet (27 inches) has an even balance, then its balance point — think of two sides of a scale being perfectly level — would be exactly 13½ inches from the bottom of the grip.

The heavier the racquet is, the more of its weight will be positioned so that the balance point will be closer to the handle. Otherwise it would be too clubby to swing. Frames like this are called *head-light*. Lightweight frames typically have a balance point closer to the head. This gives them more mass at contact to prevent twisting. Most frames are head-light to a certain degree. However, if a racquet has a balance point that's closer to the head than the butt end of the handle, it's classified as *head-heavy*.

Stiffness

A racquet's *stiffness* is basically a measurement of how much it bends when contacting the ball. It's rarely divulged by a racquet's manufacturer, but a knowledgeable retailer should be able to provide the rating. The number (called its *RA rating*) is determined with a fancy racquet diagnostic machine. Most racquets range from the upper 50s (flexible) to the low 70s (stiff). The stiffness can reveal whether a racquet favors power or control. A more flexible racquet is typically heavier, with thinner beams, and it feels softer and more comfortable at impact. Stiffer frames are lighter and more powerful, but they can feel harsh when contact is off-center.

WARNING

Stiff racquets can be a blast to play with. Literally. They offer more power from less of a stroke and provide extra help to shots that aren't perfectly struck. The ease of use can make the game more fun. However, if you've had any issues with shoulder, elbow, or wrist injuries, you're much better off using a flexible racquet. You may not get the same pop, but it will be kinder to your body. A stiff racquet will transmit more shock from impact to your hitting arm — especially when contact is off-center — and can irritate an already tender joint.

Swing weight

This is another rather techy spec that isn't essential, but it's important to know about.

As the name implies, *swing weight* is a measurement of how heavy a racquet feels while it's moving through the air. Like stiffness, it's also taken by an expensive diagnostic tool. Most retail racquets fall in a range from around 300 (low) to the 330s (high). The higher the number, the more demanding the racquet will be to swing. Rafael Nadal's racquet measured around 370!

TIP

A high swing weight is attractive to skilled players who need to hit and defend shots with greater pace — a higher swing weight translates to greater stability and more inherent power. But beginning players should consider a racquet with a lower swing weight so the racquet is easier to handle.

String pattern

If you're looking at a racquet face, the strings that run vertically (up and down) are called the *main strings.* The strings that run horizontally (left and right) are called the *cross strings.* The combination of both is what gives the racquet its string pattern. There are almost always fewer main strings than cross strings. The string pattern is presented with the number of mains first, followed by the number of crosses.

For instance, the 16x19 pattern is the most popular string pattern in current racquets. It provides a nice balance of power, spin, and control. But even within this pattern there are subtle differences in performance depending on how far apart the strings are positioned. If the strings have greater spacing, it favors more power and spin. If the strings are closer together in the sweet spot, the emphasis is for more control.

There are other patterns as well. Fewer strings — such as a 16x18 string pattern — would create a more elastic string bed that ups the power and spin output. More strings — such as an 18x20 string pattern — has tighter spacing so less string movement, which results in better predictability and control when it comes to directing shots. The 18x20 pattern is usually found only in racquets aimed at accomplished players.

TIP

At the end of the shaft, you find the grip (refer to Figure 3-1). Most grips are made of a cushioned and absorbent synthetic material. When I was on tour, most frames came stock with a leather grip. These days, that's a rarity. A synthetic grip is typically lighter, cushier, and less expensive to produce, making it more practical than leather.

Racquet grips range in diameter between 4 and 4⅝ inches around. No objective criteria exist for choosing a grip size. Some behemoths with hands the size of catchers' mitts like slender grips, while some petite players like big, fat handles to grab onto. Grip size is purely a matter of comfort. The current trend is to use a grip that's on the small side for the player's hand, the thinking being that it allows more freedom of movement in the wrist, which can be advantageous for putting spin on the ball. A bigger grip requires the forearm and elbow to do more work in the swing.

TIP

If you don't have a preference, tennis has an old rule of thumb — and I mean that literally. When you grip the racquet comfortably (but not tightly), you should be able to touch the tip of your thumb to the top (or outermost) knuckle of your middle finger.

WARNING

Using a grip that's technically a little small for your hand is fine, but avoid choosing a grip that's *way* too small. The natural tendency of some beginners is to select a small grip because the racquet seems easier to handle. But a really small grip will twist in your hand when you hit the ball off-center. That twisting is bad for your tennis and, even worse, could eventually hurt your wrist.

TIP

If you're torn between two similar grip diameters, go with the smaller one, for this reason: You can always build up the grip later with an overgrip (see "Loading Up on Tennis Accessories," later in this chapter, for more information).

TIP

The tail end of the racquet, the *butt cap* (refer to Figure 3-1), does not impact your play. The butt cap is most useful before you even start to play. Most racquet manufacturers put their logo on the butt cap. Many players use this logo to determine who gets to serve first in a match. (Chapter 5 tells you more about this tennis ritual.)

Understanding racquet composition

The advancement in racquet technology has been one of the biggest changes in the sport. We've come a very long way from the days of wooden frames. The deft shot-making and incredible ball speeds players can generate are in large part thanks to equipment innovation.

Racquets have become quite sophisticated. They incorporate space-age materials and are designed with computers. What's important for you to know is that the vast majority of racquets manufactured today use graphite in one form or another as the base ingredient. Graphite is the technological generation's equivalent of the trusty laminated wooden racquet that was so popular until about the 1970s.

Graphite is remarkably strong for its relatively light weight. It's what allowed manufacturers to create frames with larger head sizes without making the racquets too heavy. It provides terrific power, as well as good control and feel for the ball.

But graphite is just the main ingredient. It's often joined in a composite mixture with materials like carbon fiber, Kevlar, and fiberglass. Throw in plastics and other polymers that help absorb shock and dampen vibrations, and a racquet's properties can be shaped to produce desired playing characteristics.

MAC SAYS

You may still be able to find inexpensive aluminum racquets to buy, or even have an old-school wooden frame collecting dust in the attic. You can use these racquets, but doing so won't help your game any. Why make the game harder than it has to be by using ancient, outdated tools? Even if you're just starting out, I recommend using the current graphite-composite racquets. You'll learn faster, improve quicker, and just have more fun.

Feel is the sensation you get for how you're striking the ball and where it's going. Some racquet materials are more sensitive than others to things like impact and vibration, so they transmit information about them more readily. When a racquet is said to have good feel, it means that you have a better sense of when the ball is on the string bed. This helps when you're trying to hit softer or more creative shots. (Chapter 12 dives deeper into specialty shots). If a racquet lacks feel, it means there's less connection when the ball is on the strings. This can happen with the stiffer, power frames where the ball jumps off the string bed. It's great for smacking shots, but heavy-handed when it comes to finesse.

Deciding on a new racquet

Choosing a tennis racquet isn't rocket science, but it can feel overwhelming. Numerous brands offer countless choices with little separating them. And they're all generally quite good. In fact, I don't know that any reputable manufacturer makes a "bad" racquet these days.

In the end, it boils down to personal preference. All the marketing promises of supersized sweet spots and limitless power don't matter. Nor does it make any difference which touring pro uses which particular model. The ultimate determining factor is simply what feels good when you hit the ball and gives you the best results. A sharp-looking racquet never hurt either.

I SHOULD'VE ASKED FOR ROYALTIES

In the spring of 1983, I was playing with the Dunlop 200G graphite racquet; my brother John was still using his wooden Dunlop McEnroe Maxply. At the time, John was already a very successful player, and like anyone else in his shoes, he was reluctant to change a winning game. We were practicing together at the Cove Tennis Center near our home on Long Island, just days before John was supposed to go off to play in the World Championship Tennis Finals in Dallas. We were in front of our coach, Tony Palafox, and John was getting frustrated that I kept hitting my returns past him as he approached net. He got so annoyed that he grabbed my racquet to try it for himself. He immediately got about 20 percent more pop on his shots.

Two days later, he got on the plane to Dallas, taking my racquets instead of his. And four days after that, he beat his lifelong rival, Ivan Lendl, in the final of the World Championship Tennis event. John continued to use the graphite racquet, and he won Wimbledon with it. The very next year, John had his best year ever — and one of the best years ever recorded in the pro game: He won 13 of the 15 singles tournaments he played, compiling an 82-3 singles match record. All with my racquet — and his game.

As of this writing, you can expect to pay around $200 to $275 for a high-performance racquet. That said, there are certainly other options if you can't afford — or don't want to — spend that much money. Stop by a sporting-goods store or do a search on Amazon, and you'll find numerous choices below $100. My preference would be for you to consult a knowledgeable pro shop or online retailer to discover which options, regardless of price, are good fits given your athletic background and playing potential. Ultimately, you should base your buying decision on what type of racquet feels the most comfortable for the shots you like to make. (See the next section for some tips on finding a suitable racquet.)

Try before you buy: Demoing a racquet

If you're spending a chunk of change, avoid buying a racquet that you haven't tried first. I don't care if the video review you watched on YouTube was really persuasive. I don't care if the best player you know plays with it. I don't care if Roger Federer himself told you to use it. Play-test a racquet whenever you can. It's a common practice, and most good tennis shops and online retailers have demo programs in place for this purpose. Many often put the cost of the demos toward the purchase of a new racquet.

TIP

Keep the following tips in mind as you play-test a racquet:

>> **Limit variables when testing a new racquet.** You want to be on familiar ground when you try something unfamiliar. Ideally, that means the court you play on most often. Same with the strings in the racquet and grip size. If possible, try to replicate your current playing experience as closely as possible. Otherwise, it's not a fair comparison.

>> **If you have a racquet already, warm up with your own racquet.** Getting loosened up with your own racquet can help you form a fresh, accurate impression of the differences between the racquets.

>> **Give each new racquet at least 15 minutes of your time.** Your very first impressions about a racquet are valuable and accurate, but give a racquet a little time to grow on you. A rough start could just be a step backward before taking two steps forward. Ask yourself the following questions after the racquet enjoys its 15 minutes of fame, and base your decision to buy (or not) on the answers:

- Did the racquet feel as comfortable to use as your former frame?

- Could you hit your three best shots as well and as consistently as you did with your customary racquet?

- Could you serve confidently and effectively with the new racquet?

- Did you notice any change in the way your wrist, shoulder, and the muscles in your racquet arm feel?

WARNING

Fifteen minutes may not be enough time to tell you whether the relative stiffness, or some other playing property of the racquet, may eventually cause you to experience soreness or discomfort. You need to play longer with a racquet to establish the cause of any tennis injuries. It's a chance you have to take. If you do develop a sore wrist, tendinitis, or even tennis elbow, changing racquets may be the cause — especially when you change to a stiffer racquet. (You can read more about common tennis injuries in Chapter 17.)

>> **Give it a chance in competition.** If you've advanced to the point of playing matches, it's always wise to see if a potential new racquet can stand up to the pressures of competition. It's one thing to enjoy a honeymoon phase with a racquet when you're just smacking balls around in practice. Make sure it can duplicate its performance when there's a scoreboard involved before you make a commitment.

>> **Ask a regular playing partner for feedback.** If you have a player, a group of players, or a coach who you often play with, they can provide valuable firsthand testimony when it comes to a new racquet. Because they're already familiar with how you play, they can judge whether this new frame is benefitting your strokes. Say you're looking to add more power or spin to your shots — they can give a thumbs-up or thumbs-down on whether this new frame is getting the job done.

Figuring out how many racquets you need

Some questions get old really fast for pro tennis players. When I was on tour, the classic line I invariably heard in airports when other travelers saw me carrying racquet bags stuffed thick with frames was, "Do you really need that many racquets?"

For a pro player, yes — you need that many racquets. A pro needs at least six racquets, often more, in order to make sure that they always have enough freshly strung, playable frames on hand during a match. When I was playing, this was to ensure I had enough racquets handy in case I broke a string. Nowadays, players change racquets throughout the match. They're not worried about breaking a string; they want to switch the racquet out before its tension drops too much (check out "String tension: Lower for power, tighter for control," later in this chapter, for more information).

Pros are incredibly attuned to their equipment. You don't need to be nearly that finicky. Having two racquets is great, just in case you break a string during play. But recreational players rarely ever need more than two racquets. Many players get along okay with just one.

Strings: The Overlooked Necessity

Strings aren't sexy. Strings aren't flashy. Strings don't give you instant prestige. But trust me — strings are the secret ingredient to success at tennis. Think about it: Your strings should be the only thing that makes contact with the ball. Still, players will spend weeks and months demoing different frames, but they won't give a second thought to the strings used in it. Your racquet and strings are the two most important variables in the equipment equation. Don't overlook this necessity.

In this section, I fill you in on what the different types, shapes, and tensions of strings can do for your game, and the importance of frequent restringing.

A matter of materials

Just like racquets, strings have enjoyed tremendous innovation over the last couple of decades. Arguably, more so. And just like racquets, a vast array of ingredients are used to make strings. For this book, I focus on the four major categories: natural gut, synthetic multifilament, polyester, and hybrid.

Natural gut: Still relevant after all these years

Natural gut is the game's first high-performance string. It was introduced in 1875 by Babolat, a family-run business in Lyon, France, that specialized in turning natural gut into such things as surgical thread and strings for musical instruments. The tennis string has been significantly refined since those early days, but there's still an old-school vibe about natural gut. Given its long service and all the technological improvements in strings, some players may consider gut an outdated relic. Yet it still remains a viable and worthwhile string for players of all levels.

Gut is highly fibrous, which makes it exceptionally soft and elastic. This allows the ball to *pocket* (sink into the string bed) longer and propel shots deeper with less effort. It also results in a very cushioned feel at contact. If you've got arm pain, no string is easier on the joints than gut.

Gut also holds its tension better than any string, so its performance remains constant longer. For these reasons, many touring pros still use gut, most often combined with another string in what's known as a *hybrid* (see "Hybrids: Blending the perfect mixture," later in this chapter).

The downside to gut is its lack of durability. All those fibers start to fray during play, especially if you hit with lots of spin. When gut starts to unravel, the string bed can get even springier and shots more difficult to control. Plus, gut doesn't respond well and can break sooner in moist and humid conditions. Although its longevity has been improved over the years, there are certainly many other heartier strings. Throw in the high price tag — manufacturing gut is labor intensive — and recreational players tend to look elsewhere.

A string job with gut should cost you about $50 to $70, which makes it a serious investment — especially when you consider the fact that gut, which is made from intertwined natural fibers, has a tendency to unravel and snap sooner than most nylon strings.

TIP

Gut's price, high maintenance, and low lifespan give it a limited audience. If you're just starting out, it's probably best to save yourself some headaches and walking-around money. But as your game matures, it's still worth considering. Perhaps it's best to think of gut as a high-end luxury car: As long as you don't mind the occasional costly upkeep, it offers a beautiful ride.

Synthetic multifilament: The people's choice

Synthetic strings are fabricated in a variety of ways from a variety of materials. Think of this category as the Target or Walmart of the string universe — there's something for everyone. On one end of the spectrum, there are simple solid core offerings with only a few wrappings to soften the feel at contact. These are great strings for beginners because they're durable, cost as little as $4 for a set, and offer good playability.

On the other end of the spectrum sit more sophisticated multifilaments with hundreds of synthetic fibers that try to replicate the performance of natural gut, but at a lower price. These can cost more than $20 a set and are attractive to more skilled players. In between, you'll find an endless array of choices, often with an emphasis on certain playing traits, such as power, control, or durability.

Just about in the middle of the category is where *synthetic gut* is found — the catchall name for the solid-core and single-wrap synthetic models that are popular with recreational players, thanks to their combination of solid playability and low cost. Basically, it's the best bang for the buck. As players develop, they tend to look for higher-level strings or leave the category altogether.

Polyester: The skilled player's preference

Earlier, when I said that strings may have outpaced racquets in terms of advancing tennis performance, it was mainly polyesters that I was referring to. The shorthand for it amongst knowledgeable players is simply *poly*. When I was finishing my playing career, polys were just hitting the scene, and they weren't too popular. They were primarily *monofilament* (single-core) strings that were incredibly sturdy but not easy to play with. Boy, have things changed. As the strings have evolved to become more user-friendly, they've become the most popular strings on the professional tours, on college teams, and with accomplished recreational players.

WARNING

However, before we go any further, let's be clear: *Beginners should think long and hard about using polyester strings. Same with young juniors.* For reasons I explain in this section, a player needs certain skills and physical maturity to reap the benefits of polyester strings. Otherwise, the string will be too demanding, and the negatives will outweigh the positives.

The first characteristic that draws players to polys is their durability. They can be tougher to break than Roger Federer at Wimbledon. Strings snap because they grind against each other during play. Polys are less abrasive than other strings, resulting in less wear and tear. This is attractive to string-breakers and hard-hitters who need a dependable string option. However, this resiliency can actually be a detriment if you don't restring the racquet frequently enough. (I get to the benefits of restringing a little later in the chapter.)

Because polyester strings are inherently stiff, they also flex less at contact. This means less power, but a more consistent string bed, resulting in more predictable shots. So, players can take big cuts at the ball and still keep their shots inside the lines. The downside is that the firmness of the string can be a nightmare on tender joints.

The other area that is really helped by polyester strings is spin production. The stiffness and texture of the strings bite into the ball more than softer synthetics. And their less abrasive nature allows the strings to move at contact and then quickly snap back into place — often referred to as *snapback.* Throw in the faster swing speeds, and it's a platform to really accentuate the spin on the ball. This not only makes shots more lively — higher bounces and more movement — but in the case of topspin affords higher net clearance for better safety because the spin will drop the ball more quickly in the court. (Read more about putting topspin on the ball in Chapter 8.)

Hybrids: Blending the perfect mixture

Hybrids are also for more experienced and discerning players. It's not a unique type of string, but rather the combination of two different types of string in one string bed. It's a method used to balance out the playing characteristics of two strings. The most common practice is to put a firmer string like a polyester in the main strings and a softer multifilament or natural gut in the crosses.

The mains give the string bed more of its identity. They're also typically the first to break, so putting a long-lasting string there will increase the longevity of the string job. Plus, there's still the benefit of good spin production and control. By putting softer strings in the crosses, it lessens the harshness of a full string bed of polyester without suffering inadequate durability. It's not quite the best of both worlds — you always compromise something — but it's pretty darn close.

Reversing the pattern — softer strings in the mains and tough strings in the crosses — results in a more comfortable hybrid as the emphasis shifts to the more forgiving strings. Players who prefer a cushier string bed, and don't break strings often, will appreciate this setup.

A benefit of hybrid stringing is that it can lower the cost of an expensive string. Say you really like natural gut, but the high price and frequent restringing make it too costly. You can lower the overall cost by using a cheaper, tougher synthetic in the crosses. Will it play and feel exactly like a full set of gut? No. But the minimal offset in performance will be a worthwhile concession. The same practice can be done to lower the cost of any high-end string.

The finer points: Gauge, shape, and texture

The thickness of a string is called its *gauge*, and it's measured in millimeters. Gauges start at 15 and go all the way up to 20 in certain strings. The higher the gauge number, the thinner the string. The large majority of the thinnest strings are polyesters because they're naturally more durable.

This is another of those subjects that applies more to players with some experience. If you're a beginner, the gauge or shape of your string shouldn't be on your radar yet. When you have your racquet strung, go with a 16-gauge synthetic multifilament in a price range you're comfortable with. If you eventually get two racquets, you can string one with varying gauges, shapes, or textures to experience the differences, and you can keep the other strung with the standard string as your go-to frame.

If you do experiment with these nuances in strings, keep the following points in mind:

>> **Thinner strings are springier.** The 17- or 18-gauge model of a string is more lively and elastic than the thicker 15- or 16-gauge versions. This results in a softer string bed that can produce easier power. You can also impart more spin with thin strings, as they more readily dig into the ball.

>> **Thinner strings break faster.** Although thin strings are strong enough to handle the power of any player, they usually break sooner than thick strings because there's less material to wear out.

>> **Textured and shaped strings help impart more spin.** This is a feature generally found in the polyester category. Instead of the more traditional round shape, some strings are designed with a multisided profile. This gives the string sharper edges to grab the ball for more spin. Additionally, some strings have a textured coating. For instance, certain strings are labeled *rough* because they have a grittier surface. This also helps the string grab the ball at contact and accentuate the spin put on the shot.

String tension: Lower for power, tighter for control

A racquet's *string tension*, usually expressed in *pounds*, refers to the pressure under which the strings are secured to the frame. The string tension affects the playing characteristics of the racquet.

TIP

Nearly all racquets come with recommended stringing tensions, mostly between 45 and 60 pounds. The general rule is that you string *lower*, at fewer pounds of pressure, for more power, and *tighter* for better control. Beginners using a synthetic multifilament should start in the middle of the recommended tension range, which usually means about 55 pounds.

The following general rules about string tension may help you decide which tension is best for you:

>> A loosely strung racquet may feel like it has a larger sweet spot, but when you swing hard enough, it also produces a "trampoline effect," which can cause your shots to fly unpredictably.

>> A tightly strung racquet transmits a firmer feel at contact. This can mean a less comfortable hitting surface, particularly when contact is off-center. But when you hit the ball cleanly, a tightly strung racquet can give you excellent control.

>> A loosely strung racquet enables you to hit delicate finesse shots with more confidence. Those shots call for a light, feathery touch. Tight strings are under a lot of tension, so it's harder to caress the ball with them.

>> If you hit the ball hard, a tightly strung racquet can tire your arm more quickly.

>> Lower tensions soften the string bed, which lessens shock at contact. This can be helpful if you've got arm troubles.

REMEMBER

Honestly, you won't need to be too concerned with these issues until you become an experienced player. But you may as well get a taste for them now, because they'll become more important as your game grows.

THE IMPORTANCE OF RESTRINGING

If ain't broke, don't fix it. That's the approach many players take with their strings. Which is a big mistake. Never underestimate the value of a new string job. A racquet performs much better when the strings are fresh. When you want a racquet strung, you should take it to a local tennis shop or experienced stringer. If you don't know one, you can check the website of the United States Racquet Stringers Association (https://racquettech.com) for a certified stringer in your area. If you're unsure of which strings to use, a knowledgeable stringer will help.

Because strings are under tension, they begin to lose elasticity and tension the moment you install them in a racquet. Plus, every time you hit a ball, you're doing damage to the strings — perhaps not enough to break them, but the cumulative wear and tear will adversely affect its performance. When strings lose enough tension and get worn down, they go dead. Dead strings change the way your racquet performs, cut down your ability to generate power and pace, make you work much harder than you may need to on your strokes, and absorb less shock at contact. Add it all up, and using a racquet with dead strings will not only hurt your game but can even hurt your arm.

So, how often should you restring in order to avoid dead strings? Use the following guidelines to help you decide. You should restring your racquet:

- **At least as many times in a year as you play in a week:** If you play three times a week, restring your racquet three times a year.

- **After every 40 hours of play:** If you play three times a week for about two hours every session, that works out to be about every six weeks.

- **After you lose 25 percent or more of tension:** The person who strings your racquet should be able to measure the tension to see if it's time to replace your strings.

- **When your strings sound dead:** Depending on their composition and the tension they're strung at, strings make a distinct sound at contact. That sound can range from a ping to a thud. When a string gets worn down, and that sound disappears, it's definitely time to restring.

- **More frequently if you use polyester strings:** If you use polyester strings — which I strongly advise against for beginners — keep in mind that they lose tension very quickly. And when they go dead they can be particularly damaging to the arm. So, the moment they start feeling soft and stop snapping back into place, it's time for a new set.

Lacing Up Your Tennis Shoes

There's an old tennis locker room adage that when you find your perfect racquet and a dependable pair of shoes, never ever switch. They're that hard to find. That's easier with racquets because popular models don't change much from generation to generation. And a decent frame will also last for many years. But shoes aren't nearly as durable, and get revamped or phased out quite frequently. So, it pays to know what to look for in a good tennis shoe.

What makes it a "tennis" shoe

Not all athletic shoes are created equally. Your trusty running or gym shoes may serve you well on the treadmill or during a workout, but playing tennis is a different animal. Running shoes are meant for continuous straight ahead movement. But make a quick cut in them as you would during a tennis point, and you may end up with a rolled ankle. That's why tennis shoes have far greater lateral support. They also have outsoles with tread patterns that grip the court for smooth footwork. That way, they can handle all the stops, starts, and side-to-side movement. If you want to play the game well and — most important — safely, you need a pair of dedicated tennis shoes.

The different types of models

Just as with racquets, there are different types of shoes to suit different types of players. At the top of the tennis shoe pyramid sit the high-performance stability and support shoes. These are built to handle the most intense movement and take a beating in the process. They're loaded with support features and padding, which generally makes them heavier options. This also gives them a premium price tag, which can run around $150.

On the other end of the spectrum, you'll find lightweight and speed shoes. These generally don't have as many support features or as much cushioning to absorb shock. However, this keeps them trim and puts your foot lower to the court. This doesn't necessarily make you faster, but it can feel that way. They're also softer and more flexible, which can be more comfortable. The price is generally a little lower than the beefier stability shoes, but they still run upwards of $140.

In between these categories are shoes for more casual players. These lines are dressed down in terms of technology, with the focus on cushioning and comfort. They're still supportive enough for everyday play, and with price points hovering at $100 or less, they're the sensible choice for beginners.

Pay attention to the following features when picking out your tennis shoes:

» **Cut:** The cut is basically the width of the shoe. Most tennis shoes have a narrow, medium, or wide cut. A few models come in extra wide, but there's generally no variability in a particular shoe. It's important to find one with a cut that suits your foot. Otherwise, it won't fit well and cause issues when playing.

» **Cushioning:** Because tennis is a stop-and-start sport, often played on hard surfaces, good cushioning is a must in a tennis shoe. When you run in your shoes, your feet should get a soft landing when they hit the ground — rather than a thud.

» **Supportive upper:** The upper is the top part of the shoe that houses the tongue and laces. It's generally made of a combination of synthetic materials that bring varying levels of breathability, durability, and support. Ideally, you want something that flexes comfortably when you move but still provides enough toughness to feel stable.

» **A rugged outsole:** The bottoms of tennis shoes have distinct tread patterns. They're designed to have some give so that when you're moving quickly and you need to slam on the brakes, your foot slides a little bit and doesn't get stuck on the court. This prevents a dangerous tumble. This give is balanced with better grip when using short, choppy steps to get in position to hit the ball. The high-wear areas of the outsole often have a wider tread for greater durability. Some models come with a six-month outsole warranty, which is useful if you'll be playing often on hard courts.

Many private clubs, and most public or private clay-court facilities, require that you wear a shoe with a smooth outsole. Running or cross-training shoes often have ridged or lug soles featuring bumps that stand out from the sole. This type of sole can tear up clay.

» **A protected toe cap:** Many players drag their toes either when they serve the ball or as they hit their strokes. This can burn a hole on the shoe right by the big toe. A sturdy toe cap, which is beefed up rubber covering the toe of the shoe, will help minimize the damage.

» **A midsole shank:** The midsole is the area of the shoe in between the upper and the outsole. There's generally a bed of cushioning along with some sort of support shank or plate. This piece is made of a firm material, such as thermoplastic polyurethane (TPU), and serves as the shoe's "backbone" during movement.

All-surface versus clay-court outsoles

Most shoes come with all-surface outsoles. This means the tread pattern is versatile enough to be used on any court. If you're going to be splitting time between hard and clay courts, this type of outsole will do the trick. (If you happen to play on grass courts — a real rarity — there are outsoles with little "nubs" specifically for use on grass).

However, if you're going to be spending most of your time on clay courts, it's a good idea to get a shoe with a clay-court outsole. Some shoe models are offered in both all-surface and clay-court options. The clay-court outsoles typically have a tight, herringbone pattern that isn't as thick or heavy as an outsole that's designed to weather the abrasion of a hard court. The pattern allows the clay to channel through its grooves so it doesn't get caked on the outsole. This leads to more assured footing on the slippery surface. In some instances, clay-court shoes can have additional material or a tighter weave in its upper to prevent clay from getting inside the shoe. Otherwise, the build of the shoe is exactly like the all-surface version.

REMEMBER

The most overlooked and potentially important items of clothing are your socks. You just can't beat high-quality socks made of moisture-wicking performance fabrics that have added cushioning at the toe and heel. I wore two pair of socks whenever I played tennis — until I had orthotics made and could no longer fit the extra socks into my shoes. (You can read more about orthotics in Chapter 17.)

Tennis Balls: Fuzzy, Yellow, and Short-Lived

Once upon a time, you bought balls in a metal can (three per can) that you opened with a key, like a tin of sardines. You were lucky if you didn't inadvertently slice your finger open on the sharp metal edges and end up in the emergency room of a hospital instead of on the tennis court. Similarly, particularly in Europe, balls also used to come in boxes. Today, most tennis balls come in pop-top, recyclable plastic cans. Three balls to a can is still customary in the United States, and four-ball cans are more prevalent in Europe and Australia. The extra ball is a popular option for doubles.

The anatomy of a tennis ball

The generic, regulation tennis ball is about 2½ inches in diameter and 2 ounces in weight. It's made from natural rubber, pressurized air, and a wool/nylon covering called the *nap*. The only exception to these "ingredients" is the absence of pressurized air in the *pressureless ball* that was once used commonly in Europe. (Pressureless balls still have a small place in the game today, which I discuss in the nearby sidebar.)

EVERYONE LOVES OPENING A NEW CAN OF BALLS

Tennis balls are packed under 11 to 14 pounds of pressure, which is why the can makes that loud *Psshhhhh* sound when you open it. Opening a new can of balls, you notice a distinct smell, much as you do when you open a can of fresh coffee. In fact, that pleasant "new ball" smell is one of my favorite things about tennis. I think dogs love the smell, too, which is why they're also crazy about tennis balls.

In addition to the name and logo of the manufacturer, each ball is also imprinted with a number, usually between 1 and 4. At a multicourt facility, balls from one court invariably end up rolling onto other courts. The numbers on the balls give you a way to tell which balls belong to whom. For example, if you're using Wilson 3s and you pick up a Wilson 4, you know that it belongs to another court. (See Chapter 6 for the proper etiquette on retrieving balls from another court.)

The nap

The nap, a mixture of loomed wool and nylon, adds air resistance — if tennis balls didn't have that fuzzy nap, they would fly through the air like BBs, and the game would become impossibly fast. And when the ball bounces, the friction between the nap and the court surface affects the speed and height of the bounce. It also allows the racquet's strings to grab the ball for more control.

The thickness of a ball's nap makes it more suitable for some surfaces than others. You get the two following choices when it comes to the ball's nap:

>> **Regular-duty:** Regular-duty balls are better on clay and softer indoor surfaces — the nap (which is more tightly woven on regular-duty balls) doesn't fluff up as much as it does on extra-duty balls.

>> **Extra-duty:** The thicker nap of extra-duty balls are better for hard courts, where regular-duty balls go bald more quickly.

MAC SAYS

If you have to make do with just one type of ball for all purposes, I recommend regular-duty. Unless you're playing on a pure cement hard court, the nap will be sturdy enough, whereas clay can get caught in and weigh down extra-duty balls, causing them to be more difficult to play with.

Air pressure

The more air pressure a ball contains, the more *lively* the ball is — or the more it will fly. It's just like when you blow up a balloon and then suddenly let it go, allowing the air to escape. The more air that you breathed into the balloon, the more wildly and quickly it zooms around before falling to the ground. Relax — you don't have to blow air into your tennis balls. They come with the air already inside. Instead, you apply force with your racquet. When a ball has a lot of air pressure, it takes less force to make it fly farther and faster. Such lively balls are more difficult to control.

The real-life differences in the interior air pressure of new tennis balls are minimal from manufacturer to manufacturer because most balls conform to the International Tennis Federation (ITF) bounce requirements. But tennis balls lose their air pressure — in effect, go flat — in a relatively short period of time.

SHOWING THEIR TRUE COLORS

Until 1972, all tennis balls were white. Then research showed that a high-optic yellow is a more visible color, particularly on TV. Since then, the yellow ball has come to rule.

Playing with *dead balls,* or balls that have lost a lot of pressure, takes much of the fun out of playing. You won't improve your game, and you could even hurt your arm. Take it from a guy who's had several shoulder surgeries — it's no fun.

TIP

Use new balls as often as you can — every time you play, if you can afford the $3 to $5 investment. Try not to play with the same balls for more than three hours if you're reluctant to buy new ones every time you play. If your balls get wet, or you hit them over the fence and into the mud, you can wipe them clean or even throw them in the clothes dryer and then use them again, as long as they don't sit around for so long that they lose their pressure.

Dead balls are great for games of fetch with your dog. Don't have a pet? Try to donate them to a charity or recycle if possible. Some facilities even have recycling bins courtside. If you throw them in the trash, they'll end up in a landfill, contributing tons of indecomposable waste. That's not the kind of tennis legacy you want to leave.

Which ball should you play?

The three major ball manufacturers — Wilson, Penn, and Dunlop — all make a premium ball (the Wilson U.S. Open, the Penn Tour, and the Dunlop ATP) and a second-line ball. The premium balls cost up to $2 more than the second-line balls, but all of them meet the minimum required standards for tennis balls. Other brands make balls as well, but they're not as prevalent.

To most players, the difference between the balls offered by different companies is negligible at best, as is the difference between the premium label and the second-tier ball. Use them and save a lot of money until the day comes (if it comes) when you notice a difference and develop a preference for a premium ball.

TIP

Instead of concentrating on brand names, try using the balls designed for the court you're playing on — regular-duty for clay, synthetic surfaces, and grass (if you're lucky), and extra-duty for hard courts.

Dressing for (Tennis) Success

MAC SAYS

Tennis attire has more or less morphed into gym attire. So, you don't need a separate wardrobe of tennis dresses, skirts, and polos. Those are still clothing staples, and there are no shortage of options to become a tennis fashionista. But wearing basic workout gear is perfectly acceptable in most situations. If you prefer to play in a tank top and yoga tights, have at it.

That said, some private clubs still enforce dress codes, such as all-white clothing. This guideline is frequently misunderstood as snobby (I suppose because many high-priced clubs require that you wear white), but it's based in practicality. Predominantly white or light-colored clothes actually makes sense for tennis because they reflect heat, so they're more comfortable to wear on hot, sunny days.

TIP

Beyond specific dress codes, you're pretty much on your own to find out what's comfortable for you. The following tips may help you when you're dressing for the court:

>> **Lightweight moisture-wicking performance fabrics can keep you drier and more comfortable.** I think pure cotton feels nicer, but it can soak up sweat, cling to your body, and weigh you down.

>> **Have at least one old-school tennis ensemble.** At some point in your tennis career, you'll probably encounter a facility with a dress code. It could require a collared shirt, or it could be all-whites. It pays to have a couple of pieces in your wardrobe that will suffice.

>> **Wear shorts with ball storage capabilities.** When you're serving, you'll need to have two balls handy — one for the first serve, and a second in case it's a fault (Chapter 11 addresses the serve in full detail). Putting the spare in your shorts, skirt, or tights is the most practical method.

>> **Carry sweats or some type of layering.** I've learned to always have some kind of sweatshirt or light jacket on hand to keep my shoulder and arm warm before I play — and during the cooldown period after I've played. It also comes in handy when there's a chill in the air.

Loading Up on Tennis Accessories

Like most sports, tennis is awash with accessories, gadgets, instructional aids, and other novelties. Some are just for fun — like a mini tennis racquet bottle opener — but others are actually useful and even vital, including the following:

>> **Hats:** Dealing with the sun is a constant issue in tennis, both for ease of play and for skin protection. The most practical and popular hat these days is the ubiquitous baseball cap. White is the best color because it reflects heat, but the underside of the brim should be a neutral or dark color like green to minimize reflected glare. Hats made of polyester-based performance fabrics dry faster and are easier to clean.

>> **Sunscreen:** The dangers of skin cancer from frequent, prolonged exposure to a strong sun are well documented. Always use sunscreen, even if it isn't very

bright or hot. Your complexion and the time you spend outdoors should determine the sun protection factor (SPF) that you choose, but generally the higher, the better. And try to find a sunscreen designed for sports — they're less likely to run into and sting your eyes when you start sweating.

>> **Sunglasses:** Lightweight sunglasses designed for active sports can provide relief from glare, as well as protect your eyes from harsh UV sunlight. The latest models often have antifog lenses, but you should keep a cloth handy if perspiration gets on them. But remember — if you get used to wearing sunglasses, you need to readjust when you aren't wearing them.

>> **Sweatbands:** Wristbands (and if you have long hair — headbands) are really helpful. Nothing is more distracting than out-of-control perspiration that makes your racquet handle slippery, stings your eyes, and causes wet hair to fly in your face.

>> **A towel:** It's amazing how many people ignore this basic accessory that comes in so handy. Just drape it over the net post, or jam it into the chain-link fence, and you'll be able to reach for it quickly to get instant relief from perspiration whenever you need it.

>> **Grip wraps:** Two kinds of grip wraps for your racquet are available: replacement grips and overgrips. *Replacement grips* can be swapped in for the stock grip on your racquet. They're reasonably priced ($5 to $20) and come in different types, such as absorbent, tacky, and cushioned. You can swap them in when your grip is worn down, or if you want to give the handle a different feel. On the other hand, you can wind *overgrips* on top of the racquet grip. Overgrips also come in different textures and serve mostly to absorb perspiration, but they're useful to build up a grip that's too small. Overwraps are commonly sold in multipacks; you should change them when they start showing wear and stop absorbing sweat.

>> **Racquet bags:** These bags run the gamut from the basic backpack to elaborate over-the-shoulder movable lockers. They're designed to carry anywhere from 2 to 15 racquets, and they include various compartments and pockets for storing clothes, drinks, valuables, and so on.

>> **Vibration dampeners:** Have you ever noticed the little rubber doodad that some players stick between a cross string and main string down near the throat of the racquet? That's called a *vibration dampener*. It's actually too small to soak up any of the vibration created at impact, so it won't protect your arm. But it does change the sound of the strings and the feel of the ball when you hit. The sensation can make you feel like you're hitting the ball more solidly.

TIP

Andre Agassi used a plain old rubber band, tied into the strings, as a vibration dampener. If it was good enough for Agassi. . . .

Chapter **4**

Scoring in Tennis: Love Means Nothing

T he scoring system in tennis baffles many people. I've lost count of the people who ask me things like "Hey, how come you get 15 points for winning just one point (the first point)?" And the use of the word *love* as a synonym for *zero* has left countless people scratching their heads and has even spawned its share of puns and T-shirts.

Actually, the tennis scoring system is not very difficult — it's just the terminology of scoring that confuses some people. Think of knowing tennis-speak as being proficient in a unique language.

In this chapter, you discover everything you need to know about tennis scoring.

The Anatomy of a Match

You can have a lot of fun just hitting a tennis ball around, either for the exercise or as a way to practice the game. But if you actually want to play and compete, you have to be familiar with the traditional scoring system and terminology.

A tennis *match,* either between two players (singles) or four players (doubles), is composed of the following three scoring units:

>> **Points:** You win a point by being the player who keeps the ball in play the longest.

>> **Games:** You must win at least four points to win a game. If both players win three points apiece, then you play until one of you wins two points in a row starting from the deuce court. A deuce game always ends after a point in the advantage (or ad) court.

>> **Sets:** The first player to win at least six games with a lead of two games over the opponent wins the set. A match is typically played best out of three sets (some professional events are best out of five).

If you want to keep score, don't think that you need to play a complete match. You can just play points, games, or a single set. In fact, serious players don't always like to play full, standard matches — they represent a more competitive level of play that isn't always appropriate for practice or just a fun workout.

Winning Points

You win a game by winning more points than your opponent. Every point starts with one player serving the ball to put it into play and the other player receiving. If the serve clears the net and lands in the service area and the receiver doesn't even touch the serve with their racquet, the server has hit an *ace* and wins the point automatically. (See Chapter 11 for more on serving and aces.)

If the serve lands in the service area and the receiver returns the serve, the point continues, with the players hitting the ball over the net, until one of the following happens:

>> **The ball fails to clear the net.** If your shot doesn't make it over the net, you lose the point.

>> **The ball clears the net but lands outside the boundary lines.** If your shot lands outside the sidelines or the baseline, you lose the point. (See Chapter 2 for more information on the lines that define the court.)

>> **The ball clears the net and lands inside the boundary lines, but the other player can't return it successfully before the ball bounces a second time.** If your shot lands in the legal playing space but your opponent can't make it to the ball before it bounces twice, you win the point. If the ball bounces in the court and then hits the back fence before your opponent can hit it — say, on a deep lob — that would count as the second bounce.

Scoring Games

The first player to win four points, with a margin of two points, wins the game. I know, it sounds easy — but it's getting that two-point margin that often complicates matters.

Scoring points

Instead of keeping score logically (say, by counting "zero, one, two, three, four," and so on), tennis uses the following terminology to keep track of how many points the players win in a game:

>> **Love:** At the start of a game, you both have love — or zero.

>> **15:** After you win one point, your score is 15. For example, if you serve and win the first point, the score of the game is 15-love (which is the same as 1-0).

REMEMBER

It's customary and a darned good idea to announce the score after every point, just to avoid any potential controversy. But unlike the pros, you likely won't have an umpire sitting in a high chair to do that for you. In that case, it's up to the server to call out the score after every point. At the tennis academy I run with my brothers in New York, we teach our kids that it's always a good habit to call out the score. Even at high-level junior tennis and league tennis tournaments there may be roving umpires but rarely anyone to call out the score.

The server's score is always given first. So, if you serve and win the first point, you call out, "Fifteen love." But if you serve and then lose the point, you say, "Love 15." Don't call the score out the moment the point ends. Walk back to the baseline, get ready to serve, and then call out the score right before you start to serve to begin the next point. This all part of proper *tennis etiquette*.

TIP

When you call out the score, you say, "Love 15" or "Fifteen love," not "Love to 15." You may come across some experienced players who will abbreviate this point as *five* when announcing the score.

>> **30:** After you win a second point, your score is 30. For example, if you serve and win both the first and second points, the score of the game is 30-love.

If, at some point in the game, both players have won the same number of points, you get to abbreviate the score by using the collective word *all.* For example, if you win the first point, but your opponent wins the second point, the score is 15-all. If you both have two points, the score is 30-all. No one ever says 15-15 or 30-30. You get the picture.

>> **40:** After you win a third point, your score is 40. For example, if you serve and win the first, second, and third points, the score of the game is 40-love. (See "That darned deuce," later in this chapter, to find out what to do if both you and your opponent get to 40 and neither of you can reach that margin of two points.)

>> **Game:** After you win the fourth point (with a margin of two points), you win the game. For example, if you win the first, second, third, and fourth points (and your opponent wins no points), the score of the game is game-love, but you don't have to call that out. If you've kept track of the score, you both know that the game is over after the last point. Instead, call out the set score, like "Four one, chump!" Actually, better leave out that last word — it's bad sportsmanship.

TIP

Whenever a player needs to win only one more point to take the game, that next point is also called a *game point.* If the player is one point from winning the set or match, that point is known as *set point* or *match point,* respectively. But that's just standard tennis lingo — you don't call it out as part of the score unless you're trying to irritate your opponent.

REMEMBER

After one player reaches game, the serve switches to the other player. (See Chapter 11 for more information on serving.)

That darned deuce

It's quite common that neither player can reach game with a two-point margin. If players are evenly matched, it can happen numerous times during a set. When both players' scores are 40-40, the score is called *deuce.*

Switching the scoring over to deuce (instead of continuing with numbers like 15, 30, and 40) makes it easier to keep track. *Remember:* Neither player has been able to win the game with the minimum number of points (four) by a margin of two. From this point on, the only way that either player can win is by taking two points in a row starting from the deuce court. The players can take turns winning points until the cows come home, but nobody wins the game without achieving that margin of two.

Because deuce games can pile up and extend match times, no-ad scoring (see "No-ad scoring," later in this chapter) is becoming more prevalent in tennis. Basically after you get to deuce, you play one point to decide the game. Certain levels of college tennis and International Tennis Federation (ITF) circuit tournaments have adopted no-ad scoring in order to shorten matches.

The player who wins the deuce point is said to have the *advantage.* If that same player wins the advantage point, they win the game. However, if the player who lost the deuce point manages to win the advantage point, the score goes back to deuce. Rinse and repeat until someone gets the two-point margin.

TIP

The common way to announce the advantage is to say, "Ad-in" or "Ad-out." If the server (who also does the job of announcing the score) wins the deuce point, it's ad-in. If the receiver wins the point, though, it's ad-out. Just saying "My ad" or "Your ad" (depending on who won the point) is also a common practice. But no one ever says the full word *advantage* when announcing the score.

If the player with the advantage wins the very next point, it's game. But if the player with the advantage *loses* the point, it's right back to deuce. All bets are off again. Neither player can win the game on the next point when the score is deuce (as a player can if they have the advantage).

When you're serving and the score is ad-out, meaning that your opponent has the advantage, you can win the game by winning the next three points in a row. You need one point to get back to deuce, another to get you the advantage, and then the game point. In other words, you really have your work cut out for you.

TAKING DEUCES TO DIZZYING LENGTHS

It may occur to you that a single game can go on forever, as long as nobody wins two points in a row. A tennis game *could* go on forever — although one player eventually triumphs, either because one player guts it out, or the other player can't take the monotony.

No official record exists for the highest number of deuces in a game, but history has been peppered by some very famous deuce games. For example, at a crucial stage in the Wimbledon men's singles final in 2023, Novak Djokovic and Carlos Alcaraz played a 26-minute game in which they traded 13 deuces over 32 points. You can win an entire set with fewer than 32 points!

Scoring Sets

The purpose of accumulating games is to win *sets*. To win a set, you must win six games by a margin of two. (The purpose of winning sets is to win the *match*, which you can read more about in "Scoring Matches," later in this chapter.)

For example, you win the set if the set score reaches 6-0, 6-4, or 7-5. In all three cases, you've won the set with a minimum of six games and a margin of two.

In order to get a margin of two games in a set, you need to win at least one of the games that your opponent serves in the set. When you win your service game, you *hold serve*. When you win a game served by your opponent, you *break serve* — that's how you get a margin of two. (Read "The heartbreaking tiebreaker" in this chapter to find out what happens when neither player can get that two-game margin.)

TIP

Follow these tips for calling out the set score consistently every time you need to (that is, every time you serve):

>> Call out the set score right before you begin to serve any game, as in, "It's four one." You can also say, "Four to one," or just like the game score, "Four one."

>> Make sure that you call out the score loudly enough for your opponent to hear, and insist that they do the same. This habit can help prevent a scoring controversy.

>> At the end of a set, you can call the set score, as in "Six four," or just say, "That's set."

TENNIS PLAYERS LOVE BAGELS

Most of us who play tennis have a fondness for our esoteric tennis terminology. In fact, not only do we grow to love it, but we keep adding to it.

In 1972, the popular pro Eddie Dibbs made his contribution when he described winning a set by the score of 6-0 as a "bagel job." Since then, *bagel* has become the shorthand term for a love set score. You can use it as a verb: "I bageled them in the first set." Or as a noun: "We rolled a bagel." The *double bagel* — a 6-0, 6-0 score — is the ultimate sign of dominance.

Sometimes neither you nor your opponent can win six games with a margin of two games. When you get to that point (six games all), you play a special kind of game, called a *tiebreaker*, to keep the set from going on forever. Think of tiebreakers as choosing to play sudden death after both players win six games, instead of trudging through endless overtime periods.

In the tiebreaker, you play a series of points; the first player to win seven points by a margin of two wins the tiebreaker. For example, you have won the tiebreaker if your point score reaches any of the following: 7-0, 7-5, 13-11, or 29-27.

You call out the score in tiebreakers just as in a regular game. Before each point, the player serving calls out their score first, followed by their opponent's. As in "Four two," to indicate that you're ahead or "Two four" if you're behind.

When the time comes, follow these steps to play the tiebreaker:

1. **The player due to serve the 13th game serves the first point, into their opponent's deuce court.**

2. **After the first point, the serve goes over to the other player, who serves the next two points, serving first into the ad court and then into the deuce court.**

3. **After the third point, the players alternate, serving two points each — always beginning with the ad court. Basically you switch serving every odd point.**

4. **After the first six points are played, no matter what the score is, the players change ends, and continue to do so after every other six-point span. In other words, when the total amount of points equals 6, 12, 18, and so on. This continues until one player wins at least seven points with a margin of two points.**

The player who served first to start the tiebreaker, receives the first game of the new set following the tiebreaker.

WARNING

If you lose just one of your service points in a tiebreaker, the other player needs only to make sure that they win all the points they serve and that's it — you're toast. So, remember, if you lose a service point in a tiebreaker, it's especially important to try to strike back and win a point that your opponent serves before your luck — and time — run out!

When the serving player loses the game, it's termed a *service break*. Losing a single service point in a tiebreaker is often called a *mini-break*. That's because each point in a tiebreaker is so important.

THE TIEBREAKER TO END ALL TIEBREAKERS

The most famous tiebreaker of all probably was the one that my brother John and his rival Björn Borg played in the 1980 Wimbledon finals.

Borg was gunning for five straight Wimbledon titles. At one point in the match, Borg led by two sets to one. With a service break at 5-4, all Borg had to do was win his service game to take the championship. In the ensuing game, Borg led 40-15, giving him two match points — two championship points. But John won those two points and broke Borg's serve. Then, after each man held serve, they played the tiebreaker.

That 'breaker lasted 22 minutes. In the game, Borg had five match/championship points. John had seven set points. John finally won on the 34th point of the tiebreaker — Borg missed a tough shot, and John won the set.

It was all for naught for John, though. Borg won the fifth set, and the title.

TIP

One of the more notable recent changes in Grand Slam tournaments is the standardizing of the final-set format. For quite some time, only the U.S. Open used a tiebreak to break a 6-6 game score to finish the match in the final set. The other three tournaments stuck with a deuce set in which a player needed a two-game margin in order to win. In an effort to curb the length of matches, the Australian Open and Wimbledon eventually broke from that format and briefly experimented with different final-set tiebreaker scenarios. So, at one point, all four slams had alternate ending possibilities. It was confusing even for ardent tennis fans. The governing bodies that run the Grand Slams soon recognized this and decided on uniformity. In 2022, they agreed that final sets of slams will be decided by a ten-point *match tiebreak*. It's the exact same format as the standard tiebreak, only the winning score is to ten points with a margin of at least two points. (See Chapter 20 for more information about Grand Slam events.)

Scoring Matches

Depending on the kind of match you play, you may need to win a different number of sets in order to bag the entire match.

The best-of-three sets

The *best-of-three sets* is by far the most common match format, at every level of the game. As a recreational player, this is the longest type of match you will ever play. The name is slightly deceiving, because you don't have to play three sets — the first player to win two sets is the winner.

A best-of-three sets match can end in one of three ways:

>> **One player wins the first and second sets.** For example, if you win the first two sets 6-0, 6-4, you've got the match.

>> **Each player wins one set, necessitating a third set to break the tie.** For example, if you win the first set 6-0 and your opponent wins the second set 6-4, you get to play a third, decisive set.

TIP

Instead of playing out a full third set, many leagues and tournaments use a ten-point tiebreak instead. This is a tiebreaker played first player to ten points with a two-point lead. It saves time if you're in a tournament or you need to play multiple matches in a day. It's also a real test of nerves.

The best-of-five sets

In the *best-of-five sets* format, the first player to take three sets wins the match. A match like this can be over after as few as three straight sets or as many as five sets, which can make for some long, long matches. (The pro record for the longest best-of-five match is 11 hours and 5 minutes, set by John Isner and Nicolas Mahut in the first round of Wimbledon in 2010. It had to be played over three days and the final-set score was 70-68! It was sheer madness. If you want to know why all the slams agreed to institute a final-set tiebreak, this match is Exhibit A.)

The best-of-five format is now used exclusively in the men's Grand Slam singles tournaments. The Davis Cup competition and the final match of some big tournaments, like the ATP Tour World Championships, used to also be best-of-five sets. (Chapter 20 tells you all about these exciting events in tennis.) However, the pro game has gotten so physical and demanding, it's just too tough on the players to use outside of the majors. Plus, some five-setters can take up to five hours, which can be a nightmare for tournament and TV scheduling.

Alternative Scoring Systems

Lots of people play tennis, for all kinds of reasons, with varying degrees of competitiveness. In some play (such as charity events or practice), you just don't want to have long matches. Name a need, and there's a scoring system to meet it.

Alternative scoring systems have a great advantage for beginners, too. If you aren't in great shape or you don't have the time to play a best-of-three match, you can have a quicker match with one of the alternative scoring systems and still get the spice of competition into your tennis.

In this section, I tell you about a few alternative scoring systems that you're most likely to run into.

No-ad scoring

Many colleges, high schools, junior tournaments, and leagues use streamlined *no-ad scoring*, with numerical scoring. You count 0, 1, 2, 3, and 4, allotting one point per point. If the score in any game reaches three points all, a single sudden-death point is played for the game. The returner gets to choose which side the opponent serves to in that three-all, sudden-death situation. No-ad scoring offers no deuce or advantage points.

At six-all in the set, you play a standard tiebreaker to decide the set (see "The heartbreaking tiebreaker," earlier in this chapter, for more information).

Some players believe that no-ad scoring makes them concentrate better, because those three-all points are awfully important. It also adds elements of strategy — which side the returner chooses to receive — and drama. One thing is for sure: No-ad tennis matches are a lot faster than deuce tennis, which really suits team competitions and other formats in which time is of the essence.

The pro set

If you want to play a quick, competitive mini-match, the *pro set* is your ticket. The pro set consists of only a single set in which you must win eight or ten games by a margin of two (instead of six games, as in a conventional set). If the score reaches eight-all or ten-all, you play a conventional tiebreaker to determine the outcome.

The fast set

This format is popular in professional exhibitions, 10 and Under (10U) tennis, and occasionally in junior tournaments when rain delays hamper the schedule. The set is played to just four games with no-ad scoring. A tiebreak is played at 3-3. With fewer games and no-ad scoring, the importance of each point is elevated. Because the sets go so quickly, best-of-five sets can even be used. The Next Gen ATP Finals, which pits eight of the top 21-and-under male players in a round-robin format, uses fast sets.

Reading Line Scores

TIP

When you watch tennis matches on TV, the umpire tracks the score on a scoreboard. That's the thing that usually flashes on the screen before going to a commercial.

The scoreboard breaks down a match by sets and games. Each column of numbers represents a set, telling you how many games each player won in that set.

If the scoreboard shows only two columns, the match was over in two sets, or *straight sets.* For example, on a good day, my ESPN colleague Brad Gilbert could beat me straight sets with a score like the following (but only if BG didn't stay up too late the night before drinking his beloved Bud Ice):

Player	Set 1	Set 2	Set 3
Gilbert	7	6	
McEnroe	5	4	

Or I might put up a better fight and win the match in three sets, like this:

Player	Set 1	Set 2	Set 3
Gilbert	6	6	4
McEnroe	3	7	6

We *split* the first two sets, winning one each. You may notice that the second set ended 7-6. This score indicates that the set was decided by a tiebreaker.

If I were playing in a Grand Slam event, all of which use the best-of-five format, against Brad, the scoreboard would look a little more like this:

Player	Set 1	Set 2	Set 3	Set 4	Set 5
McEnroe	7 (11)	6	4	5	6
Gilbert	6	4	6	7	0

See that number 11 in parentheses after my score in the first set? That number tells you the score in the tiebreaker, which was 13-11. Line scores often show only the lower score of the tiebreaker, because you can always figure out the precise score by simply adding two points to the number that appears in parentheses. The tiebreaker score appears this way because if the winner took the match with the minimum number of points, 7, you wouldn't know whether he won the tiebreaker easily (as in 7-0) or by a close score (as in 7-5).

I won the next set a little more easily, 6-4. I then lost the next two sets, which forced a fifth and final set. I breezed through it 6-0, just to show BG who's boss.

IN THIS CHAPTER

» Serving and receiving by the rules

» Knowing when to switch ends of the court

» Calling a ball out

» Getting clear on how you may lose the point

» Calling a let not related to serving

» Knowing the rules of doubles tennis

Chapter **5**

Rules and Regulations

Would you believe me if I told you that the rules and regulations of tennis actually make the game more fun? Well, it's true. Knowing what to do, and how and when to do it, helps you feel like you're really getting into the game. It gives you a sense of the history, tradition and style of tennis.

Servin' 'Em Up

In singles, play begins when either you or your opponent serves. (Check out "Discovering Doubles Rules," later in this chapter, for information on serving in doubles.) At the end of each game, the serve goes over to the other player for the next game. The serve alternates between players in this fashion until the end of the match; a tiebreaker represents the only exception to this serving rule. (Chapter 4 tells you all about serving and playing tiebreakers.)

Deciding who serves first

You determine who serves first by using a convention called the *spin*, which you can do in one of two ways:

>> **Spinning the racquet:** Racquets usually have the logo of the manufacturer printed on the bottom of the *butt cap*. (See Chapter 3 to find out more about the parts of a racquet.) You can view the logo right-side up or upside down. (For example, Wilson racquets have a *W* on the butt cap, which you can read as a *W* or as an *M,* depending on which way you look at the letter.) Spin the racquet, and then ask the other player to call out "Up!" or "Down!" If they correctly call out the way the logo falls, they get to choose whether to serve first or receive.

>> **Tossing a coin:** One player tosses the coin, and the other player calls out "Heads!" or "Tails!" The player who wins the toss gets to choose whether to serve first or receive. This is the more formal approach; it's generally only done in tournaments with an umpire.

Stick with the racquet spin. If neither you nor your playing partner has a racquet with an appropriate butt cap, settle it the schoolyard way: Rock Paper Scissors.

TIP

If you win the spin, knowing your opponent's game can help you decide what to do next. If you haven't played against your opponent before (so you don't know their strengths and weaknesses), make sure that you warm up with them before the spin. (Chapter 17 gives you the full scoop on warming up.)

If you win the spin, you can do one of the following:

>> **Serve first.** Serving is generally an advantage, and winning the first game puts your opponent in an immediate hole. Plus, if you keep winning your serve, your opponent will always be playing catchup on the scoreboard. However, if you lack confidence in your serve, or you're really good at returning, you can choose for your opponent to serve first.

>> **Receive the serve.** If you know that your opponent doesn't have a strong serve, breaking their serve first thing in the match can put a little pressure on them. Also, receiving first allows you to warm up and get in the flow of the game before you serve. Lastly, if you're playing someone with a terrific serve, you may have your best chance to break in the first game, before your opponent is fully warmed up.

>> **Instead of serving or receiving, choose the side of the court.** If there's a bright sun or a steady wind, you may want to choose the end of the court where you feel most comfortable in the opening game. Or you can also choose to take the tougher side. You'll be changing ends after the first game,

so your opponent will have to play two games under tough conditions at the very start of the match, while you only play one. But don't get too psyched, because you'll have plenty of chances to screw up on the tougher side — you change ends after every odd-numbered game (see "Trading Ends of the Court," later in this chapter).

>> **Defer to your opponent.** Turning the choice over to your opponent can be a good idea if you want to get them off-balance and wondering, right off the bat. It's also a good idea if *you're* off-balance and wondering. If you're really confused about what to do, this decision sure takes the burden of responsibility off your shoulders.

After you make your choice, your opponent can then choose one of the other options. For example, if you elect to receive, your partner can choose from which end they want to serve first; if you choose to take a certain end, your partner can choose to either serve or receive.

Choosing sides

After you and your opponent take the appropriate ends of the court, play begins. The first point of each game begins on the deuce side of the court for both players. The next point begins on the ad court. (See Chapter 2 for more information on the layout of the court.) When you serve the ball, it's directed diagonally from your deuce or ad court, to your opponent's deuce or ad court service box.

Getting the point started

Each point starts with a serve. The player serving stands behind the baseline on one side of the court and tries to hit the ball into the service box on the opposite side. For instance, on the first point of a game, the server hits the ball from the deuce side of their court and aims the shot at the deuce box of their opponent. (Chapter 11 goes into more detail about hitting the serve.)

TIP

FINDING YOURSELF ON THE WRONG SIDE OF THE COURT

When facing the net, the right-side service box is called the *deuce court* because all deuce points are served into that side — it's mathematically written into stone. If you catch yourself serving into the wrong box and you aren't sure why, you let the score stand as is and move over so you can serve into the correct court.

In the best-case scenario, you step up to the line and pop in an *ace*. Aces are serves that are so fast, well placed, or both, that your opponent can't even touch the ball with their racquet. End of point.

You can serve an ace on either the first or second serve. But most second-serve aces are the result of unintentionally great serves. The main objective of the second serve is to get the ball in play in order to avoid double-faulting and losing the point.

Avoiding foot faults

Tennis has very strict rules about where you can stand when you serve. Otherwise, you could stand right in front of the net, serving straight down into your opponent's court.

The following rules govern where and how you serve on both the deuce and ad sides:

TIP

>> In singles, you can line up to serve anywhere between the centerline on the baseline (on the correct side, of course) and the singles sideline of the court. For a serve in doubles, you can stand anywhere from the centerline to the doubles sideline. (See "Discovering Doubles Rules," later in this chapter, for more about doubles rules.)

Most players in singles tend to serve close to the center mark, because this position enables better court coverage after the return.

>> You can stand as far behind the baseline as you want when you serve.

>> You can't take a walking or running start, like a javelin thrower.

>> Your foot can't touch the centerline at any point during your service motion. In fact, you can't even swing your leg in the air over the line.

>> You can't touch the baseline with any part of your foot or step inside the court until after you hit the serve. You often see pros land inside the baseline after they serve, but when they make contact with the ball, their feet are actually off the court and in the air.

WARNING

Breaking any of the preceding rules results in the dreaded *foot fault*, meaning that your serve automatically becomes invalid. If you foot fault on your first serve, you can use your second serve to give it another try. If you foot fault on your second serve, you lose the whole point.

In professional tournaments, the line judges and umpire watch for foot faults and call them as soon as they happen. (See Chapter 19 for more information on professional play.) In most matches that you play, you and your opponent must "police" each other's feet. This can be tricky, because the last thing you want to do when receiving serve is concentrate on your opponent's feet rather than their shot.

TIP

Some recreational players, especially beginners, are chronic foot faulters. Don't allow it to irritate you or throw off your concentration. Most of the time, it's just an unfortunate bending of the rules by an inexperienced player with little effect on the ensuing point. However, if an opponent's blatant foot-faulting really bothers you, you're within your rights to stop play and bring it to their attention. Just do it nicely. You can say something like, "Your first serve is really strong today. Except sometimes your foot goes way inside the baseline before you hit it." Most players want to play within the rules and will look at this as constructive criticism. But if it continues to be a problem, ask a friend or bystander to provide an objective viewpoint by watching your opponent serve.

Avoiding faults and double faults

Tennis gives you two chances to make good on your serve; you always have two serves at the start of a point.

Sometimes, you step up to the line, your serve clears the net, and then it lands inside the correct service box. If so, you've successfully put the ball in play. Congratulations!

But if you mess up on the first serve — and you will, a fair amount of the time — it's called a *fault*, which means that your serve doesn't count. You have to try again with your second serve. Any of the following events constitutes a fault:

>> **You commit a foot fault.** No matter where the ball goes, if you commit a foot fault, the serve doesn't count (on either first or second serve). However, this rule is rarely enforced in social tennis.

>> **You miss the ball entirely.** Even if you don't make contact, if you swing, it's a fault. If you halt your swing because, say, you weren't happy with your toss, you get a *do-over,* meaning that you can serve again without using up your serve.

>> **Your serve fails to clear the net.** Serves can go funny places if you don't hit them properly, and the net gobbles up many of them.

>> **Your serve clears the net but lands outside the boundary lines of the correct service box in your opponent's court.** These serves usually land beyond the service line, or outside either of the sidelines. They can be very close, but close means no cigar in tennis.

>> **Your serve *ticks* (or hits) the net and lands outside the boundary of the correct service box.** Whether the ball drops in is just a matter of fate. (See the following "Calling lets during the serve" section to find out how to count a serve that ticks the net and lands *inside* the service box.)

If you miss your second serve as well, you've committed a *double fault.* When you double-fault you automatically lose the point before it even gets started.

MAC SAYS

Unfortunately, most players serve up their share of double faults — especially beginning players. Double faults aren't the end of the world, but they are a major bummer. When you hit a double fault, just put it behind you mentally and move on.

Calling lets during the serve

A serve that ticks the net, drops over, and lands inside the boundary of the correct service box is called a *let.* (See the preceding section to find out how to count a serve that lands outside the service box.)

You get a do-over when you serve a let, regardless of whether the let occurs on your first or second serve. However, if your second serve is a let, it doesn't wipe out your previous, first-serve fault. You still have only your second serve to hit again.

Your opponent is responsible for yelling "Let!" if your serve hits the net and lands in the service box. However, a let can be called when any of the following things happen during your serve:

>> **Your serve clips the net and hits your opponent without bouncing.** However, if you hit a *clean serve* (one that does not touch the net) that hits an opponent without bouncing, it's your point. It doesn't matter whether the ball was heading in or out. This is much more common in doubles when one of your opponents is typically positioned close to the net. (See "Discovering Doubles Rules," later in this chapter, for more information.)

>> **You serve, and the receiver isn't ready.** The returner must be ready to accept your serve, and they have the right to say they weren't. If you hit a serve when they're not ready, they can immediately call a let. You can consider your opponent ready to receive your serve if they stand in the ready position and look right at you. If you have any doubts about whether they're ready, just ask.

Receiving the Serve

The returner can stand anywhere they please, meaning anywhere on — or off — their entire half of the court. They can even go sit down on a courtside chair, although they'll probably get aced a lot.

TECHNICAL STUFF

They can even walk up into the service box to field the serve from really close to the net — but that's considered very unsporting and is frowned upon. Returning the serve from this position can also be really tough, so you may as well forget this ploy.

TIP

Most players receive near the baseline, at about the midway point between the center hash mark and the singles sideline of the service court in question. Players adjust their positions based on an understanding of their own game and their opponent's game. (Turn to Chapter 13 to read more about the various strategies involved with receiving.)

Trading Ends of the Court

Players change ends of the court to ensure that both players have to deal with the weather conditions on either end of the court, such as the sun or wind, or defects in the surface. Pros may also have to deal with loud, annoying people in the crowd — I've heard a few of them in my day — but it's not generally a concern for recreational players.

Each time the number of games played in a set adds up to an odd number, the players change ends of the court. For example, after the first game, the cumulative number of games played is one, so the players change ends. After the next game, the number of games totals up to two, so the players stay put. Then after the next game (now a total of three games), the players again change ends. During change-overs, players can take a quick break, towel off, and grab a drink.

If a set ends in an even number of games (say, 6-4), you don't change ends until after the first game of the next set.

Calling the Lines

If the ball lands on any of the court boundary lines, the shot is good, just as if the ball landed inside the court. (Chapter 2 outlines all the lines that define the court.) Only those balls that land completely outside the lines can be called *out*.

In professional play, either electronic line-calling or a whole host of linespersons call the lines. Most matches at lower levels don't have these benefits, leaving the person receiving the ball to make the calls. Of course, this rule leaves plenty of room for judgment and plenty of opportunity for abuse and plain old error. When your opponent repeatedly makes errors when calling the line, you can question their calls; turn to Chapter 6 for tips on how to do so.

Looking at Other Ways to Lose the Point

Besides double-faulting, letting a ball bounce twice before you hit it, or hitting the ball outside the boundaries, you can lose a point due to a number of other, and thankfully less common, factors.

Getting struck by or catching the ball

You lose the point if the ball hits you or anything attached to you — like your racquet, your clothes, or even your hair.

If the ball hits you, you should fess up and give your opponent the point (see Chapter 6 for more on tennis etiquette). If you think that your opponent was hit by your shot and they don't cop to it, ask them politely if they're mistaken — something along the lines of "Are you sure the ball didn't hit your hand?"

Strictly speaking, catching the ball before it bounces, no matter where the ball appears to be headed or where you're standing, causes you to lose the point. Never do so in a league match or tournament — a stickler for detail has the right to call you on your catch.

REMEMBER

Sometimes you can safely assume that your partner will have no issues with your catching a ball that's obviously out — it's a pretty common understanding among friends in casual games. But even in the friendliest of matches, you should avoid catching the ball before it bounces — unless it's going way, way out. Catching the ball can lead to disagreements, even among friends, so it's best to eliminate the practice.

Intentionally hitting the ball twice

You can't deliberately hit the ball with your racquet more than once (notice the use of the word *deliberately*). If, in the course of a normal swing, the ball happens to hit your racquet twice, it's okay. Play on!

Sometimes it's hard to judge a double hit. If the ball glances off a part of your racquet and you alter your swing in order to make contact again to successfully get it over the net, that's clearly a deliberate double hit. But if the ball strikes the frame and subsequently caroms into another part of the racquet during your normal swing and goes back over the net, that's an unintentional double hit.

Touching the net or your opponent's side of the court

You also lose the point if your racquet (whether it's in your hand or flying out of it), anything you wear, or any part of your body touches the net, net posts, or your opponent's court while the ball is in play.

You must also wait until the ball crosses the net before you return it — if you reach over to return the ball before it crosses the net, you lose the point.

However, if you hit the ball from your side of the court and, on your follow-through, the racquet crosses over the net and into your opponent's court, the ball remains in play — as long as you don't actually touch the net. Also, if a ball with crazy spin hits the court on your side and then bounces back over the net, you can reach over the net to hit it. (Chapter 7 tells you more about spin.)

But you can't, under any circumstances, touch the net with any part of your body or anything attached to it until the ball has bounced twice.

Hitting an obstruction

Your shot may hit a permanent court fixture such as a light, curtain, or water cooler. If that object stands outside the lines of the court, you lose the point — even if the ball caroms back into your opponent's court.

REMEMBER

The only exception to this rule is if the ball hits the net posts or any part of the net. A ball that bounces off the net (or net posts) and lands in your opponent's court is a good shot, and the ball remains in play.

Although the ball is supposed to go over the net, sometimes a shot pulls you way off the court on either side, and you still have a chance to return the ball. The ball can pass outside the net post, lower than the net, and if it lands inside your opponent's court, it's good. The ball is still in play.

Throwing the racquet at the ball

In an act of desperation, and probably a healthy dose of frustration, you may throw your racquet at a ball you know you have no chance of returning. Or, butterfingers, the racquet may fly out of your hands in the course of a normal swing. Chances are slim that your racquet will actually hit the ball and cause it to go over the net in a legal play. However, if the improbable comes to pass, you must relinquish the point.

MAC SAYS

Throwing your racquet at the ball is strictly illegal, whether on purpose or by accident. Throwing your racquet in a fit of anger after losing a point is simply bad form and can damage your equipment.

Stopping Play with a Let

In addition to calling a let when a serve clips the net, you can call a let and stop play in some other instances. Either player has the right to call a let; as soon as a player calls a let, the point starts over. The let call is like pressing the Pause button and rewinding to the start of the point.

You should call a let when any of the following things happen:

>> **A ball rolls onto your court.** A ball from a neighboring court may shoot across your court during a point. Some players choose to endure this annoyance (unless the ball rolls right under their feet), especially if it's a frequent occurrence. Either player can call a let in such cases, even if one player is willing to play on.

>> **Your shot hits a stray ball.** You may find yourself playing a point with a ball lying inside the boundaries of the court. This is usually the result of a first-serve fault into the net. (Some servers don't like to pick up loose balls between serves.)

It's extremely rare, but if a ball in play hits another ball lying inside the boundaries of the court, the ball is still in play. If the ball is returned successfully, play on. However, if you can't tell which ball bounced up and became live, you play a let.

>> **A distraction breaks the concentration of either player.** You toss the ball to serve and a car horn blares just as you're about to hit the ball. Or someone's unreasonably loud cell phone starts ringing while the ball is in play. If any of these sudden and unexpected distractions is too disruptive, you can play a let. Such a let is called an *interruption let.*

Discovering Doubles Rules

The rules for playing doubles differ from singles rules in a few important ways. First, the doubles court is larger, so the boundaries of legal play differ from those of a singles court. (See Chapter 2 for all the details on the playing area for doubles.) Beyond the court size, doubles offers a few other, more complicated rule differences.

Taking sides: Deuce versus ad

The members of a doubles team must choose to receive serve in either the deuce or the ad court. After choosing a side, each player returns serves from only that side of the court for the duration of the set. The returners can change the court in which each player receives at the start of each new set, but only then.

The receiving team can take up any positions on the court, as long as the person designated to return the serve actually makes the return. In other words, you can stand arm-in-arm with your partner while one of you is returning (if that's your idea of strategy).

TIP

The receiver usually stands along or just behind the baseline to return serve. The player not returning the serve often sets up along the service line in the other half of the court to be closer to the net. This is an advantageous position to pick off any weak shots by the serving team. It has also become increasingly common for both receiving players to start the point along the baseline, especially if they're more comfortable hitting groundstrokes.

Establishing a serving rotation

Just as players set their respective receiving positions, they also determine a serving order. Like singles, the teams take turns serving each game, observing a four-player rotation established at the start of each set. For example, say that Player A and Player B are playing against Player C and Player D. Players A and C decide to serve first for their respective teams. The serve then rotates in the following order: A, C, B, D, A, C, B, D, and so on.

TIP

Either member of a team can serve first. However, the smart strategy is to let the better server on the team serve first. If there isn't a marked difference between the servers, it's often best to have the more confident net player handle those duties to start the set, while their partner serves.

At the beginning of each new set, either player can serve the first game for their team — even if it breaks the rotation established in the previous set. For example, even if I serve the last game of the first set for my team, I can also serve the first game of the new set when it's our turn to serve again. The same holds true if we're playing a match tiebreaker instead of a full third or final set. The tiebreaker would constitute a new set; therefore, the same serving rotation rules apply.

Choosing a serving formation

The server in doubles needs to observe the same positioning rules as in singles pertaining to the centerline and the court into which they're serving. They can serve from anywhere behind the baseline on that half of the court. The server's playing partner generally stands in the other half of the court up close to the net in between the singles sideline and the center service line. If you extend your hitting arm, your racquet should just about touch the net. Better doubles teams often experiment with different formations, but this is the classic starting point.

TIP

In general, doubles servers stand farther from the center mark than they do in singles because they have a partner there to cover half the court. (See Chapter 13 for more on doubles strategy.)

Receiving the serve

After the designated server hits the serve into the appropriate box, and the designated returner puts it back in play, the point is on. Now any player can hit the ball. Only one player on a doubles team can hit a given ball on each of its trips over the net. For example, you and your partner may end up trying to hit the same ball; if both of your racquets hit it, you automatically lose the point. But you don't lose the point if your racquets collide and only one of them hits the ball.

You don't have to take turns hitting the ball. If one player chooses to cover the entire court and take every shot, that's okay (except when it comes to serving and returning). The players can also move around all over the court after the serve — there's no rules about keeping to your side of the court. In fact, a player can decide to take a seat after the serve. It's not illegal, just lousy teamwork.

Playing tiebreakers

The doubles tiebreaker follows the same format as in singles (which I explain in Chapter 4), except now all four players participate in the rotation. After one team serves the first point, the teams take turns serving two points each — essentially switching on all odd-numbered points — until one team wins the tiebreaker. They must observe the same serving order as in the previous portion of the set.

For example, in a tiebreaker between the team of Player A and Player B against Player C and Player D, the serving rotation would progress as shown in Table 5-1. (Players A and C have served first for their respective teams.)

That's it. Player C just hit an ace to end the tiebreaker, 7-4.

TABLE 5-1   ## Serve Rotation in a Doubles Tiebreaker

Point Number	Player
1	A
2	C
3	C
4	B
5	B
6	D
7	D
8	A
9	A
10	C
11	C

Chapter **6**

Tennis Etiquette

ennis etiquette provides guidelines of conduct that make playing the game easier, friendlier, and more fun. No matter at what level you play the game, following proper tennis etiquette reminds you to think of tennis as a game, rather than as a direct confrontation between individuals who have a lot of ego on the line. There's nothing wrong with being competitive, but it shouldn't come before good sportsmanship and decorum. *Remember:* In the end, playing tennis is about having fun and getting some exercise.

Respecting the Ball and Your Equipment

Knowing and following proper etiquette when you retrieve balls is a service you do for yourself and your opponent. By following a routine with the balls, you avoid interrupting the rhythm of the game with unnecessary delays.

TIP

Beginners spend more time picking up balls because they make more errors, play shorter points, and haven't figured out how to pick up balls efficiently. Just follow these general guidelines for retrieving balls, and you'll find yourself spending the minimum amount of time chasing them down:

>> **Retrieve the balls that end up on your own side of the net.** If you hit the ball into the net, it only seems fair that you have to retrieve the ball. At our academy in New York, we make sure that all the kids clean up any balls that go into the net. Mostly it's done for safety reasons — there are often multiple kids on every court — but it also makes them run a bit more and teaches them respect for other players.

>> **If you hit the ball to Mars, go get it yourself.** If you make a mess of a shot and it flies wildly outside the boundary of your court, go get the ball yourself, even if it's technically on your opponent's side of the net.

>> **Make sure that the server has two balls when needed.** If the server already has two balls, you can just hang onto the third ball. Keep it in your pocket or place it in a spot where it won't interfere with play. Or you can toss or hit the third ball across the net to the server, where they can keep it out of the way until called upon.

The server always needs to have at least two balls in their possession before starting a point; they may need to replace one in the event of a first-serve let (see Chapter 11 for the details on serving). But don't interrupt play to pick up the ball after a first-serve fault, unless:

- **The ball distracts the players.** This situation is a judgment call. Don't be shy about asking your opponent to pick up a ball if it's in a distracting or potentially dangerous place.

- **The ball poses the danger of injury.** The farther from the net that a ball is lying — say, around the service line — the greater the chance that you'll inadvertently step on it during the ensuing point and turn an ankle. Make your court a safer place by clearing away unwanted balls.

- **The server needs or requests the ball.** The server has the right to ask you for the extra ball. You may have to do some legwork, but don't complain about it. If anything, the added time may disrupt the server's rhythm and their chances of hitting a successful serve.

When the server hits a fault, you can let the ball go by, return it softly up to the net where it will be out of the way, or catch it and quickly put it somewhere where it won't interfere with the ensuing point.

When you return a ball across the net for the next point, try to alert your opponent it's on the way — saying something like "Heads!" — so as to not hit them by mistake. And don't launch it. Players sometimes get frustrated after losing a tough point in a tight match. It's tempting to slam a ball into the court, at a curtain, or across the net. Same with smacking your racquet against the court. I dive deeper into the problems with equipment abuse in a few pages, but just know it's a bad look that reflects poorly on you and negatively affects the spirit of the match.

TIP

If, for some reason, you can't quickly retrieve a ball after a first-serve fault, or if in doing so you cause an interruption (for example, you try to tap the ball to the back fence, but it rolls onto another court by mistake, and you have to retrieve it), start the entire point over. Tell the server, "Take two" — meaning "take two serves."

If the server hits a second-serve let and getting them another ball to hit takes an unusually long time (or constitutes an interruption), offer the server two new serves. In casual games or matches, the server may even turn down this generous offer because they didn't feel too put out. That's the kind of opponent you want to befriend.

REMEMBER

It's a good idea to keep constant track of all the balls. The best way to do this is by making sure the server has them before the start of every point. It may seem like a hassle to be so diligent, but it's easy for a ball to get lost under a bench, behind a curtain, or on a neighboring court.

Keeping Track of the Score

The server keeps track of the score. Generally, the server should call out the score just before serving the next point, just to avoid misunderstanding. Call the score loudly enough for your opponent to hear it. If your opponent isn't calling the score loudly enough, tell them politely to pump up the volume. If you're receiving serve, it's also perfectly acceptable to confirm the score with your opponent before the point begins. In junior tennis, we often see kids try to change score (in other words, cheat!), so it's very important for competitive players to call out the score to avoid this problem.

Inevitably, at some point, you'll get into a situation where you don't agree on the score. The server calls out, "40-30" and you may be tempted to say, "What?! It's 30-all!" Don't lose your cool like that. Just say, "Are you sure? I have it at 30-all." Most of the time, the error is just a slip of the tongue. But if your opponent insists, check which side they're set to serve — because the server has to alternate sides after every point, you can usually figure out who's right about the score.

If your opponent's position and the point count are in sync but you're still convinced that you're right, walk up to the net and tell your opponent in a friendly and calm manner, "I really think we've got the wrong score here." Then, with the help of your opponent, mentally replay the points from the last point played, if you can.

If you agree on the last two points but have different versions of how the point before them ended, make your cases but don't belabor the issue. At that point, you can suggest playing over from the last point you both agree on, starting over from deuce (if the controversy occurred at a higher score, like 40-30, or ad-in), or starting the game over. You can also accept the score if it turns out that you're no longer dead certain that you're right.

Making Those Delicate Line Calls

Tennis is one of the rare sports in which the players must officiate themselves. Determining whether a ball lands in bounds or out of bounds is — by far — the area of greatest potential controversy between opposing players. Mistakes will occur, trust me on that. You'll make some errors, and your opponent will make some errors when calling a ball in or out.

REMEMBER

Often, you may feel absolutely sure that your call is right, or that your opponent's call is wrong. Even when you're that convinced, keep two things in mind. First, your eyes can play tricks on you in competitive situations. Second, each player is the ultimate authority on their side of the net. If you feel that you were wronged, prove it by winning the next point. As it's often said in sports: The ball never lies.

Ninety-nine percent out is 100 percent in

TIP

When I competed, I had a motto: If I'm not sure of the call, the ball is in. A tennis match could never be that important that I would intentionally cheat. To avoid controversy over a call, keep the following tips in mind:

>> **Make your call instantly.** Nothing is worse than playing an opponent who hems and haws before making an "out" call. Hesitancy implies uncertainty. If you don't make the call instantly, you must play on.

Give your opponent the benefit of the doubt. Even if it appears that most of the ball was outside the line — balls leave distinct marks on clay courts in particular — touching just a sliver of the line means it was in.

>> **Make your call decisively.** Prefacing your out call with phrases like "I think," "I guess," or "I'm pretty sure" isn't fair to your opponent. You have an obligation to be firm with your out call. Even if you're correct, you'll give the impression that you're being a bit cagey.

>> **Make your call loudly.** You're making the call for the benefit of your opponent, who happens to be all the way on the other side of the net. However, don't overdo it — yelling the call could be construed as rubbing their face in it.

>> **Keep the call simple.** Just call, "Out!" when the ball lands beyond the boundaries. "No!," "Deep!," and "Long!" are acceptable alternatives. But don't ever call a ball "in" during a point, because it can be distracting. It's understood that your silence means it was good. And avoid injecting any commentary into your calls. Saying things like, "Sorry, you just missed," when they miss an easy shot is just pouring salt on a wound.

>> **Don't make calls on your opponent's side of the net.** Even if you think you're being generous by calling a let serve or an out ball on yourself, don't make the call. That's their job. There may be times when an opponent asks your opinion on a call because they didn't have a good view of it. When they ask you, you can certainly offer your assessment.

When you start playing regularly, you'll get hip to some of the sign language that often substitutes for verbal communication between experienced players. Here are the most common examples:

>> When a ball lands out, players often just raise their free arm and point an index finger in the air to indicate that the ball was long, or point to the left or right to indicate that it was out along the sideline.

>> When a ball lands just inside or on the line, players will hold their hand with the palm down facing the court to indicate the shot was in.

>> When returning serve, you can hold two fingers up, like the peace sign, to indicate that the server should take two serves because of an interruption or distraction.

>> When you aren't ready to receive the serve, just hold up your free arm in the common halt gesture.

When you question your opponent's calls

If you think that your opponent made a bad call, don't rush to judgment. If you feel that you were cheated, consciously or otherwise, file the potential bad call away under the heading *Accident.* Be prepared to accept one accident per set. Think of it as a strike one.

If you get another bad call soon after the first, politely but firmly say to your opponent, "Are you sure of the call?" That's strike two.

REMEMBER

Questioning a call politely sends the message that you won't be abused. Be aware of your opponent's reaction, but don't read too much into it. Cheaters can be either blasé or overly defensive. Honest players are rarely either — they tend to be reasonable and eager to straighten out any misunderstanding.

If you get yet another bad call, consider it strike three. Feel free to calmly say something like "I clearly saw that ball in. Would you reconsider your call?" or "Are you sure about that, because I definitely saw the ball in?"

If they act offended that you're questioning the call, mention that you've had silent but firm doubts about at least two earlier calls as well. If your opponent becomes belligerent, resist getting into an argument. You always have the option of walking away from the mess. But you can also play on, making the best of a bad situation.

WARNING

Sometimes bad calls can really sting and impact your chances of winning. Other times, a few bad calls don't do nearly as much damage as coming mentally unglued because of them. But don't start making flagrant bad calls of your own for revenge. That can get really ugly.

REMEMBER

If you count three questionable calls during a tournament, where someone is in charge, you can excuse yourself and go to the tournament director or organizer to make a formal complaint. Often, the person in charge can send someone out to monitor your match. This person is there not to call lines, but to act as an appeals judge, or cop, if you get into yet another controversy. Unfortunately, in recreational play, you don't have that kind of recourse most of the time. If you're too furious to play on and you're not having fun, tell your opponent, "This just isn't fun for me anymore. I have to stop now."

WARNING

No matter how good your intentions, never make a call and then ask your opponent, "How did you see it?" It isn't a fair position to put them in, because it's like saying, "I really want to take this point, but I'm not sure it belongs to me. Will you help me take it from you?" When your opponent looks pained after a call or shows some sign of mistrusting you, it's okay to say something friendly like "The ball was close, but I'm positive it was out."

When your opponent questions you

Honest players can tolerate being questioned about their line calls. If you're sure of your call, you should have no trouble saying so. Don't be overly anxious or plant any doubt in your opponent's mind by launching into long-winded explanations, even if you're angered at being questioned. Tell your opponent firmly and politely that you're sure of your call. Just say, "I'm sorry, but I never had a moment of doubt. The ball was clearly out."

TIP

If you're playing in a tournament, offer to bring an official out to the court to monitor the match when it's clear that your opponent mistrusts you. Make sure it's an impartial observer, rather than a friend or family member.

Don't get all bent out of shape and take the dispute personally. Accept disagreement as part of the stress of competition and focus on the quality of your play.

You know what? Sometimes, *you* may make a bad call without realizing it until after you've ended the point. (A little voice inside your head may tell you so.) In such cases, be decent about your mistake. Tell your opponent, "I'm sorry. I may have made a bad call. Let's play two." In effect, it's a let.

If you're sure that you blew a call on a ball that you couldn't have returned anyway, give your opponent the point. One great thing about giving your opponent a reasonable benefit of the doubt is that it frees up your mind to focus on the task at hand — playing good tennis.

Freely given courtesy is the essence of etiquette, and very often the favor will be returned.

REMEMBER

When you're playing a match against someone whom you don't know well, never catch the ball with your hand or racquet before it bounces. Technically, your opponent can claim the point. You can discuss the issue before you play if some reason (like a low fence behind the court) makes catching the ball a real time-saving issue. But as a rule, avoid that habit.

THE SMOKING GUN

On a clay court, the ball often leaves a mark when it hits the court surface. If you want to dispute your opponent's call, ask them to show you the mark, and feel free to have a look at it yourself. Under tennis etiquette, this practice is perfectly acceptable whenever you're convinced that a call was wrong.

Taking Two Serves

When a distraction occurs during a point, you should stop immediately and say, "Let's replay the point." If you ignore the distraction and play on, don't ask your opponent to play two after you lose the point, even if the distraction threw you off. Immediately ask to play two, or don't ask at all. Either player can stop the action to take two, no matter who is serving.

If your opponent gets uppity when you ask to play two, politely explain why you did it. There's no reason to question your claim of a distraction. Both you and your opponent have the prerogative to stop play and take two.

Showing Good Sportsmanship

Good sportsmanship includes qualities like being a gracious winner, tolerating errors in others, and taking defeat in stride. But the most important component in sportsmanship may be your willingness to put the means (playing) above the ends (winning). Appreciate and enjoy the journey more than the destination.

It has been said that you can learn a lot about a person by the way they behave on a tennis court. That's probably because sports serve as ways to grasp the important lessons of life — teamwork, coping with frustration, accepting victory modestly. One very important aspect of sportsmanship is seeing the person whom you're playing against as your opponent, not as your enemy.

The standard of sportsmanship on the pro tour these days is pretty high. For example, players often make gestures of apology with a little wave of their hand or racquet when they make a lucky shot. Serious altercations between players are rare. This lack of open conflict during a pro match tells you something very important about sportsmanship: If the best players in the world (people whose reputations and livelihoods depend on their tennis results) are good sports, the very concept must be valuable.

It's perhaps best summed up by the quote from Rudyard Kipling's poem, "If" which is inscribed by the entrance to the Centre Court at Wimbledon: "If you can meet with Triumph and Disaster, and treat those imposters just the same. . . ."

Those lucky letcords and other opportunities to apologize

I'm a respectful person, but I'm not in the habit of apologizing at the drop of a hat. Yet I still keep up the old tradition of apologizing when I win a point because the ball hits the net or the *letcord* (the steel cable on which the net hangs) and goes by my opponent for a winner. I also apologize when I hit my opponent with a ball.

MAC SAYS

These apologies are often just little signals between players, so subtle that spectators may not even notice them — a raised hand or a concerned look that's acknowledged by an opponent with a reassuring nod or thumbs-up. It's fascinating that most players continue to do this, even though no rules demand it. I think it proves that most people have an innate sense of fairness. Be nice. When you hit an opponent with the ball, say, "I'm sorry. I didn't mean that. Are you okay?" You don't have to march up to the net, offer to shake hands, or take your opponent to Starbucks out of atonement. A little gesture is all it takes.

Not embarrassing your opponent (or yourself)

Play hard. Play to win. Try to grab every point. But don't gloat when you're in command, and don't go berserk every time you make a decent shot. What goes around, comes around and you wouldn't like it if your opponent rubbed it in your face whenever they make a great shot.

When you hit a winner at a crucial time in a match, it's natural to react with spontaneous emotion. Even the pros are apt to clench their fists or cry out, "Yes!" or "Come on!" Being an international sport, *"Vamos!"* is also a common celebration. Just remember, a little of that goes a long way. Don't be a jerk, acting like you just won Wimbledon, every time you win a point.

And unless you're playing with an opponent who's also a good friend, keep the chitchat to a minimum. Some players enjoy casual conversation; others prefer to be all business. Don't comment on an opponent's errors, even if you want to console them — that's patronizing. Just say, "Well done" or "Too good" if your opponent makes a terrific shot. If your opponent played poorly and you want to express your sympathy, wait until the match is over and then make it short and sweet. Say something like "I could see you were having a rough day. Tough luck." Most losing players don't expect to get a pat on the back; they're content to go back to the drawing board.

REMEMBER

Don't be condescending to your opponent by giving away points or showing pity. Just respect your opponents as individuals. Their degree of talent or struggles with the game have nothing to do with the amount of respect they deserve.

Venting anger

Some players are naturally hot-headed and expressive on the court. Others aren't. If you're an emotional person, when frustrations bubble up blowing off a little steam can be necessary and helpful. Slapping yourself on the thigh or chiding yourself under your breath after missing an easy shot can be cathartic. But there are limits.

Expressing genuine and extended anger on the court is always a distraction to your partner or opponent. You also may be robbing them of some of the pleasure of playing. And making a big scene may be an imposition to players on other courts near you as well. It just makes what should be an enjoyable experience awkward and uncomfortable. And ultimately, a meltdown almost always ends up upending your game.

If you do happen to blow a gasket, the first thing you should do is figure out why all the fuss. Often, your tension is rooted in something else, like what a coworker said as you were leaving the office. Sometimes it's a reaction to the pressures of a match. Other times, the expectations you're putting on yourself may be the cause. Sometimes, like when you're playing with much better or much worse players, those expectations are out of line with reality.

IT'S ALL IN THE FAMILY

I asked my brother John, who is legendary for his flouting of tennis etiquette, to write this chapter, but he politely declined, reasoning that people consider me the "quiet" or "polite" McEnroe.

In some ways, John and I are as different as night and day. Like most players, I tend to play worse when I get angry, which gives me great incentive to control my temper. John was blessed — and cursed — with the ability to raise the level of his game when he got angry or felt cheated. His anger, no matter how petty or absurd the cause, was always an emotion that automatically lifted his game. That's a truly extraordinary ability, given the way that most people's games fall apart when they succumb to temper. And temper isn't exactly an emotion that's likely to make you popular. I've often wondered how two kids from the same gene pool could end up having such radically different personalities.

TIP

If your anger is getting the better of you, try to focus all that negativity in a positive way. Use it to tighten up your concentration or take it out on the ball. Pour it into the effort to get to every shot that your opponent hits.

Never take out your anger on your opponent, even if it's a regular playing partner. It could cost you a friend. If you're playing with someone you don't know well, getting angry could cost you a bloody nose. *Remember:* Tennis is not supposed to be a contact sport.

Pros have a great incentive to keep their tempers under control. They can be disqualified or even fined for violating the tour's code of conduct. (See Chapter 19 for more information on the WTA and ATP tours.)

As a pro, you can incur fines for infractions that include cursing; stalling between points; smashing your racquet on the ground (it's officially called *racquet abuse*); and berating officials, your opponent, or even spectators. If you act up or otherwise violate the tour's code of conduct, you get a warning. The umpire announces it, just like they call the score. If you commit another infraction of any kind during the match, you automatically lose the game being played. And if you violate *The Code* again, you're outta there — disqualified — with the other player automatically winning the match.

Avoiding gamesmanship

Gamesmanship is the willingness to exploit (and even break) the rules in underhanded ways in an attempt to garner a win. It's the polar opposite of sportsmanship.

To be clear, this isn't cheating in the strict sense that your opponent consciously makes bad calls. Gamesmanship is more subtle than that. Gamesmanship is about mind games.

Watch out for — and refrain from engaging in — the following typical tricks of gamesmanship:

>> **Stalling:** Nobody likes to have to wait while an opponent reties a perfectly well-tied shoelace or takes an usually long towel break. Stalling is a way for opponents to dictate what's happening on the court. Recognize stalling for what it is: a childish attempt to assert control. Use the free time to catch your breath or contemplate your strategy.

CURSING

You may curse, and you may not mind when others curse in your presence. If that's the case, and you're in a secluded court with no one else around, then fill up your swear jar.

However, cursing up a storm on a public court or at a club where others are playing is a different story. If you do so, players on adjacent or nearby courts may rightfully take objection to your outbursts.

Cursing isn't just a way to vent your anger; it's also an attention-getting device. You should aim to grab attention with stellar play rather than a foul mouth. Keep the dialogue — vulgar or otherwise — to yourself.

>> **Verbal provocation:** When your opponent says, "Gee, I heard you're having a lot of trouble with your forehand" or "I don't care what they say, you've got a heckuva volley" as you're about to start the match, that's gamesmanship. The best response is to ignore the comment instead of stewing over it and get the better of them on the scoreboard. Then, after the match, you can reassure them that your strokes are doing just fine.

>> **Noise:** A player who takes an extra loud, deep breath or stomps their feet every time you're about to hit a serve can be pretty distracting. Usually, actions like that are intended to break your concentration. Same goes for excessive and extended grunting when hitting shots. Once spotted, these ploys become predictable and repetitive, so it shouldn't bother you. Surprises are what throws you off.

Instead of getting upset by gamesmanship, recognize it for what it is. Your opponent is telling you that, deep down, they don't feel that their game is good enough to win the match fair and square. Gamesmanship is a poor substitute to draw on when forehands and serves won't get the job done.

Being a Supportive Doubles Partner

In doubles, the player closest to the ball makes the call during a point. When the ball is served, the returner's partner typically makes the call on the service line. The returner has the better view on wide serves by the singles sideline and generally makes that call. When one or the other player isn't clearly closer to the ball, the important thing is consensus. If the partners disagree about a call, they should concede the point to their opponents. When your doubles partner makes a call, accept their judgment and back up your partner if the other team challenges the call.

However, if your partner does make a bad call, you can reverse it. Do this tactfully, turning to your partner first, saying something like, "I saw the ball in. We should give them the point." Then tell your opponents the news. Just say, "Sorry, I had a better vantage point. It's your point."

Changing the call can be demoralizing to your partner. Don't do it unless you're dead certain.

Try not to get engaged in independent discussions with your opponents in issues that involve your partner. If some potential for conflict exists between you and your partner, retreat to discuss the issue together, without the other team overhearing.

If you want to get the best out of your partner, it really pays to compliment good racquet work as often as it occurs. When your partner makes a good shot, say so — "Great shot" or "Nicely done" will do. When your partner makes a bad error or poor shot choice, don't pull a long face or in any other way show displeasure. Doing so only pumps a little air into your opponents. It can also make your partner mad, and justifiably so.

But if your partner is making errors for some discernible technical or tactical reason, wait until an appropriate time, like a changeover, and make your point as part of your overall strategic discussion. You can say something like, "They're loving that wide serve against you. Maybe take a step or two to your right to take it away and force them to serve down the middle."

Ending the Match with Class

After match point, win or lose, shake hands with your opponent. It's the customary way to acknowledge your opponent's efforts and put a bow on the match. The loser typically offers congratulations — "Just too good today" — and the winner accepts graciously — "Thanks, well played." In a tournament, the loser often wishes the winner good luck for the rest of tournament. It also doesn't hurt to compliment your opponent on some part of their game.

In doubles, as soon as the last point ends, the partners on either side of the net shake hands with each other. Then all four players go to the net, and the opponents take turns shaking hands with each other. On the way up there, you can say a few kind words to your partner, like, "Wow, you really carried us today. I owe you one!" or "You made me look good out there." If you lost, just be supportive, as in, "Well, it wasn't the result we wanted, but it's always a pleasure playing with you." If you're a regular doubles team, you'll have plenty of time later, when the sting of defeat has worn off, to discuss what happened.

I also like the idea of players walking off the court just as they walked on — together. This long-standing habit has disappeared on the pro tour, partly because winners often do live TV interviews right there on the court. But the players at Wimbledon are still expected to walk off the court together, which is nice.

2

Playing the Game

Chapter **7**

Mastering the Fundamentals

Some pros and coaches tell everyone to hit strokes a certain way — their way. I beg to differ. I'm convinced that to be a good tennis player, you need to be a *comfortable* player — a player who does what comes naturally, as long as it doesn't interfere with the basics of hitting a good stroke. The closer you come to tapping into the strokes most suitable to you, the more easily and completely you'll master the game.

Watching the pros on TV may have shown you that you can hit a tennis ball lots of different ways. But how do you figure out which way fits you best? Although strokes can vary and look quite different, they usually have basic similar essentials. In this chapter, I show you the fundamentals of tennis that you can use to develop your own style of hitting the ball.

The Basic Strokes

Four primary types of strokes build the foundation of your game. Any shot you hit — other than a desperate, diving, anything-goes swipe — is derived from one of these strokes.

REMEMBER

There are other strokes — lobs, overheads, and drop shots — but they won't form the foundation of your game. To read more about them, head to Chapter 12.

Groundstrokes

The following two shots are your *groundstrokes* — so called because you use these strokes when you hit a ball that has bounced off the ground. Specialty shots, such as the drop shot and lob, are variations of the groundstroke. (You can learn more about these shots in Chapter 12).

The forehand

The bread-and-butter shot for most players, the forehand is the most natural of your strokes because it's a pretty straightforward swing at the ball, from the side of the body where you're most accustomed to performing tasks.

To envision a forehand, imagine that someone throws a ball to your right side, expecting you to hit it back with your hand. If you're a right-hander, your natural reaction is to hit it back with the palm of your right hand, from the right-hand side of your body. In fact, if I throw the ball at your body, your automatic impulse would be to step to your left and then hit the ball.

The majority of players find that the forehand comes more naturally to them, and most players hit the forehand when they have a choice in the matter. Unless your opponent is very crafty, or you're one of those rare players who prefers to hit backhands, the majority of the shots that you hit in any given match will be forehands.

TIP

Turn to Chapter 8 to see how to hit successful forehands.

The backhand

You hit the backhand on the side of your body where you don't perform the majority of your tasks. If you're a right-hander, you hit the backhand on your left side; if you're a left-hander, you hit it on your right side.

If you weren't holding a racquet and I tossed a ball to your backhand side, you would naturally hit the ball with the back of your hand. In order to do that, you would bring your hand around your body.

The backhand stroke almost always feels less natural than the forehand. And the mechanics of the swing typically makes it less powerful. But when you become familiar and confident in the backhand, it can be a very effective shot.

Turn to Chapter 9 to get more acquainted with the backhand.

Serve

You use the *serve* to begin every point. As long as you hit the ball out of the air before it bounces on the court, you can hit the serve any way you choose. In fact, many beginning players serve underhanded, as do some pros trying to pull a fast one on their opponents. But you get the best results by tossing the ball up over your head and then taking a full swing at it. As you develop, the serve takes on an increasingly enhanced role, and you could make the case that it's the most important shot in the game.

Turn to Chapter 11 to read more about the serve.

Return of serve

The *return of serve* resembles groundstrokes, but you're often required to use slightly different technique on either your forehand or backhand side to quickly adjust to the incoming serve.

The quality of your opponent's serve will often dictate a player's approach and strategy with their return of serve. As with the serve, this shot grows in importance as you advance in playing level.

Turn to Chapter 13 for detailed information on the return of serve.

Volley

The *volley* looks like a short punch with your racquet, comparable to a jab in boxing, hit with little or no backswing. You use the volley when you play up near the net, on either your forehand or backhand side. It's a staple of players who feel confident advancing forward and hitting shots around the net. The volley also figures prominently in doubles.

There are subtle variations, but the standard volley is typically hit directly out of the air. Most of the time, you use the volley to end points, because you have a great chance to hit a winner when you're up at the net — the angles are easier to make, and clearing the net isn't as challenging.

TIP

Chapter 10 gives you the full scoop on hitting volleys.

The Essential Grips

Before you can hit any sort of a shot in tennis, you need to have your racquet in your hand, ready for play. How you hold your racquet, referred to as your *grip*, significantly impacts any stroke you make.

You have a variety of choices when it comes to your grip. You don't have to pick just one grip. Most players use different grips on their various strokes because some grips are just better for some strokes than others.

At first, changing grips for different shots may seem confusing and awkward, but with practice, changing grips becomes second nature. In fact, almost all the pros change their grips — and they play a faster game than anyone else.

MAC SAYS

I recommend that you first understand the differences between the grips, and then, as your experience and confidence grows, incorporate into your strokes the grips that feel most comfortable. Even if a grip is considered optimal for a particular stroke, it's perfectly fine to use slight adjustments if that makes the shot more effective and comfortable.

TECHNICAL STUFF

Yes, the grip introduces a confusing bit of tennis terminology. You grip your racquet on the racquet's grip, which is the part of the racquet right above the butt cap. (Refer to Chapter 3 to explore the various parts of the average tennis racquet.) So, the grip can be a reference either to the physical part of the racquet that you hold, or to the specific way that you hold the racquet to hit different shots.

Choosing from the grips

The handle, or *grip*, of the racquet is an octagon. It features eight flat surfaces with *bevels*, or ridges, between them. (See Chapter 3 for more information on the anatomy of a racquet.)

When you grip the racquet for a stroke, your hand doesn't fit into a predetermined place on the handle. Each shot dictates that you hold the racquet a certain way. I get into the finer points in the chapters addressing those shots, but for now, here are the four broad grip categories:

>> **Continental:** The continental grip is so versatile that it could technically be used for every stroke (although that hasn't been standard practice since the days of long tennis pants). It's the preferred grip for serving, volleying, and hitting slice shots. Beginners almost always find this grip uncomfortable.

>> **Eastern:** This grip is generally considered the easiest one to use when learning the forehand. With a slight adjustment, it allows you to hit a pretty good backhand, too. The eastern grip allows you to brush up the back of the ball for topspin or hit flatter to drive the ball through the court. Usually, beginners find this grip the most comfortable one to start with.

>> **Semi-western:** The semi-western has become the preeminent forehand grip for better players. It's easier to apply more topspin to the ball than it is with the eastern grip, giving shots more net clearance, control, and margin for error.

>> **Western:** The western is an extreme grip that can help generate tons of topspin. However, it isn't very versatile and requires a significant grip change to hit different types of shots.

THE EVER-CHANGING ROLE OF THE GRIP

The grips represent four different placements of the hand on the racquet handle. Moving your hand slightly on the handle of the racquet, in either direction, always takes you away from one grip and closer to another of the four grips. I'm talking about fractions of an inch here — they may not feel very different, but they make a big difference in how you hit the ball.

Players manage to find a zillion niches in between the standard grips, seeking optimum comfort. That's the key — comfort with your strokes.

Your favorite grips may change with time. The most comfortable grip when you're a beginner may lose its appeal as your game flourishes. Always be comfortable, but keep an open mind about grips as your game improves.

TIP

When you first start playing the game, experiment mostly with the eastern, semi-western, and continental grips. The western may feel the most comfortable on the forehand side, but transitioning to the backhand and volley grips from it is really tricky. Over time, you may find yourself gravitating toward the western grip for your forehand. That's fine, but don't rob Peter (your backhand) to pay Paul (your forehand). If you use a western forehand grip, you have to change the grip to hit backhands.

Finding the grip: Using the bevels

There are various ways to find the different grips, but perhaps the simplest is using the position of the base knuckle of your index finger as a reference point. Where you place that knuckle along the eight bevels of the handle is how you arrive at each particular grip. This is clearer when you look at the diagram of the racquet handle in Figure 7-1. You'll notice the eight different sides or bevels. Lining up the base knuckle with the appropriate side and then closing your hand around the handle is how you'll find the grip.

FIGURE 7-1:
The racquet
handle.

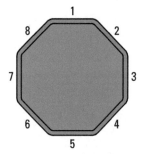

© John Wiley & Sons, Inc.

TIP

No matter which grip you use, keep the following tips in mind:

>> **Don't strangle the handle.** Squeezing the grip of your racquet too hard tightens the entire hitting arm and makes hitting fluid, natural strokes more difficult. It can also make your forearm and wrist ache.

>> **Apply only as much pressure as you need so the racquet doesn't fly out of your hand when swinging it.** You don't squeeze the handle of a hammer the minute you pick it up; you just hold it good and tight as you hit the nail. Hold the racquet just securely enough so that it doesn't yield when the ball hits it.

The following sections take a closer look at how you find each of the main grips.

Continental

The continental grip can be used for both the forehand and the backhand, so no grip change is required between strokes. It's the only grip that can make that claim. When looking down on the grip, the V created by your thumb and forefinger will be directly on top of the handle.

Bevel locations

Righty: 2

Lefty: 8

Eastern

Some people call the eastern forehand grip the "handshake" grip because you can also find it by, in effect, shaking hands with the handle of the racquet. You can also place your hand flat on the strings and slide down to the grip. Or you can even lay the racquet flat on a table, close your eyes, and pick it up. They all work. What you're essentially doing is rotating that base knuckle clockwise (counterclockwise for lefties) one bevel from the continental grip.

Bevel locations

Righty: 3

Lefty: 7

The eastern backhand grip is a one bevel shift from the continental grip in the opposite direction. If you're looking directly down at the grip, this puts the base knuckle on the very top of the handle. Whether hitting a one- or two-handed backhand, this is the grip for your dominant hand.

Bevel locations

Righty: 1

Lefty: 1

Semi-western

Shifting the base knuckle clockwise (counterclockwise for lefties) one bevel from the eastern forehand grip gets you to a semi-western forehand grip. This naturally closes the racquet face more at contact, which allows you to brush up on the ball at contact to create topspin. (Chapter 8 details topspin forehand technique).

Bevel locations

Righty: 4

Lefty: 6

The semi-western or extreme eastern backhand grip is not a common grip and not something I'd recommend for most players — certainly not a beginner. It can be quite effective at putting topspin on the ball, but it requires lots of wrist action, a lengthy swing, and excellent timing.

Bevel locations

Righty: 8

Lefty: 2

Western

A full western grip puts the base knuckle on the very bottom of the handle. The palm of your hand should be almost completely under grip. If a player were so inclined, they could flip their hand over and play an eastern backhand using the same side of the racquet face. For that reason, and due to its extreme nature, there is no backhand equivalent.

Bevel locations

Righty: 5

Lefty: 5

Working the Face of Your Racquet

I always tell people that the ball will do what the face of the racquet tells it to do. The angle at which your racquet face meets the ball is the biggest factor in determining the direction in which the ball will travel. (The only exceptions are shots that use spin, which are created by intentionally brushing under or over the ball. You can read about hitting spins later in this chapter.)

For example, if you hit the ball with the face of your racquet *open*, or pointing upward, the ball flies upward, as you see in Figure 7-2.

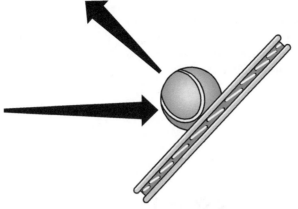

FIGURE 7-2:
Sending the ball
up, up, and away
with an
open face.

When you want to hit a lob, you strive to make your racquet face open. (See Chapter 12 for more information on the lob.) But if you hit your groundstrokes and volleys with the racquet face too open, most of them will fly high in the air and land behind the baseline.

In Figure 7-3, you see that the ball travels downward when you hit it with a *closed* face, pointing downward.

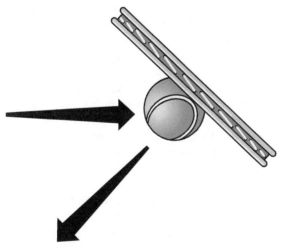

FIGURE 7-3:
Your closed-face
racquet drives
the ball down.

TIP

As a beginner, you should strive to hit your groundstrokes and volleys with a square face, as shown in Figure 7-4. To hit the ball with a square face on your forehand and backhand, the racquet face should be perpendicular to the ground at the moment of contact.

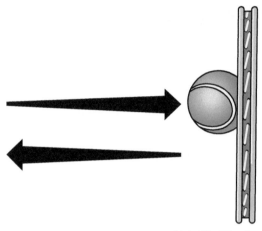

FIGURE 7-4:
Giving the ball a square deal.

© John Wiley & Sons, Inc.

Tennis would be a lot easier if one, natural grip allowed you to swing in a way that gave you a natural, square face on impact every time, on both the forehand and backhand side. But it doesn't work that way. A grip that allows you to hit a forehand naturally — with a square face — won't work on the backhand side, and vice versa.

REMEMBER

Most of the grips, as well as the arc of your stroke, dispose you toward one or the other of these angles on impact, often requiring that you make some adjustment with your wrist in order to hit the ball with a square face. That's why it's important to keep a relaxed hold on the grip, to allow some "play" in the wrist. Think of your wrist as a flexible joint that sometimes must be adjusted to enable you to hit with a square face.

This business of adjusting your wrist isn't nearly as complicated as it may sound. Try taking nice, slow swings with your racquet, using the various grips. Don't worry about your form for now; just bring the racquet back and then forward at about waist level. (You can refer to the very next section for a little more info on your swing.) As you swing, watch the face of the racquet. At what point, if any, is it "square" or perpendicular to the ground? Gently roll your wrist in either direction, and you'll see how little it takes to open, close, or bring square the face of the racquet.

The Elements of the Swing

Figure 7-5 shows you the path the ball travels when you hit it with a good, controlled swing. The shot travels in an arc because it must get high enough to clear the net, and then the shot falls fast enough to drop inside the lines.

A poor swing combined with an erratic racquet face can cause the ball to either land in the net or sail clear over your opponent's baseline.

A big swing and solid contact are fine as long as you add the control to keep even the hardest of your shots inside the lines.

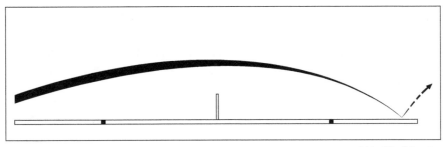

FIGURE 7-5: When you're hitting a groundstroke, the ball should travel in an arc across the net.

© John Wiley & Sons, Inc.

In this section, I describe some stroking fundamentals that apply to both of your groundstrokes. (See Chapters 8 and 9 for more specific information on how to hit sweet shots with your forehand and backhand.) Feel free to grab your racquet and follow along as I take you through the various stages of the perfect swing.

Stance

When hitting a ball, some measure of footwork is generally required. You have to move to the ball to get in position and then adjust your feet into a stance while executing the swing.

A *squared stance* is when you step toward the ball with your lead foot so that your feet are lined up parallel to each other and perpendicular to the baseline. If you were standing on a clockface, your back foot would be at 6 o'clock, and your front foot would be just about at 12 o'clock.

If your front foot steps across your body to around 2 o'clock, this is a *closed stance*, because it closes your hips and limits upper-body rotation.

An *open stance* is when the lead foot steps to the side so your feet are almost parallel to the baseline. To use the clock analogy, it would be having your feet at 3 o'clock and 9 o'clock.

Because tennis is a game of movement and improvisation, most shots are hit with the feet somewhere in between these stances. Ideally, there would be enough time for the lead foot to step forward to some degree — often called a *semi-open stance* — so there's weight transfer into the shot.

Backswing

As you move for the ball, bring your racquet back. This comes very naturally, because you must use your shoulders to turn toward the ball, and that automatically helps you bring back the racquet. The two motions go hand in hand.

REMEMBER

Failing to bring the racquet back quickly enough, whether you're standing still for a shot hit directly to you, or running for one, is one of the biggest, most common, and most preventable mistakes made by beginners.

Practice turning your shoulders and getting the racquet back in one smooth motion in front of the mirror, keeping the racquet at about the same level as your waist. Don't hyperextend your racquet and arm behind you. You want to be loose and relaxed, and let the shoulder turn do most of the work.

Swing path

In order to cover the ball, you have to sweep over it with the racquet face traveling low to high. The only exception to this technique is shots hit with the spin called *slice*, which you can read about later in this chapter.

MAC SAYS

HEY, THEY CAN DO THAT — THEY'RE PROS

When you watch the pros, it may look like they aren't getting the racquet back right away. They seem to time their swing so that it's just one, smooth motion. That's why they're pros. All of them learned to bring the racquet back early, and many of them still do it just like I describe in this book. Some of them can instinctively wait until the last moment without losing their timing or accuracy.

When you first start out, don't worry that your shots don't look smooth. Tennis is a game of rhythm — the more you play, the more rhythm you get. Worry about getting your racquet back and hitting good shots, and you'll end up looking just fine.

For both the forehand and backhand strokes, your racquet starts out at about waist level and ends up slightly above the shoulder. Think about it this way: On a good shot, you don't just make contact — you fit the ball into a good, long, low-to-high swing. You don't strike the ball as much as you envelop it in a stroke that causes it to travel in an arc.

Of course, some balls bounce low, so sometimes you need to drop your backswing even lower than waist level. You may also need to bend lower on such shots. But even when that happens, you should still finish high, with your racquet over your opposite shoulder.

I show you how to hit smooth, low-to-high strokes on your forehand and back-hand sides in Chapters 8 and 9.

Trunk rotation and weight transfer

Another common mistake of beginning players is they *arm* the shot — they try to power the ball with just the hitting arm. Even if they turn the shoulders during the backswing, they don't uncoil their upper body when bringing the racquet forward to contact. In an attempt to generate more swing speed, they take wild swipes at the ball that draw poor contact.

REMEMBER

Using a controlled, relaxed swing that incorporates the upper body and weight transfer into the swing produces easier depth and power on shots with less effort. It also produces a steadier racquet face that makes cleaner contact with the ball, making your shots more consistent as well.

I find that many players make the mistake of trying to emulate the pros they watch on TV by swinging as fast as they can. There's a reason pros are pros — they have unique ability. You must learn proper technique and timing before trying to use what I call *racquet speed.* Just as you crawl before you walk, you've got to slow down to learn how to speed up.

Strike zone: Finding the perfect contact point

You should go out to meet the ball on every groundstroke. You can see in Figure 7-6 that you make contact with the ball in front of your body, forward of your lead leg.

FIGURE 7-6:
Your racquet is
the welcome
wagon going out
to meet the ball.

© John Wiley & Sons, Inc.

TIP

No matter how big or small you are, strive to make contact when the ball is out in front of your body. How far in front will depend on the type of stance you're in. But ideally you want to hit the ball when it's just in front of your leading hip. That's your left hip on the forehand shot and your right hip on the backhand side. (Opposite hips for lefties). If you let the ball travel too far back, you're increasing your odds of hitting an errant shot.

Many beginners get timid and let the ball travel too far back or too close to their bodies before they make contact. Strive to meet the ball in front of you, with your arm and racquet comfortably and loosely extended. The rule is "Play the ball" — don't let the ball play you!

TIP

Keep your head still at and through the moment of contact. This gives you a better chance of hitting the racquet's sweet spot. Don't worry one bit about where the shot is going. Your swing and timing determine where it will go. If you move your head, or jerk it up to see where the ball is going while you're making contact, the shot will fly astray.

Follow-through

From the moment the ball leaves your racquet, you're in the finishing stage of your stroke, or the *follow-through.*

One of the most common errors made by beginners is the failure to follow through. It may seem like you're no longer affecting the flight of the ball on your follow-through — after all, the ball has left your racquet. But abruptly stopping the swing after contact will hamper the shot and potentially hurt your arm.

Your follow-through should be a relaxed deceleration of your hitting arm as the racquet extends toward the target. As you improve, and your swing both speeds up and lengthens, the racquet should finish around the opposite shoulder.

TIP

Keep these follow-through tips in mind when directing your shots:

>> **If you want your shot to go across the court, come farther around on your follow-through.** Shots that go across the court are called *crosscourt shots*. To drive the ball crosscourt, strike it closer to its outside edge of the ball and extend the racquet farther across your body.

>> **If you want the shot to go straight, finish farther out in front of you.** This kind of shot is called a *down-the-line shot*. For down-the-line shots, hit directly on the back of the ball and follow through more forward than around your body.

Putting Shape on Your Shots

On a *flat shot,* an eagle-eyed player can practically read the label on the ball as it approaches. However, almost all shots invariably have a slight amount of spin. If you were to slo-mo a spin shot right after you hit it, you'd see the writing on the ball rotating as it makes its way over the net.

Balls hit with a lot of spin travel differently than flat balls, and they do different things when they bounce, which can be beneficial to you and really create problems for your opponent.

You won't be experimenting much with spin until you have some good practice time under your belt. Creating spin demands hitting a specific portion of the ball, altering the path of your stroke, using more of your wrist, or all of the above.

To prepare you for the fateful day when you can start putting some spin on your shots, I want to give you a brief overview of spin. I tell you how to incorporate spin into your shots in the chapters that address the specific strokes.

Attacking with topspin

When you put *topspin* on your shots, the ball spins toward your opponent. That's why it's sometimes referred to as *overspin*. When the ball bounces, it leaps high on the bounce toward your opponent. This high, quick bounce can wreak havoc with your opponent's timing. Because topspin naturally brings the ball down into the court, it also allows a player to hit the ball higher over the net — thus creating more margin for error.

The disadvantages of topspin are that, like any kind of spin, it slows the ball down. This can make it more difficult to hit the ball by your opponent. Hitting with very heavy topspin can also cause the ball to fall shorter in the court, making it tougher to hit the ball deep and keep your opponent pinned to the baseline. But overall, hitting with topspin is a massive plus that is something to work toward. It helps with consistency and keeping shots deep in your opponent's court, which is a fundamental strategy. (Chapter 13 tells you more about strategy.)

Cutting with slice

Slice causes the ball to spin backward. The ball rotates in the opposite direction of topspin. Slice is also referred to as *underspin*. When a slice shot is hit well, the ball *skids* — or bites the court — and stays low after it bounces. This can force opponents to have to stretch and alter their swing in order to return it. The slice can be particularly useful to players who like to attack the net and volley, a strategy I discuss in Chapter 13.

The slice can be a useful weapon, but it does have some disadvantages. Slice shots typically travel with less pace. This becomes even more noticeable when the slice is hit poorly or out of desperation just to get the ball back in play. These shots tend to float and travel through the air slowly. Instead of biting and staying low, the ball will kind of just bounce straight up. This is what's sometimes called a *sitter,* because the ball just sits there. Your opponents can do almost anything they want with a juicy sitter.

Key Components of a Perfect Swing

Preparation is the key to making good strokes and shots. In order to make good stroking habitual, you have to get accustomed to habitual preparation.

Focused footwork

Just standing there, with the racquet dangling alongside you, is lazy tennis. It gives you that much more to worry about when the ball is on its way.

Prepare yourself by getting into the ready position. Wait for the ball with both hands on the racquet. Keep your playing hand on the grip and cradle the throat of the racquet gently with your free hand if you play your shots one-handed. Keep the racquet squarely in front of you, with the head of the racquet above the level of your wrist.

TIP

If you have a two-handed backhand, keep your hands close together on the racquet handle so you won't have to go looking for your grip when you start for the ball.

Just before a point begins, and in the brief periods when the ball travels from racquet to racquet, always face the net. Stay on the balls of your feet, leaning slightly forward. And keep your feet moving, bouncing on them lightly the way a prizefighter does. That way, you're ready to go in either direction when the time comes.

TIP

I often tell people not to move directly to the ball, but to the place where you want to hit it. When you move and position yourself like this, it creates good spacing to hit the ball effectively.

Always try to get back to the middle of the court after you hit a shot so you have the same distance to travel in either direction for the next shot. If you hit a shot from the right side of the court and then just stand there, waiting for a return, you leave the whole left side of the court open for your opponent.

Bounce on your feet even when you're waiting for your opponent to serve. When they begin their service motion, you should be up on the balls of your feet and ready to go. Being ready to move is especially important when your opponent has a fast, powerful serve. You need every split second at your disposal!

TIP

As soon as you see where the ball is going, push off with the opposite foot. So, if the ball is headed to your left, you push off with your right foot. A quick start is vital to getting to the ball in time. Because you're facing the net, the best way to get a good powerful start is by pivoting and turning your body toward the ball as you push off.

A steady head

Ever play fetch with a dog who loves to chase a tennis ball? The dog not only retrieves the ball until your arm goes numb, but also watches it as intently as they can through all the fakes and changes of direction and false throws. That's how you want to play tennis.

Get in the habit of watching the ball come off your opponent's strings, and then watch it until you make contact with the ball. Sounds like a no-brainer, right? But I'm amazed at how often even top players get either distracted or lazy and take their eyes off the ball.

TIP

One neat little trick that may help you focus on the ball is to keep your head still and your eyes fixed on the point of contact for a split second after you hit the shot, almost as if you're posing for picture. If you want a perfect example of this, look at still photos or watch videos of Roger Federer — he was perhaps the best ever at doing this. Fed would complete his follow-through, and his eyes were still glued to the point of contact.

Watching the ball not only allows you to prepare faster but also enables you to execute your own shot better. If you don't watch the ball, you may not even make contact with it.

REMEMBER

Even if you can't remember the score from point to point, you must have at least enough concentration to watch the ball on every shot. You need this form of concentration to play good tennis. It's nonnegotiable.

A smooth and relaxed sequence

I've talked about all the key fundamentals in the swing like backswing, contact point, and follow-through. Although each element is important, none of them works in a vacuum — they all need to link together in one fluid motion. Squeezing the racquet too tightly, lurching at the ball, or having too much tension in the body can cause any of those links to get stuck. The swing looks herky-jerky, and it's difficult to consistently hit good shots.

Take the stance for example. Having a soft knee flex in your stance is an important part of hitting a good tennis stroke. Keeping your knees slightly bent puts you in a mild crouch that makes it easier to get a fast start for the ball. If you play stiff-legged, with your knees locked, you can't tap into all your power sources or move quickly.

On the other hand, jumping wildly out of your stance as you hit the ball isn't good either. On a typical good stroke, you naturally and subtly transfer your weight forward as you swing, rising slightly. Don't exaggerate this effect by popping up like a jack-in-the-box as you make your stroke. You should only rise up about an inch or two.

REMEMBER

It's often said that better players have a way of making the game look effortless. That starts with having a smooth, connected swing sequence. The racquet accelerates easily, the face stays steady, and contact is cleaner and more repeatable.

The Pre-Match Warm-up

A thorough warm-up is a very important hedge against injury, and it's a nice way to get loose and ready for a match or a structured practice.

REMEMBER

Before you even start your warm-up, stretch and warm up each of the muscle groups that I tell you about in Chapter 16.

During the warm-up, you want to get your body, and all your strokes, ready to play. You can achieve that goal in a typical warm-up that lasts no more than ten minutes by following these steps:

1. **Both players stand at the baseline, exchanging groundstrokes for at least three minutes.**

   Hit the ball to both sides of your opponent and expect the same in return. Don't hit hard shots or try to show off your best strokes. Just keep the ball in play so that both of you can warm up your groundstrokes and your arm and leg muscles.

2. **Move up to the net to hit volleys for at least two minutes.**

   It doesn't matter who moves up to the net first — you'll both get your turn — but only one player at a time is at the net during the warm-up.

   Return your volleys to your opponent at the baseline. Your opponent should hit groundstrokes right to you, so both of you can keep the ball in play.

3. **Ask for lobs, either by saying so or by just pointing a finger in the air, so that you can hit a handful of overheads.**

   At this point, your opponent begins to feed you lobs, and you hit returnable overheads back to your opponent. Hit your overheads at about 40 percent of your maximum arm speed at first, and add pace in increments as you warm up your shoulder. (Crushing a real hard one on the last ball is okay.) Your opponent should hit you lobs that you can reach comfortably, although the harder you hit your overhead, the more difficult it is to do that.

4. **Return to the baseline, while your opponent gets to practice the volley and overhead for about the same amount of time as you did.**

5. **When your opponent returns to the baseline, hit serves to each other.**

You can do this simultaneously, although taking turns is more efficient; one player serves, and the other one catches the ball. That way, you don't have to run around picking up balls all the time.

After serving to one court for at least a minute, both players go to the other side of the court and hit more practice serves for at least a minute. It's not uncommon for one player to be happy with their serve, while the other needs a few extra warm-ups before feeling ready.

6. **When you feel properly warmed up, ask if your opponent is ready to play.**

Either player can ask, and it's perfectly okay to ask for another minute or two to work out a few kinks. But don't prolong the warm-up any longer than that. The warm-up is just that: a brief prelude to playing, not a practice session.

In doubles, you warm up much the same way. The big difference is that each of the four players takes either the deuce or ad side on one side of the court and warms up with the player directly opposite. So the player on one deuce side will warm up the opposing player in the ad court. You warm up simultaneously, with each pair of opponents using half the court and whichever ball is handy. That means that there are two warm-ups going on at the same time. If you're beginners, this can get a little confusing because the balls may be flying all over the place. But trying to warm up four players by using one ball at a time is far less efficient.

When it's time to volley, both players on one team should move up to the net and then return to the baseline after taking their share of volleys and overheads. When you're all ready to take your warm-up serves, serve diagonally, not to the partner opposite you. Change positions with your partner at the baseline so that you hit some serves to both service boxes.

WARNING

Be extra careful not to hit atomic shots when warming up in doubles with two separate warm-ups going on at once. Because both players on the other side of the net are concentrating on their own warm-ups, they're vulnerable to being hit by stray shots from the other players. Take special care when you hit overheads and other hard shots.

REMEMBER

After you play tennis, don't forget to allow your muscles to cool down for at least ten minutes. To do so, follow the stretches I show you in Chapter 16.

IN THIS CHAPTER

» **Finding a forehand grip**

» **Preparing to hit**

» **Taking a good stance**

» **Making your backswing**

» **Swinging away**

» **Using spin**

Chapter **8**

The Forehand: Your Money Shot

For most players, the forehand is their go-to shot. A strong, steady forehand is the anchor of your game. If all else is coming unglued — you can't find the box on your first serve and your backhand has gone AWOL — the forehand should be your security blanket. Without a reliable forehand, you'll end up as roadkill on the great tennis highway. And as you develop your game, the forehand will grow into a weapon you can use to control and finish off points.

In this chapter, I show you how to get on the road to developing a forehand you can count on.

ONE HAND IS BETTER THAN TWO

If you've seen players with deadly two-handed backhands, you may have been moved to wonder, "Hey, that works great! How come they don't do the same thing with their forehands?" Well, Monica Seles did that. So have some other terrific players over the years, like Fabrice Santoro (1990s to 2000s), and Marion Bartoli (2000s). But the two-handed forehand has become virtually extinct. Your support arm — the left one if you're a righty — helps power a two-handed backhand, but it's actually in the way when you hit a two-handed forehand. You also have diminished reach and racquet maneuverability.

Players who have been successful with the two-handed forehand triumphed in spite of the shot. Most beginners, even 6- and 8-year-olds, are strong enough to hit good, effective forehands with one hand the minute they pick up a racquet. In fact, I suspect you won't see another successful pro player with a two-handed forehand.

Finding Your Forehand Grip

You can hit a solid forehand with any of the common grips, although the semi-western is probably the most popular and effective choice. (See Chapter 7 for more information on the various grips.) The grip is well-suited to put topspin on the ball (see "Hitting with Topspin," later in this chapter), yet it's not so extreme that it's difficult to quickly switch to a backhand or volley grip.

That said, beginners can certainly start with an eastern grip because it can feel more natural. And you can still hit a pretty darn good forehand with it. But I'd advise against starting with a continental grip. Yes, you can conceivably hit both your forehand and your backhand with one grip, eliminating the need for grip changes. However, you won't be able to put much topspin on your shots — the backhand can really only be hit with slice — and you'll severely limit your growth as a player.

As you become more comfortable with your forehand, I recommend taking a peek at the semi-western grip because many players find that it helps them hit great, powerful forehands. It's an excellent compromise between the driving shots of an eastern grip and the heavy topspin of a full western grip. It's the one I use on my own forehand, and I'd suggest it for just about any player.

Letting It Rip

The forehand swing is a simple proposition if you have good control of the racquet face. In fact, the path of the swing when you hit your basic forehand is almost a mirror image of the backswing, except for a gradual low-to-high trajectory and the follow-though.

REMEMBER

The success of your forehand depends less on following a precise angle in your swing than it does on observing the keys to preparation and your fundamentals. You can read about them in Chapter 7.

TIP

You don't have to swing hard or fast in order to hit an impactful forehand. A lot of the pace and accuracy comes from hitting the ball on the sweet spot, with a firm, smooth stroke. (Chapter 7 talks about finding the sweet spot.)

Okay, grab your racquet and follow along as I walk you through the basics of the forehand. The description is for right-handed players; lefties should apply it to the opposite hand and feet.

1. **Hold the racquet at about waist height in front of you, with your right hand assuming your forehand grip on the handle of the racquet. Bend your knees slightly and feet slightly shoulder-width apart (see Figure 8-1).**

   Stand just inside the baseline, near the centerline.

   I recommend either the eastern or semi-western grip for beginners. (Chapter 7 tells you all about finding the different grips.)

REMEMBER

   The heel of your palm should rest against the raised butt of the racquet. Support the throat of the racquet lightly with the fingers of your left hand.

2. **As the ball approaches, turn your shoulders to the right, allow the racquet head to drop, and draw it toward the back fence with a smooth, pendular motion (see Figure 8-2). At the same time, pivot on your right foot and take a comfortable step forward toward the ball with your left foot.**

   When you're first learning, it's okay to immediately get the racquet back as soon as you see the ball coming to your forehand side. This may cause the racquet head to stop briefly as you wait for the ball before starting your forward swing. Ideally, though, as you improve, the goal is to time the shot so the racquet head never stops after you start your swing. You'll get more racquet head speed and better results from one smooth, integrated motion.

FIGURE 8-1:
You and your
racquet are ready
for action.

FIGURE 8-2:
Turn and get your
racquet back.

Many beginning players find it helpful to point at the ball with their left arm while they make their backswing.

If you have to run to set up for the shot, push off with the foot opposite the side the shot is coming to. Avoid running to your position helter-skelter and then setting up your stance with a separate motion. You should start your backswing as you close in on your hitting position.

3. **Slow down your backswing when the head of the racquet is slightly below the level of your waist and your arm is comfortably extended (see Figure 8-3).**

    Don't stretch your arm backward — stay nice and relaxed.

FIGURE 8-3:
Stop your backswing when your arm is comfortably extended.

© John Wiley & Sons, Inc.

4. **Pause for a moment.**

    As you improve, your goal will be to eliminate this step, but it can be a helpful training tool as you learn the stroke. The pause can range from a split second to two seconds or more, because the ball has to arrive in the area where you'll make contact. The important thing is to prepare quickly enough so that the backswing and forward swing are two separate and distinct motions, not one hurried one.

5. **Begin your forward swing with your shoulders rather than your arm leading the way (see Figure 8-4).**

   This swing ensures that your shoulders and upper body get out of your way so that you can make a smooth, free stroke.

FIGURE 8-4:
Begin your
forward swing.

© John Wiley & Sons, Inc.

   Your arm should be relaxed when you swing, and your wrist should be firm but neither locked nor under stress from gripping the racquet too tightly.

6. **Make contact with the ball when it's just about in front of your left hip, with your arm comfortably extended and a slight bend in the elbow (see Figure 8-5).**

   The ball should be at about waist height.

FIGURE 8-5:
Finally, the
moment
of impact.

© John Wiley & Sons, Inc.

7. **Follow through, finishing the stroke with the racquet above the level of your shoulders, and in the direction you want the ball to go (see Figure 8-6).**

   As the swing speed on your forehand increases, it may need more time to gradually decelerate. At that point, the racquet should follow through over your left shoulder.

8. **Get back into the ready position (see Step 1) for your next shot.**

FIGURE 8-6:
Your
follow-through.

Hitting with Topspin

Smart, percentage tennis is about managing errors. Most matches are won by keeping the ball in play more than by hitting spectacular winners. The more aggressively you play, the more likely you are to make errors.

Topspin allows you to swing harder and closer to the lines while still having a reasonable level of safety on your shots. Flatter balls aimed for the lines are low-percentage shots. Adding topspin to your forehand adds a degree of control to your shots, allowing you to hit close to the lines more consistently.

Giving yourself more margin for error

On any shot, the net is always the first obstacle to overcome. After you do that, the next hurdle is getting the ball to drop down inside the lines. Topspin helps with both. (You can read more about topspin in Chapter 7.)

The higher over the net you hit the ball, the deeper it will generally go in your opponent's court. If you use topspin, you can hit the ball harder and higher over the net and use the spin to bring the ball back down into the court. You can hit high, arcing forehands over the net that land deep and jump up on your opponent. In a sense, you get to be more aggressive and safer with your shots at the same time. That's a great advantage!

TIP

To start putting more topspin on your forehand stroke, slightly modify your technique in the following ways:

>> **Instead of swinging the racquet through contact in a gradual low-to-high fashion, try brushing up more on the back of the ball.** If the back of the ball were a clockface, you would try to hit it from 6 o'clock to 12 o'clock. A simple way to learn this sensation is to take a ball and pin it between the top of the net — the net cord — and the strings of your racquet. Then roll the ball over the net by sweeping up the back of it with the racquet face. This helps relay the brushing motion needed to apply topspin.

>> **Keep your wrist loose and relaxed.** This helps to brush up the ball and put topspin on it. However, make sure your wrist isn't so floppy that you lose control of the racquet face.

>> **Try a semi-western or western grip.** You can hit good topspin forehands with an eastern grip, but using a semi-western or full western can really enhance the shot. These grips slightly close the racquet face at contact, which encourages a more natural brushing motion.

After you get good at putting topspin on the ball, you can increase your output with your equipment. Certain racquets and strings are designed to promote spin production. (You can read more about gear in Chapter 3.)

Producing a "heavy" ball

When a forehand can produce shots that combine speed with heavy topspin, you've really got something. The ball zips across the net, bounds high off the court, and pushes opponents deep behind the baseline. All the spin on the ball makes it a real load to return. You may even hear an announcer like me say, "That player hits a heavy ball." Even though its weight is technically the same, when the ball hits your racquet strings, it just *feels* heftier. If an opponent ever tells you that you've got a heavy forehand, you've got my permission to puff out your chest.

Defending with the Slice Forehand

The slice forehand used to be more of a staple shot. When the game was much slower and played more often on grass, the control and low bounce produced by a slice stroke were very much appreciated. Advances in equipment and harder surfaces have sped the game up, and slicing the forehand has fallen out of favor. This shift also coincided with more players adopting western grips on the forehand, which aren't conducive to hitting a slice but produce a more powerful shot.

Like all slice shots, the forehand version is hit with a high-to-low swing path, with the strings brushing under the ball. If you don't play with either already, you should shift your grip to an eastern forehand or continental grip. (Chapter 7 covers the different grips.) Before you start your forward swing, raise the racquet head to around shoulder height, open the face slightly so that the hitting surface angles up, and produce a slice by cutting under the ball with a long, smooth stroke. Make sure not to chop down on the ball; you still want to make a full follow-through out toward your target.

TIP

The slice forehand is easier to execute, but don't use it as a substitute for your drive or topspin forehand. It's primarily a defensive shot that comes into play mostly on three occasions:

>> **When you're out of options:** Whether you're scrambling to retrieve a shot by your opponent (this is called making a *get*) or stretching to return a wide serve, you may not have enough time to set up to hit your standard forehand. Instead, all you can muster is to hack the ball back with a slice and buy yourself a little time to get back in position. This shot is often referred to as a *squash shot* because it resembles the forehand stroke often used in that racquet sport.

>> **When you want to throw your opponent a curveball:** If you've been feeding your opponent a steady barrage of topspin forehands, mixing in the odd slice can throw them off-balance.

>> **When you want to hit a drop shot:** The *drop shot* is an offensive stroke (see Chapter 12 for the details).

Chapter **9**

The Backhand: A Perfect Complement

There was a time when the backhand was seen as a necessary evil. It was a shot you hit only because you couldn't hit a forehand. Well, times have changed. The backhand still can be more challenging to learn than the forehand, but it has evolved into a more formidable stroke. Even if you have a strong forehand, your life as a tennis player will run more smoothly if you develop a strong backhand to go with it.

Now, you can try to "run around" your backhand as often as possible to hit more forehands — that's a legitimate strategy that you can read about in Chapter 13. But consider this: Most of your opponents will try to hit to your backhand as a basic strategy. So, if you have a good backhand and know how to use it wisely, your opponents will find themselves playing not to your weakness, but to your hidden *strength.*

One of the reasons the backhand has become a more dependable shot is the wider adoption of the two-handed grip. Not long ago, it was debatable which style — one-handed or two-handed — was more advantageous. However, the pluses of the two-hander have proven more beneficial in the modern game. If you want proof, look at the best players in the world. At the end of the 2000 season, there were eight men and three women ranked in the top 20 of their respective tours using one-handed backhands. At the end of the 2024 season those numbers dropped to three men and zero women. And I don't see the trend reversing course.

Now, this doesn't mean you have to play with a two-handed backhand. I'd recommend it, but the one-handed backhand isn't a lost cause. In this chapter, I lay out the pros and cons of each, and you can decide for yourself.

Understanding the Backhand's Split Personality

You can hit the backhand with two hands on the grip or with one hand, depending on which way feels most comfortable to you. If playing with patience and consistency appeals to you, you'll probably gravitate to the two-handed backhand. If you're drawn to imaginative play, you may have the personality of a one-handed backhand player. Keep in mind, even if you hit most of your backhands with two hands, you can still hit certain shots with one hand — a kind of best-of-both-worlds scenario. Read on to see what I mean.

The two-handed backhand

The two-hander is an ideal backhand for beginners who lack the arm strength or the coordination required by the one-handed backhand. The two-handed backhand offers the following advantages:

>> **Ease:** The two-handed stroke is generally shorter and less complicated, making it easier to learn. The extra hand also helps when contact is outside the sweet spot or the timing of the shot is a little off.

>> **Stability:** You have more strength with two hands than one, and you can keep the racquet face steadier as you swing and follow through. This is especially true when returning a high-bouncing ball that gets up around the shoulders.

>> **Readiness:** You can prepare quickly and do more in less time by using the two-handed stroke. You can hit the two-handed backhand with good power by using just a short backswing and quick upper-body rotation into the ball.

>> **Power:** Most beginners find that, for making power, two hands are better than one. You can get a lot of oomph into a two-handed backhand without sacrificing control.

DISPELLING THE FEAR OF THE BACKHAND

The backhand may seem uncomfortable at first, but only for the following reasons:

- **You haven't formed the habit yet.** If you're right-handed, you accomplish most of your daily tasks from your right, forehand side, so working on the other side feels (and sometimes looks) as comfortable as sitting in the middle seat on an airplane.

- **You haven't fully developed racquet control.** The normal challenges inherent in using an extension of your arm (the racquet) are compounded on the backhand side, making controlling the racquet that much harder.

- **Your muscles aren't quite strong enough.** At first, you may lack the strength to hit a good backhand, even if you understand the mechanics. Conditioning can help you out with your strength, which you can read about in Chapter 16.

All of these reasons may deter you from developing a good backhand. However, you can overcome them with practice and patience, and the results are worth the effort.

Strategically speaking, you may choose to pursue the two-handed backhand if you fall into one or more of the following categories as a player:

>> **You like to outlast opponents in long baseline-to-baseline rallies.** If so, you'll love the steadiness of the two-handed backhand.

>> **You like to push your opponents into making errors.** If so, you'll like the consistency of the two-handed backhand.

>> **You try to win points by reacting to an opponent's aggressive shots (rather than seizing the initiative).** If so, you'll enjoy the stability of the two-handed backhand. These players are known in tennis lingo as *counterpunchers.*

Using the two-handed backhand has the following disadvantages:

>> **Hitting on the run is more difficult.** Running to a far corner of the court and making a shot when you're pressed for time can be awkward when you have two hands on the grip.

>> **Your reach is limited.** You have a shorter reach with the two-hander, especially on balls hit low and wide on your backhand side.

>> **Volleying is harder with two hands on the racquet.** Maneuvering and making reflex-driven shots isn't as easy with the two-hander.

>> **You can't vary your shots as much when you use two hands.** For example, you can hit a slice backhand (a shot that I talk about later in this chapter) more easily and effectively with only one hand on the racquet.

>> **Getting comfortable hitting one-handed shots takes longer.** Many two-handed players still try to learn to hit backhand slices, volleys, and drop shots with one hand, which I definitely encourage. But it won't come as naturally as it would to a player who uses a one-handed backhand.

MAC SAYS

If you're just starting out with the game, I highly recommend that you play-test the two-handed backhand (despite the preceding list). As I mention earlier, the two-handed backhand has become the preferred method for the overwhelming majority of the top players in the world. Most accredited coaches start teaching their students the two-handed backhand. If it doesn't turn out to be the right fit, you can always change later to the one-hander, when you've got more experience under your belt.

The one-handed backhand

Although the one-handed backhand lacks the stability provided by using two hands, it's a more fluid and stylish shot (as opposed to the mechanical appearance of the two-handed backhand).

More important, the one-handed backhand has the following qualities going for it:

>> **Versatility:** One-handers have lots of stroking options, including the use of the one-handed slice backhand, which is such an effective stroke that some players don't hit any other backhand at all. (You can read all about the one-handed slice backhand at the end of this chapter.)

You can also easily improvise on the run with a one-handed stroke because you aren't quite as tied to the racquet. One-handed players are more comfortable rotating their forearms or flicking their wrists to return a shot in a desperate situation. Two-handed players are more limited.

>> **Reach:** You have better reach with a one-handed stroke, especially when hitting balls that are low and away from. You can also get to some shots more quickly because you don't have to hit the one-handed backhand from quite as close to your body as you do the two-hander.

>> **Spin:** With just one hand on the handle, there's a lot of freedom for the wrist to help the racquet face brush up or cut under the ball to create a good amount of spin.

Even though the two-hander is the more popular choice, if the one-handed backhand feels comfortable, and you find that you can make consistent contact and hit the ball with an acceptable amount of power, it could be a good fit for your game.

Even if the one-handed backhand doesn't come to you naturally, first thing out of the gate, you still may want to develop a one-handed backhand if you recognize yourself as one of the following types of players:

>> **You like to mix up the game and use a variety of spins and shots.** If so, you may prefer the one-hander.

>> **You like to attack the net and win points from the forecourt.** If so, you may like the one-hander. When you're up at the net, the ball gets to you faster, and you have to react so quickly that the more maneuverable one-handed volley (which you can read about in Chapter 10) is undoubtedly the better tool.

>> **You have a lot of finesse, or *feel*.** If so, you may want to use the one-hander. Think of it this way: When you're swinging an ax to chop down the old tree in your backyard, you use two hands. When you're painting a self-portrait, you use one hand on the brush.

The disadvantages of the one-handed backhand have become more noticeable as the speeds and spins of the modern game have increased. What used to be minor hinderances that could be overcome are discouraging more and more players from adopting the stroke:

>> **Not enough power:** It takes a strong shoulder, forearm, and wrist to meet the ball with enough resistance to drive the ball back with any kind of authority. This goes double when you're trying to return a shot with good pace and spin on it. You can hit a one-handed backhand as hard as a two-hander, but it does take more effort.

>> **Erratic contact:** Being a more refined shot, the timing and footwork on a one-hander are more demanding. The racquet face can be more difficult to control with just one hand. Add it up, and consistency can be more challenging than it is with a two-hander.

>> **Trouble with the high ball:** Hitting with topspin has become an integral part of today's game (Chapter 7 dives into topspin). These shots bound high off the court, and returning them often requires contact around shoulder level. Hitting the backhand at this height can be kryptonite to a one-hander. The added strength and stability of a second hand on the racquet makes these shots much easier to return with a two-handed backhand.

Hitting the Two-Handed Backhand

When you hit the two-handed backhand, your hands serve different functions. If you're a righty, your right hand is your *racquet hand,* and your left hand is your *support hand.* Your racquet hand goes on the bottom of your grip, and your support hand goes right above it, in the way I describe in the next section of this chapter.

WARNING

If you get confused and reverse your hands, you aren't hitting a two-handed backhand at all — you're hitting a two-handed lefty forehand. Nobody short of a wily opponent trying to con you out of your sneakers would recommend that you do that. Just remember: Your racquet hand is always at the bottom of the racquet when you hit two-handed backhands.

MAC SAYS

THE TWO-HANDED BACKHAND COMES INTO ITS OWN

There was a time when the two-handed backhand was considered a novelty.

Cliff Drysdale, my frequent colleague on ESPN broadcasts, was famous in the early days of the pro tour (in the 1970s) because he hit the backhand with two hands. It didn't hurt that Cliffy was a stylish guy who also wore a pristine white tennis glove on his right racquet hand.

Then came Björn Borg, Jimmy Connors, Chris Evert, and Tracy Austin. All of a sudden, the two-handed backhand became all the rage, and I was one of the young players who adopted it with the blessing of various teachers and coaches. My first racquet (not counting hand-me-downs) was a Bancroft that featured an extra-long grip to accommodate two-handed players.

I was three years old when I started playing tennis, and I wasn't strong enough to swing a racquet with a one-handed backhand like my brothers did. Besides, John and Mark were lefties, and they taught me how to bat in baseball as a lefty. That's probably how I developed a natural predisposition toward the two-handed backhand shot that became my best stroke.

To this day, I bat and play golf lefty, but I do everything else right-handed. Weird, huh?

Finding the two-handed grip

When hitting the two-handed backhand, my first choice would be to hold the racquet hand down at the bottom of the handle, using the continental grip. I think it's the easiest way to learn the stroke, and it produces the most effective shots. It also allows you to simply take your support hand off the frame to hit slice backhands or volleys without changing grips.

That said, just like with the forehand grip (see Chapter 8), it's not my way or the highway. You can hit a very solid two-hander with your racquet hand turned more toward an eastern backhand grip. It's not as versatile as having your racquet hand in a continental grip, but it has become a popular choice because it naturally closes the face of the racquet more at contact, making it easier to brush up the back of the ball to produce extra topspin.

The racquet hand is the most important element in your grip, but your support hand does a lot more than just go along for the ride when you use a two-handed backhand. I get into the details a little bit, but the input from your nondominant hand and arm go a long way in determining the quality of your two-handed backhand. In terms of the grip, I advocate holding the support hand in an eastern forehand grip. (Chapter 7 has the details on how to use this grip). I think this provides the most racquet head stability at contact.

However, once again — is there an echo in here? — there is not one perfect way to position the support hand. Shifting the support hand closer to a semi-western forehand grip is also acceptable. It will also help put more topspin on the backhand and has been the choice of many effective two-handers. You should experiment to see what's the best fit for your stroke.

To assume my preferred two-handed grip, follow these steps:

1. **Place your racquet hand on the bottom of the grip of the racquet, with the heel of your hand resting against the raised butt of the racquet.**

2. **Adjust your hand to assume the continental grip.**

    You can see how to do this in Chapter 7.

3. **Now place your support hand on the grip of the racquet, above your racquet hand in an eastern forehand grip.**

4. **Slide your support hand down until it touches your racquet hand.**

    This position prevents you from having a gap between your hands. Having a hairbreadth of space between your two hands is okay, but the farther apart you place your hands on the grip, the more it limits the racquet's extension through contact and the power you can put into the shot.

Using your nondominant arm

If you followed the steps in the preceding section, you notice that your two hands are on the grip at different angles. Your racquet hand is in the continental grip position, and your support hand is in the same position that a left-hander would use for an eastern forehand grip, albeit higher up on the racquet.

This two-handed grip, which places the palm of your support hand behind the grip of the racquet, allows you to hit firmer shots, provides more resistance on impact, and stabilizes the racquet at the moment of contact. To a great extent, the extra oomph that you get from your powerful two-handed backhand comes from the backup provided by your support hand.

For instance, Rafael Nadal is a natural righty, but his uncle taught him to play tennis left-handed. So his support hand on his two-handed backhand was in all other instances his dominant one. Being strong, coordinated, and comfortable using his right hand helped his two-hander become a real weapon.

Here's the good news: You don't have to switch your playing hand in order to hit a strong two-hander. Smacking a two-handed backhand takes only a smooth turn of the shoulders and hips away from the ball and a brisk turn back toward contact with your racquet along for the ride. That kind of efficiency makes the two-handed backhand a solid, dependable stroke. To swing away and hit a two-handed back-hand shot, follow these steps (which assume you're right-handed — if you're a leftie, you know what to do):

1. **Assume the ready position with your knees bent and feet slightly more than shoulder-width apart (see Figure 9-1).**

    Chapter 7 tells you all about the ready position.

2. **Hold your racquet comfortably at waist height with the two-handed backhand grip.**

    Keep the racquet head slightly higher than the level of your wrists and your elbows away from your body (see Figure 9-2).

3. **As the ball approaches, pivot on your left foot as you rotate your shoulders to the left, bringing your racquet into the backswing position.**

    You'll know you're making a full turn when your right shoulder is just about underneath your chin (see Figure 9-3).

4. **Keep your arms slightly bent with a little tension as the racquet moves into position.**

    Having soft, relaxed wrists will help drop the racquet head to around knee level. If you're using the proper grip, at this point the racquet face should be slightly closed to the court.

FIGURE 9-1:
The ready
position for the
two-handed
backhand.

FIGURE 9-2:
As the ball
approaches,
prepare for
the stroke by
getting your
racquet back.

FIGURE 9-3:
Step into the shot
with your knees
slightly bent.

© John Wiley & Sons, Inc.

REMEMBER

Even though you don't need much preparation time for the two-handed backhand, you must watch the ball, get your racquet back quickly, and keep your knees lightly flexed. (Chapter 7 tells you some other universal fundamentals to observe with all your strokes.)

Your swing comes naturally as you uncoil your shoulders and step toward the ball.

TIP

Try to keep your hands back as you turn your shoulders toward the ball, allowing the racquet head to gradually build speed into contact.

5. **Step toward the ball and swing smoothly, leading with your right shoulder, following a low-to-high path.**

   Accelerate through contact and extend the racquet toward the target. A good point of reference: If your left shoulder just about reaches your chin, that's full shoulder rotation.

   You want to make contact at a point about even with your right hip. You should feel a transfer of weight to your right thigh as you start the swing.

   Uncoil your shoulders. Let your shoulders lead your swing through its arc rather than relying on just your arms. The shoulders add firmness to your stroke.

TIP

During your swing, keep your support hand firm behind the racquet handle. You generate more power and have better extension through contact with an active support hand. A classic drill to learn how to incorporate more *off-arm* (your nondominant arm, or the arm of your support hand) in a two-handed backhand is by hitting the shot with the racquet hand essentially removed from the stroke. Assume the two-handed backhand grip, only now use just the tips of the thumb, index, and middle fingers of the racquet hand to gently hold the butt of the racquet. It serves only as a guide as you swing. Hitting two-handed backhands in this fashion — essentially a lefty forehand — teaches you how to more effectively incorporate your off-hand in the swing.

6. **Finish with the racquet head pointed up and away, at about a 45-degree angle to the net (see Figure 9-4).**

   As you improve, and your swing picks up more speed, it should naturally decelerate over your right shoulder.

FIGURE 9-4:
As you bring your racquet forward to make contact with the ball and follow through, your eyes should never leave the ball.

© John Wiley & Sons, Inc.

You've just hit a successful two-handed backhand. Who knows? With some practice, it could develop into your money shot.

Hitting the One-Handed Backhand

The one-handed backhand is versatile and graceful. When hit properly, it's a thing of beauty. But it can be a tough shot to learn, even more than the two-handed backhand. Plus, it's more difficult to hit consistently, making it a less practical shot. Hence, its drop in popularity over the past several generations. However, some players still find success with a dedicated one-handed backhand. And even if you opt for the two-hander, knowing how to hit the one-handed slice (which I cover later in this chapter) will give you a more well-rounded stroke.

Finding the one-handed backhand grip

If you're going to drive the one-handed backhand, or hit it with topspin, the eastern backhand grip suits the shot best. The continental grip is superior when you want to put slice on the ball. (Chapter 7 tells you all about the different grips.) Becoming familiar with both grips is key to having a dependable one-handed backhand.

Extending through contact

Hitting a one-handed backhand resembles winding up to throw a Frisbee. Just as in that motion, you step forward and extend your hitting arm in a line toward the target. Where the two-handed backhand requires more shoulder rotation into the shot, the shoulders on a one-handed backhand stay more perpendicular to the net. The off-arm stays behind the body and often extends out toward the back fence. This helps to maintain balance and hit the shot with good pace and depth.

REMEMBER

The first few steps of the one-handed backhand are similar to what you do with the two-handed backhand. The major differences between the two shots are how you hold the racquet and the role of the shoulders during the swing.

Follow these steps to hit an effective one-handed backhand (again, these steps are written assuming you're right-handed):

1. **Assume the ready position with your knees bent and feet slightly more than shoulder-width apart (refer to Figure 9-1).**

    Chapter 7 tells you all about the ready position.

2. **Hold your racquet comfortably at waist height with the eastern backhand grip.**

   Keep the racquet head slightly higher than the level of your wrists. Lightly support the throat of the racquet with your nondominant hand.

3. **As the ball approaches, step forward toward it with your right foot, pivoting with your left foot (see Figure 9-5).**

   You can step straight toward the ball, or use a slightly closed stance as though you're stepping toward the left net post. At the same time, rotate your shoulders to the left, bringing your racquet back as you do so. The hitting elbow should be slightly flexed.

   Keep your left hand on the throat of the racquet, where it will stay until you begin your forward swing. Doing this aids in bringing the racquet back properly and helps keep your left hand from just dangling there uselessly.

FIGURE 9-5:
Get your racquet back while keeping your left hand on the racquet.

© John Wiley & Sons, Inc.

4. **Continuing to use your left hand as a guide, drop the racquet head below the level of the incoming ball (see Figure 9-6).**

The racquet face should be slightly closed to the court. As the ball approaches start your swing, leading with your right shoulder, following a low-to-high path, and accelerating smoothly through the stroke.

FIGURE 9-6: Make contact at a point out in front of your right hip, while your arm goes out to meet the ball.

© John Wiley & Sons, Inc.

You should feel a transfer of weight to your right leg as you start the swing.

You want to make contact at a point out in front of your right hip. As your racquet arm comes around to meet the ball, the hitting arm straightens out. Your left shoulder stays back, and your left arm swings back as a counterbalance to your forward motion. It should feel as though you're squeezing your shoulder blades together.

5. **Follow through and finish high (see Figure 9-7).**

Keep extending toward the target after the ball has left your strings. The one-handed backhand is a long stroke, ending high, with the racquet head pointing up and away from you at a 45-degree angle to the net.

REMEMBER

When you're extending through contact, try to keep your chest pointing to the side fence as long as you can. This helps get a fuller extension and better depth on shots.

FIGURE 9-7:
Finish up high, with your arms extended in a line in opposite directions.

Dressing Up Your Backhand with Slice

Whether you hit your backhand with one hand or two, hitting it with slice never goes out of style. A dependable slice backhand will help get you out of trouble when you're scrambling, throw in a change of pace to disrupt your opponent's rhythm, or serve as a security blanket when your backhand drive is misfiring. (Chapter 7 tells you about the fundamentals of slicing.) The backhand slice also has a lot in common with the backhand volley (see Chapter 10) and the backhand drop shot (see Chapter 12). So, developing a good slice is a building block for those other shots.

If you're playing with a two-handed backhand, hitting your slice that way is fine. However, the slice is generally hit more effectively with just one hand on the racquet. The support hand being on the handle and the shoulder rotation of the two-hander limit the extension out through contact, which makes it more difficult to put underspin on the ball. It can often turn into a sidespin shot, which isn't as desirable.

That's why even players who hit the backhand slice with both hands on the grip will often take the support hand off after contact and follow through with just one hand on the racquet. Or better yet, learn to hit the one-handed slice. Many great players, like Carlos Alcaraz and Aryna Sabalenka, primarily use a two-handed backhand and have developed terrific one-handed slice backhands to go along with it. I believe this is the ideal scenario.

The slice backhand offers the following practical and tactical advantages:

>> **The slice stroke has a lower degree of difficulty.** You hit under the ball, instead of through and over it, as you do on the topspin backhand. That takes less effort.

>> **Slice slows the ball down.** The more spin a ball has, the slower it travels. Slice shots generally are the slowest and don't bounce as high either. Those two qualities can mess with an opponent's timing.

>> **Slice shots travel in a flat trajectory.** You don't have to lift the ball over the net in an arc and then get it to drop back down inside the boundaries of the court the way you do with your other shots.

WARNING

Slice backhands make poor *passing shots* (the shots you try to hit by an opponent who is crowding the net — see Chapter 13.) Slow pace and the flat trajectory give your opponent two big advantages: more time and an ideal height, at about a foot above the net, to hit a winning volley.

Basically, you hit the slice backhand just as you would hit your standard backhand (both one-handed and two-handed backhands), changing only the following things about your stroke (again, assuming you're right-handed):

1. **As the ball approaches and you rotate your shoulders to your left, bring your racquet back above your left shoulder.**

   If it's not already in place, find the continental grip with your right hand.

   Your shoulders and feet should be in a line, perpendicular to the net. The stance somewhat resembles the stance you take when you step up to the plate and get ready to swing a baseball bat, only now you're hitting on the opposite side of the plate. In both cases, your hands are up around your left shoulder. The racquet head should be pointing at the back fence, at about a 45-degree angle.

Your support hand should cradle the throat of the racquet — or remain on the grip for a two-handed slice — and help get it into position. When your backswing is complete, your right shoulder is close to your chin, and your right elbow points in the same direction as your right foot.

2. **Turn the racquet face as you bring it back so the hitting surface ends up facing upward, as shown in Figure 9-8.**

    The hitting wrist should be slightly bent and relaxed. This position makes it easy and natural to brush your strings under the lower portion of the ball, producing backspin.

© John Wiley & Sons, Inc.

FIGURE 9-8:
Hold your racquet at a 45-degree angle to the fence when you slice your backhand.

3. **Swing forward with a gradual high-to-low motion.**

    If you're hitting the slice with one hand, release the racquet with your left hand as you do this. On slice shots, the racquet doesn't drop down below the ball and come up. Instead, it starts from above the ball and moves forward and slightly downward into contact at a point just in front of your right shoulder. Just as it was set in the backswing, the racquet face should be slightly open. This helps the racquet "slice" under the ball.

TIP

Don't chop at the ball. Many beginners have a tendency to exaggerate the slice's high-to-low swing path. After contact, their racquet head can end up just above the court. You still want to drive the racquet head through contact. An effective slice puts some underspin on the ball, but not too much. An excess of slice will cause to ball to float over the net and pop straight up after the bounce instead of staying low.

4. **Follow through until your racquet arm is fully extended, allowing the racquet head to decelerate before it stops around chest level.**

   If you're using two hands to hit the shot, this is where the support hand leaves the grip, so the hitting arm can fully extend. The support hand on a one-handed slice has already left the racquet and should extend toward the back fence as it would on any well-struck backhand stroke.

Chapter **10**

The Volley: An Exclamation Point

The volley is probably the most underutilized stroke in singles tennis. Today, tennis has shifted away from a serve-and-volley game toward one where the players mostly trade groundstrokes from the baseline. Players still come to the net at opportune times — it's just not often done after the serve. Most often, the volley follows successfully recognizing and attacking the midcourt ball (which I describe in more detail in this chapter). If you learn the proper technique to hit the shot and the best ways to approach net, you'll have a leg up in competitive play. In this chapter, I clear up any confusion you may have about this effective stroke and its uses.

A Half-Stroke with Punch, Possibility, and Risk

Compared to groundstrokes, the volley seems like a tiny half-stroke. You don't make a big backswing when you volley. Read that last sentence again because it's the most important thing you need to remember about the volley. In fact, with volleying, it's a disservice to call it a backswing. Your racquet should never go back behind your body the way it does on a groundstroke. The face should travel back only as far as your shoulder turn. That positions the frame just in front of your body. The swing itself is nothing more than uncoiling your shoulders as you step toward the ball.

Try to avoid lunging at or swatting at the ball. You intercept the ball with the racquet using almost a catching motion and let the energy in the ball and racquet strings take care of the rest. This is often called *punching* or *blocking* the ball back. This is all easier said than done. Comfort with the volley takes time and practice. Ultimately, you want to be able to control the ball with the most efficient technique possible. For the best volleyers, less is more.

TIP

Except in spirited doubles exchanges, you rarely hit more than one or two volleys during any given point. That's because you typically want to volley from a position within a few feet of the net, which allows you to create either the pace or angle needed to get the ball past your opponent.

Okay, volleying sounds like a pretty good situation to be in. You come to a commanding position at the net and hit a relatively easy stroke that can be almost impossible for your opponent to reach and return. You may be wondering, "If it's such a no-brainer, why don't players try to volley every point?" Well, consider the following factors:

>> **You have to approach the net on a good shot.** You can't impulsively rush up to the net just because you want to volley. If you try it, you'll often be badly out of position and vulnerable to your opponent's counterattack on your way to the net. You have to come to the net behind a weak shot by your opponent or the right kind of shot by you. The key to making your trip to the net successful is moving forward from a midcourt shot (see the "Taking the Net: Getting There Is Half the Fun" section, later in this chapter).

>> **You have a lot of territory to cover and less time to do so.** When you're back on the baseline there's more time to gauge where the ball will bounce and the speed of your opponent's shot. At net, everything happens more quickly, testing your technique and control over the ball. You must react quickly as your opponent tries to hit the ball by you with a *passing shot* (when the ball zips by out of your reach on either side of you; see Chapter 13), "handcuffing" you with a shot right at you, or *lobbing* the ball (hitting it way over your head so it drops behind you; see Chapter 13), forcing you to retreat from the net.

>> **You can get intimidated pretty easily.** Although you take the initiative at net when you choose to volley, if you're not confident you can control the ball, you can feel like a sitting duck. Even a ball hit right to you can seem like a huge challenge if you don't have belief in the stroke. Throw in an opponent smacking passing shots by you or sending lobs over your head, and you can quickly lose faith in the strategy.

Except for those times when you're drawn to the net against your will — for example, when your opponent hits a drop shot or weak short ball — you use the volley to dictate play and to pressure your opponent. Only come to the net when you're comfortable you can control the volley. As your control becomes better, you can take the initiative more often and attack the volley.

The Volley Grip

When volleying, I recommend using the continental grip because it allows you to hit both backhand and forehand volleys without changing grips. (See Chapter 7 for more information on the various grips.) You'll appreciate that versatility when you're at the net, the ball zooms toward you, and you have to react to either side in a split second. That's no time to be worrying about changing your grip!

That said, although the continental grip is my first recommendation, I'm not opposed to minor variation. I recognize that many players find the continental grip uncomfortable and unnatural, especially when they're first starting out. If that's you, a slight turn of the hand toward the eastern grip may feel more stable. If that's ultimately more effective, and transitions between forehands and backhands are smooth, then happy volleying! But I still recommend making it a practice priority to get comfortable with the continental grip for the volley.

Hitting the Forehand Volley

The volley stroke looks deceptively easy because you don't do very much to hit it. But sometimes, doing very little is much harder than it looks.

The biggest temptation you face when volleying is the urge to make a long backswing before you hit the ball. As I explain earlier, there's no bigger volley-killer than taking a long backswing. When your opponent hits a high, floating shot, it may warrant a longer backswing to create more power. But in most playing situations, you just don't have the time to bring your racquet back and then forward again to hit the volley.

It's also important to maintain your composure and make a disciplined, short, controlled stroke in quick exchanges, which you'll encounter more often in doubles. When you're up at the net (not to mention those occasions when you and your opponent both end up there), everything happens extra fast. It can be exciting — in fact, it can get you overexcited. Hitting a successful volley means keeping your head — and controlling your racquet head — to execute the shot.

Hitting the volley is just like catching a ball. When someone tosses you a ball, you don't swing your arm into position to catch it. You just reach out for the ball, intercepting it with your opened palm and fingers. That's exactly what your volley is: reaching out to catch the ball, with the racquet face serving the same role as your palm.

After you get accustomed to curbing your instinct to backswing and use that fundamental catching technique, the volley stroke is nearly foolproof. Follow these steps to hit solid forehand volleys:

1. **Take up position about three feet from the net, with your feet spread about the width of your shoulders.**

   In a real playing situation, rather than a warm-up or practice, you have to get to the net during the point. To better your chances of success, you should do that under the right circumstances. I give you some advice on how to get into position in the "Taking the Net: Getting There Is Half the Fun" section, later in this chapter.

2. **Adopt the continental grip with your dominant hand.**

3. **Hold the racquet with the head up, directly in front of you, racquet face perpendicular to your chest, with the butt cap of the racquet about even with your belly button.**

   Gently cradle the throat of the racquet with the fingers of your left hand.

4. **Flex your knees slightly, until you can feel the tension in the quad muscles of your thighs, with weight on the balls of your feet.**

   In Figure 10-1, you can see the player set and ready to hit a forehand volley.

5. **As the ball approaches on your forehand side, ideally waist to shoulder height, pivot on the balls of your feet and turn your shoulders slightly to the right.**

   This rotation of your upper body automatically brings the racquet back to a point even with your right shoulder. No farther!

   Stamping your lead foot lightly but noticeably as you meet the ball can help you hit better, crisper volleys on either side. If you concentrate on stamping your foot, it helps you step into the ball and time your stroke.

6. **Time the stroke to meet the ball in front of your body.**

   Take a small step forward with your nondominant foot and drive the racquet forward, with the head up and the hitting surface facing the ball square on (see Figure 10-2).

FIGURE 10-1:
Preparation is key
to hitting a
good volley.

FIGURE 10-2:
Turn your body
as you punch out
your volley.

Meet the ball with the racquet face when it's about even with your leading, right shoulder. The continental grip necessitates angling your wrist back slightly to provide a nice flat surface for the ball. Just cock your hand slightly, so the palm faces the ball. At contact, give the handle a little extra squeeze with your bottom three fingers to maintain a steady racquet face.

7. **Continue to drive the racquet straight forward through the point of contact until the ball has left your strings, with a controlled, smooth follow-through.**

   The follow-through on the volley is short but definite, like the stroke itself. On your volley, you don't come across your body as you do with most forehands, even when you want the ball to go crosscourt. You stand so close to the net that you can put the shot to any part of your opponent's court by slightly varying the angle of the racquet face and punching in the direction you want the ball to go.

TIP

Many beginners find that they can resist the temptation to backswing if they keep both hands close to the racquet handle as they meet the ball. Try it. When you reach forward for the ball, release your free hand but keep it moving toward the ball, close to your racquet hand. In effect, you reach for the ball with both hands.

Hitting the Backhand Volley

All players should strive to hit their backhand volley with one hand because it affords greater reach when stretched or digging out low volleys, as well as quicker reactions during rapid exchanges. Plus, it provides better feel for the ball on the strings, which helps when you're trying to hit *touch volleys* (more softly hit volleys that bounce closer to the net than the baseline).

Can you hit your backhand volley with two hands? Absolutely. In fact, I played my pro career with a two-handed backhand volley. So, I'm not opposed to the stroke, and I give you the finer points in this section.

Players who use the two-handed backhand groundstroke often prefer to volley with two hands on the racquet. Beginners, in particular, appreciate the added stability. But, although you can hit close, comfortable volleys with two hands on the racquet, the volleys that require more improvisation are problematic. So, practice hitting as many of your volleys as you can with one hand. I wish I had added the one-handed backhand volley to my game.

As with the forehand volley, it's best to hit the backhand volley with a continental grip. On the backhand side, the continental grip actually gets your forearm and hand out of the way, allowing you to lead your stroke with the racquet head. However, it can also feel less stable at impact because less of the hand is behind the handle at impact. Just as with the forehand, a subtle shift toward an eastern backhand grip can strengthen the wrist and get more support from the thumb. (See Chapter 7 for more information on the various grips.)

To hit a backhand volley, you follow most of the same steps that I outline in "Hitting the Forehand Volley," using the right foot (rather than the left) to step into the volley (see Figure 10-3). It's a valuable lesson that's worth repeating.

FIGURE 10-3: With the one-handed backhand volley, step into the volley with your right foot.

TIP

Your left hand is a terrific timing aid on the backhand side. Holding the throat of the racquet as you turn your upper body helps keep you from taking too long a backswing, and releasing the racquet as you begin your forward motion with the racquet adds punch and authority to the shot.

Follow these steps to develop a dependable backhand volley:

1. **Take up position about 3 feet from the net, with your feet spread about the width of your shoulders.**

2. **Adopt the continental grip with your right hand (if you're a right-hander) and gently cradle the throat of the racquet with the fingers of your left hand.**

   If you're hitting a two-hander, the left hand should be in an eastern forehand grip.

3. **Hold the racquet with the head up, directly in front of you, racquet face perpendicular to your chest, with the butt cap of the racquet about even with your belly button.**

4. **Flex your knees slightly, until you can feel the tension in the quad muscles of your thighs, with weight on the balls of your feet.**

5. **As the ball approaches on your backhand side, ideally waist to shoulder height, pivot on the balls of your feet and turn your shoulders slightly to the left.**

   The rotation of your shoulders automatically brings the racquet back to a point just in front of your left shoulder.

6. **Time the stroke to meet the ball in front of your body, about even with your right shoulder.**

   Control the racquet head with your hand. As you get comfortable with this, practice taking a small step forward with your dominant foot. One-handers should release the racquet with their left hand; two-handers keep both hands on the grip until contact. Drive the racquet forward, with the head up and the hitting surface facing the ball square on.

7. **Drive the racquet forward with control through the point of contact until the ball has left your strings, with a smooth follow-through.**

   If you're using two hands, your left hand will stay in front of your body at contact and follow-through. For the one-handed backhand volley, the left arm should travel farther back behind you.

Concentrate on extending the left arm back as you follow through on the one-handed backhand volley. This puts your shoulders perpendicular to the net and encourages a fuller and straighter extension through contact. The result is a more penetrating volley with less of a chance of chopping down on the ball, a common pitfall of many well-intentioned backhand volleys.

WARNING

As a beginner, you may find that even with the two-handed volley, the racquet can twist and shudder in your hand at the moment of contact. This isn't necessarily an issue of strength or stability. It happens when the ball strikes the strings outside the sweet spot. (See Chapter 3 for more info on the sweet spot.) Whether you hit the volley with two hands or just one, an off-center hit can cause the racquet to do weird things in your hands.

Taking the Net: Getting There Is Half the Fun

There's an old adage that the only time most recreational players venture to the net in singles is to congratulate an opponent after a match. That's even something we've said during my ESPN commentary about players who stay glued to the baseline: "They only come up to the net to shake hands."

But in all seriousness, many players are reluctant to volley because they don't have the necessary skill. So, they're much more comfortable employing a wait-and-see approach from the baseline. They don't work on the volley enough to make it a reliable shot, so they avoid using it as much as possible. Going to the net requires belief in your ability to control the volley. Then it becomes a great tactic to put pressure on your opponent.

Even if you prefer playing from the baseline, being able to volley effectively makes you a more well-rounded player. Plus, it's always good to have options. Against certain opponents, your mere presence at net can cause them to buckle under the pressure of producing passing shots and lobs. And if you play doubles, you start many of the points up close to the net. So, if you plan on having any success and not letting your partner down, learning to volley is a must. (Turn to Chapter 13 to read more about doubles play.)

Establishing the best times to move forward can take the guesswork out of when to come to the net. It's not uncommon for an opponent's shot to drag you inside the court against your will. This area somewhere between the baseline and service line has often been called *no man's land* because it's nowhere you want to be for very long. Executing this midcourt shot is key to set up a winning volley. At the pro level, how players handle the midcourt ball is a big factor — it can be the difference between being top 10 or top 100.

No matter the playing level, it's always more advantageous to come to the net on your terms. Deciding to come in to the net because you want to, with confidence in your volley skills is a great move. Many call the volley high risk — but think of it as a percentage shot if you know the right times and best ways to approach the net to tip the odds in your favor.

Recognizing the transition (midcourt) ball

Going forward to the net at the right times means taking advantage of an *opportunity ball* (a shot that allows you to move forward inside the court and up to the net). Sometimes these balls are fairly obvious; other times, it takes some know-how to identify. After you get good at spotting these chances, you'll know whether it's time for an approach shot, or if staying back is the proper course.

TIP

Here are some tips for this critical step in establishing a solid net game:

>> **Know your "go" zone.** The best time to transition to the net is off an opponent's short ball, primarily because the ball has already drawn you well inside the court and you're already much closer to the net. To erase indecision, you should establish a predetermined landing area that's a green light (go!) to hit an approach and move forward. A good rule of thumb to start is from the net back to a few feet behind the service line.

>> **Look for a vulnerable opponent.** Sometimes a forceful shot on your part puts your opponent in a compromising position. Telltale signs are hurried movement, poor balance, and rushed technique. If you spot an opponent under duress, you can expect a weak reply and an opportunity to move inside the court. This is what tennis players call *anticipation*. Even before your opponent returns the shot, take a couple of steps forward and get ready to pounce.

>> **Aim your approach shot deep.** Because you ideally hit your approach shot from well inside the baseline, you may have to shorten your backswing or lower your target window over the net in order to keep the ball from going long. The top priority is to put it in the court. As you get more comfortable, aim for the approach shot to land within a few feet of your opponent's baseline. This gives you more time to establish an offensive position at the net, as well as force your opponent to hit a passing shot from deep in the court.

>> **Attack your opponent's weaker side.** When possible, it's always best to direct your approach shot to your opponent's weaker stroke. For novices, this is typically the backhand. If that side is particularly shaky, you can draw errors just with your presence at net. You won't even have to hit a volley. The only time it makes sense to approach an opponent's stronger side is if they're way out of position. Otherwise, approaching down the middle can be an effective tactic. When you're pushed into a corner by the approach, the opponent has

more angle to hit a passing shot. From the middle of the court, the angle has to be created, which is more difficult.

>> **Use spin to your advantage.** Some better players can hit the approach shot for a winner, but most of the time it's meant to set up the next shot. And when you're able, adding spin to the ball can make it even more effective. Putting slice on the approach keeps it lower after the bounce, forcing your opponent to hit up on the passing shot, resulting in a high volley. And hitting a looping, topspin shot can push an opponent well behind the baseline and into an unfavorable defensive position.

Following the approach shot

You identified the midcourt ball, and you hit the approach shot. Now it's time to get moving. Even if you've done those first two steps correctly, taking a mad dash to the net can often sabotage the point. Getting in the right position after the approach gives you the best chance at successfully intercepting your opponent's next shot and hitting a winning volley. It also forces your opponent to hit a more difficult shot. That's a win-win.

REMEMBER

Sometimes, you may miscalculate your shot or your opponent's power and end up having to hit your volley from the area of the court well inside the baseline, but behind the service line. This area is called *no-man's land* because you're too far from the net to volley effectively but too close to it to hit good groundstrokes that clear the net and still fall into the boundaries. Making good shots from no-man's land is one of the most challenging assignments in tennis. To avoid hitting from no-man's land, get to the net quickly or stay at the baseline until you can make your way to the net.

Organizing your feet at the net

TIP

Your footwork and positioning are key to successful net play. Keep these tips in mind to get the most out of your volleying game:

>> **Run with controlled steps.** Don't go loping up to the net with long, gangly strides like a Saint Bernard. Your first few steps can be lengthier to cover ground, but as you close in to the net, using shorter steps will keep you better balanced and capable of changing directions. When you go to hit the ball, you should be slowing down to be on balance and in a good position to hit the ball.

>> **Head in the direction of the approach shot.** The simplest, highest-percentage play is to follow your approach shot. For instance, if you hit the

approach deep toward the singles sideline of your opponent's ad court — which would be a righty's backhand side — you should move forward and take a position just about in the middle of your deuce-side service box. This puts the court's geometry in your favor. You're covering your opponent's best shot (down the line), while daring them to attempt the more difficult option (crosscourt) that you can still move to intercept. And if a lob goes up, you've got plenty of time to retreat to hit it.

The rookie mistake is to hit the approach, run straight to the center of the court, and straddle the center service line. This would appear to put you in the best position to cover your opponent's return shot, but it only makes sense if the approach shot is directed down the middle. Otherwise, you're giving up too much valuable court real estate. The down-the-line passing shot in particular will be wide open and your opponents will be happy to take advantage.

>> **Perform a split-step as your opponent is about to hit the ball.** As you move forward, there's a temptation to just keep charging and get yourself right on top of the net. However, chances are, your opponent's shot won't be hit directly at you. And if you're barreling in at top speed and the ball is hit away from you, good luck changing directions. So, as your opponent's racquet goes into the backswing, perform a *split-step* (a small hop onto the balls of your feet). Don't take a big jump. Don't slam on the brakes. Think of it as gathering your momentum. This gets you in better balance and ready to spring in any direction.

Lifting Low Volleys and Half-Volleys over the Net

When you get accustomed to hitting volleys from up close to the net, they may seem like child's play. But in real playing situations, you'll inevitably find yourself in a jam — playing too far from the net, extending to reach a shot, or falling prey to your opponent's skill or luck.

The lower a ball drops below the level of the net before you hit it, the tougher it is to make the shot. Even tougher are balls dropping so quickly that you can't even hit them out of the air and have to let them bounce. That's because you must lift the ball over the net and still get it to fall into your opponent's court.

TIP

Low volleys and *half-volleys* (hitting the ball after it bounces) are often returned defensively, with little pace. Remember these two keys to hitting good low volleys:

» **Get down low with the ball.** Your racquet head should ideally be above the level of your wrist when you volley. You're asking for trouble if you try to make volleys the lazy way, by dropping the racquet head toward your shoe tops. You have to get down really low by bending your knees, not bending at the waist. Try to keep your chest facing the net. When you have to hit a low volley, bend your knees as you step into the ball with your *leading leg* (if you're a right-hander, your left leg on the forehand side, your right leg on the backhand). You can see how low you need to get to hit a good low volley in Figure 10-4.

» **Open the racquet face.** The lower the volley, the more you have to tilt the hitting surface of the racquet upward in order to achieve the first objective of your volley: getting it back up over the net.

REMEMBER

Don't worry about power on your low volleys and half-volleys; it's not a priority. Concentrate on placing these volleys deep into your opponent's court instead of going for extreme angles or a lot of pace. After you develop good control over these types of volleys, you can also return them short in the court like a drop shot (see Chapter 12).

FIGURE 10-4:
Getting way down low for a low volley.

© John Wiley & Sons, Inc.

Adding Touch to Your Volleys

When you have an easy, high volley that you want to hit hard for a winner, the crisp, flatter volley is your best choice. But at other times, spin and *touch shots* (delicate shots that are hit shorter in the court) can come in handy on your volley. Along with the hard, drive volley, these skills will help you attack more areas of the court.

The only spin that matters on the standard volley is slice. Almost all volleys — even the ones hit hard through the court — have some manner of slice or under-spin on the ball. The slice adds control to your shot, and it produces a shot that stays lower when it bounces than a typical ball that's hit flatter. (You can read more about the nature of slice in Chapter 7.)

TIP

Slice is especially valuable when you're fielding a low volley (below the level of the top of the net) because getting under the ball, the way you do when you use slice, is the safest and surest way to complete the first job you have: lifting the ball high enough so that it clears the net and still ends up falling inside the boundaries of your opponent's court.

Add it all up, and you see that hard flatter volleys are great for ending points with winners. But when you need control, either to return a tricky shot or to set up a winning volley on the next ball, using more slice helps. Slice also makes life more difficult for your opponents because of the low bounce it produces. If the ball stays down, instead of taking a normal, high bounce, it's much harder for your opponent to hit a good passing shot or lob.

Slice really shines on the backhand side. Hitting with underspin comes very naturally on the backhand because the continental grip makes it easy to swing the racquet with the face in an ideal *open* position — that is, with the hitting surface tilted upward.

On slice shots, the racquet travels at a slight high-to-low angle as you drive it forward to meet the ball. The strings make contact on the lower portion of the back of the ball and then brush under it to create slice. You don't have to start your swing from a higher position, but you have to make it travel at a slightly more downward angle as the racquet travels forward to meet the ball. The degree of tilt, combined with the point at which you make contact with the ball, determines the degree of slice you generate. Changing the point of contact and brushing under the ball can make a big difference in how the ball behaves after it leaves the racquet.

Touch shots are a more advanced option. It takes lots of practice and comfort with the volley before adding a touch shot to your playbook. Instead of punching through the volley, you're almost trying to catch the ball on the strings. At contact, you soften the wrist and gently slide or cup the racquet underneath the ball. This helps take pace off your opponent's ball so you can finesse the shot over the net shorter in the court. By turning your racquet face, you can angle the ball away from your opponent, or hit a *drop volley* (a volley hit short in the court that bounces at least twice before reaching the opponent's service line) or, as I like to call it, the dropper!

The value of these touch shots is that they force opponents to defend inside the court. Many players, especially beginners, are quite content scurrying side-to-side behind the baseline. Hitting the volley deep means they don't have to run as far to retrieve it — they're already back behind the baseline — and it's going right into their comfort zone. However, if the volley is hit shorter in the court, they have to run farther to return it, and it brings them to a part of the court they'd rather avoid. Another win-win situation.

To get a good sense of how slice works, think of the racquet face as a platter and the ball as a juicy yellow apple. The racquet travels under the ball, allowing you to serve up a delicious winner!

Swinging Volleys: Finishing with a Flourish

The swinging volley is another advanced shot (lots of pros use it) and one you don't need to learn right away. But it's something worth knowing about and working toward. Plus, it's a lot of fun to hit. The swinging volley falls in the volley category, but it mostly incorporates groundstroke technique. It comes in handy when you're standing inside the baseline near the service line and your opponent's shot comes floating over the net without much pace. It's not high enough to hit an overhead (see Chapter 12), but it's too high and soft to hit a forceful volley. In order to drive the ball with more pace, you need a bigger swing. So, you're taking the ball directly out of the air like you would for a traditional volley, only with a groundstroke.

Remember these two keys to execute a successful swinging volley:

>> **Make contact with the ball above net level.** Because you're inside the court when hitting the swinging volley, you're closer to the net. If you let the ball drop too low before you hit it, there's a greater chance you'll put it in the net. To avoid this, look to make contact around shoulder height. It's higher than you would on a standard groundstroke, but the elevated contact point lessens the chance of making an error in the net.

» **You still may need to swing up on the ball.** With the higher contact point above net level, it may seem natural to hit down on the ball. In other words, you make contact on the top half of the back of the ball with a high-to-low swing path. However, this technique often dumps the shot in the net. You still need to brush up the back of the ball with low-to-high motion, using topspin (see Chapter 7) to safely bring the ball down inside your opponent's court. Because you won't have to hit the ball as far as when you're on the baseline, it's fine to take a shorter backswing. Otherwise, swing away as you would on a regular groundstroke.

Chapter **11**

The Serve: The Most Important Shot in the Game

A powerful serve is the most impactful single stroke in tennis. Hitting a clean service ace really puts the competitive wind in your sails. The serve can be an atomic, preemptive first strike. It's the knockout punch of tennis shots. But that's the prize at the end of the road. Before you're banging aces by your opponents, you've got to learn to put the ball in the box.

Each point begins with either a first or second serve, and if you don't put one of them in the correct service box, the point is over before it even starts. (Turn to Chapter 5 to discover the rules and regulations of the serve.)

When you do put the serve in the box, the speed and placement of your serve can dictate the way the rest of the point develops. For example, if your opponent has a very weak, defensive backhand, the ability to consistently place your serve to that side gives you a terrific advantage at the start of a point.

REMEMBER Your opponent only has to break your serve (make you lose a game that you serve) once and then win the rest of their service games to win a set. Due to the strategic importance of winning all the games you serve, you can't put enough time into perfecting your serve.

In this chapter, I cover the fundamentals and form you need to develop a dependable and formidable serve.

The Ball Is Entirely in Your Hands

When you serve, you can do what you want, when you want, any way you want (within the rules, which you can read about in Chapter 5), from the moment you toss the ball up until you hit it. It's the only shot in which you're not reacting to your opponent's shot, putting you in complete control. Your opponent can't do anything to interfere with the mechanics of your serve.

So, technically, if you were so inclined, you could throw the ball over your left shoulder, spin in a circle, and then hit the ball over the net with the grip of your racquet. But other than showing off some impressive coordination, you wouldn't be making much of an impact with your serve.

TIP Instead of expressing your artistic individuality in your serve, you'll be better off patterning your serve on an upward-throwing motion. The fundamentals of the serve aren't too different from throwing a baseball or a football. Both motions start from a stationary position and incorporate leading with the nondominant arm, rotating the shoulders, and transferring your weight forward as you deliver an object to a target with a limber arm. This is one of the reasons many coaches have their students practice their serves by playing catch. But instead of throwing a ball, you're throwing the racquet up to a contact point above your head.

Serving Essentials

Developing a throwing action is just one part of the serve. The stroke is a coordinated, rhythmic motion that requires input from just about every part of your body. Which can make it tricky for beginners to get the hang of. In order to do it with consistent success, you have to become skilled with the following basic steps:

1. **Regularly toss the ball with your nondominant arm to a place where you can hit it easily and effectively.**

2. **Get your racquet into a good position to hit the ball.**

3. **Make solid contact.**

4. **Follow through.**

Before you start putting things in motion, though, you've got know how to hold the racquet and how to stand.

Your service motion should become a habit. Show me a player who's always tinkering with their service motion, and I'll show you someone who isn't comfortable serving.

Grip

If you want to maximize your serve, you need to hit it holding the racquet with a continental grip. (Chapter 7 tells you all about your grip choices.) It allows the server to more easily accelerate the racquet to pick up extra speed and spin, and better direct the serve to specific targets. With very rare exceptions, the best servers use the continental grip.

The catch is, it's not easy. In order to square the racquet face at contact with a continental grip, you have to rotate your hitting forearm and wrist (often called *pronation*). Otherwise, you'll be swinging at the ball with the side of the racquet, rather than the strings. This doesn't always come naturally to players.

For this reason, it's not uncommon for developing players to use more of an eastern to semi-western forehand grip to start serving. This grip automatically squares the face at contact without any need to maneuver your forearm or wrist, so it's easier to serve the ball over the net. It's a faster way to develop a serve that can routinely find the service box and get started playing points.

The downside is, using this grip puts a low ceiling on your serving potential. The hitting wrist and forearm are much less involved, which limits how much pace and spin you can put on the ball. The grip is sometimes called the "frying pan" grip because when you serve, it looks like you're hitting the ball with the back of a frying pan. As you can imagine, you can only go so far with a serving grip like that.

Although it's pretty easy to pop a ball into the service box with an eastern forehand grip, it makes it hard to use spin on your serve. And applying spin is critical to serving success as your game improves. (You can read more about spin serves later in this chapter.)

Serving is a huge part of the game, but it often gets short shrift during lessons. Instructors want to keep students moving and engaged so they get a good workout. Make sure to set aside a little time after every workout to hit practice serves and concentrate on experimenting with your service grip. If possible, move toward the continental grip as you become comfortable with the serve.

Stance

Every serve begins with you adopting a stance at the baseline. There are two predominant stances that most players use when hitting the serve:

>> **Platform stance:** The platform stance is when you keep your feet about shoulder-width apart throughout the entire motion. It provides a stable base and is a good foundation to build the rest of the serve.

>> **Pinpoint stance:** The pinpoint stance is when the player slides or brings their back foot up right behind their front foot during the motion. Sort of like standing on your tippy-toes to get taller, it encourages good weight transfer up and into the shot. However, moving the feet like this takes more balance and coordination, imposing a higher degree of difficulty.

Both stances have been proven successful at all levels. It's just a matter of choosing the one that feels comfortable and produces the most reliable results.

Your foot can't cross over the baseline and touch the court until you hit the ball. Same goes for crossing the center hash mark on the baseline. Not observing this rule is called a *foot fault*, which automatically makes your serve invalid. (Check out Chapter 5 for more information on the rules regarding serving.)

My serve has never been overpowering. Instead of concentrating on pace, I focus more on placement and consistency, which can get you very far. For those reasons, I use more of a platform stance, which gives me good balance and allows me to do lots of different things from the same basic position. I think the platform stance is the easiest stance to learn, and a similar service stance should work for you. You can always alter your stance as the nature of your natural serving style emerges.

Follow these steps to take a good, basic service stance on the deuce side of the court.

1. **Stand with your feet behind the baseline, just to the right of the center hash mark, facing the net.**

Most singles players stand close to the hash mark when they serve. In doubles, most people serve from about the middle point between the singles sideline and the hash mark. (Chapter 2 points out the pertinent lines on the tennis court.) However, as long as you're serving from the proper side of the hash mark, you can stand anywhere you like.

2. **Spread your legs to about the same width as your shoulders.**

3. **Take a comfortable step back with your dominant leg, pivoting on your front foot as you do so and allowing your entire body to turn with the step.**

   Notice that you're now facing in the direction of the right net post, with your chest at an angle to the net. Your feet should still be about shoulder-width apart, and both pointed toward the net post. The heels of your feet should be in line and perpendicular to the net.

WARNING

Avoid facing the net head-on (called *open stance* in tennis lingo), because that stance prevents you from getting the power of rotation from your torso and shoulders into the serve. The more you rely on just your arm for your serve, the less power you have and the more stress you put on your arm, inviting fatigue and injury.

Experienced players line up at the baseline at varying angles to the net before they serve. Some players start with their feet very close together. Others take a wider stance. Some stand almost square to the net, while others, like my brother John, start with their shoulders perpendicular to the net, facing the sideline. The serve stance is a matter of comfort and personal style, which develops with experience. Start with the fundamentals, and then you can evolve over time.

Preparing to Serve

Bowlers, golfers, batters, free-throw shooters, and, yes, even tennis players, almost always have a routine and little rituals they go through before they take a swing or a shot. The routines vary, but they all have the same, dual purpose: to get you into a comfortable position and to help you focus on the task at hand.

Establishing a preset routine

Player have any number of routines when preparing to serve. It could be taking a couple of deep breaths, wiping your brow with a wristband, adjusting your clothes, or even bouncing the ball between your legs. Many routines involve bouncing the ball with your nondominant hand a certain number of times — three to five is a good number — just inside the baseline as you take up your service stance. What you do isn't nearly as important as establishing the ritual. It's a way to reset from the previous point, relax, and shift your focus to hitting a good serve.

Visualizing the target

After you perform your pre-serve ritual, bring the racquet and ball together in front of you, holding both of them lightly, with the racquet head at about waist level. Touch or "kiss" the frame, or the strings, with the ball. Come to a standstill (see Figure 11-1), and let your mind clear. Picture in your head executing the serve you want to hit. It could as simple as a serve to your opponent's backhand. You can envision not only where you want the ball to go, but what to expect from your opponent's return.

FIGURE 11-1:
Setting up and getting ready to serve.

Establishing a pre-serve plan is a valuable tool. (Chapter 13 dives deeper into strategies and tactics.) Unless your opponent does something unexpected, like change their usual receiving position, stay committed to the serve you want to hit.

TOO MUCH OF A GOOD BOUNCE

Some pros bounce the ball the same number of times every single time they get ready to serve. I always bounced it three times — it just felt right.

Novak Djokovic famously has no set number. He will bounce the ball as long as it takes him to feel relaxed and ready to serve. It can be just a handful, but often, especially when matches are tight, he can reach a dozen or more on the bounce meter. It used to drive some opponents stir-crazy, but he's been doing it for so long, they've now just come to expect it. Besides, the tours have a 25-second serve clock courtside that counts down between points. If Djokovic spends too much time bouncing the ball and the clock strikes zero, he gets one warning. After that, it's a fault. (Chapter 19 covers some of the recent innovations in the pro game.)

Your opponent can move around as you prepare to serve, as long as it doesn't create a flagrant distraction. A returner can't jump around and wave their arms like crazy as you toss the ball to serve. But they can do lots of other things that can, but shouldn't, throw you off. Good returners keep their feet moving as they await your serve. They may change their position along the baseline dramatically, to make you think twice about where you're going to serve. Sometimes they may take a few steps into the court, or back from it, to make you think twice. That's legal, and they can do it at any point, even after you've tossed the ball. You shouldn't be debating legalities in your own mind as you're preparing to serve.

Don't worry about the returner — just shut them out of your mind. You never want to start your service motion unsure of where you want to hit the ball, and you don't want to change your mind about where it's going after your motion starts. If you become distracted, or you're unsure, repeat your bounce routine.

Always try to start your service motion from the same position. The key to serving success is consistency, and the keys to consistency are routine and repetition.

Taking It One Step at a Time: The Serve Sequence

The serve is probably the quirkiest of all shots. Players are prone to infuse deep knee bends, fancy windups, and happy feet that give their deliveries a unique charm. You can introduce lots of extraneous motions and flourishes into your serve, but the best serves — like all good strokes — are streamlined, efficient, and economical. Here are the integral parts of an effective serve.

Tossing the ball consistently

A consistent ball toss is the anchor of any good serve. If your toss is all over the place, you'll be chasing your serve all over the place, and your motion will look more like an interpretative dance routine than a tennis stroke.

It's called a toss, but it's really more of a lifting action. With your nondominant arm relatively straight, you raise the ball using the shoulder instead of your elbow or wrist. It's an underhand motion very similar to the one you would use to toss, say, a handful of rice, up into the air over your head. But because the positioning of the ball is so important in a service toss, you should concentrate extra hard on tossing the ball gently, with complete control over it. Tossing a ball just a few feet over your head isn't very hard, but using your nondominant arm makes it a little more complicated. It's something you can easily work on and practice outside the court. The key is to toss it accurately and consistently.

To make your tosses as uniform as possible, you need to concentrate on the following two factors:

REMEMBER

>> **Height:** Make your toss 2 to 3 inches higher than the maximum reach of your racquet. (Some top pros toss the ball noticeably higher than others, up to a foot or more above their maximum reach. You can do that, too, but the higher your toss, the harder it is to time your stroke properly.) This much is for sure: No good servers toss the ball lower than the maximum reach of their fully outstretched racquets.

You can always compensate for tossing the ball a little too high, but tossing the ball too low generally ends in disaster.

>> **Placement:** Unless you want to hit one of the spin serves that I describe later in this chapter, your toss should be about a few feet in front of your body and slightly to the right of the hitting shoulder. This advice holds true when you serve to either side of the court.

After you determine where you'd like to toss the ball, follow these steps to get the ball airborne:

1. **Hold the ball just with your fingertips.**

   Start with just one ball in your hand. Keep a second ball in your pocket.

   Cradle the ball like an egg — think of it as a precious object. Don't squeeze it tightly in your palm. Let it rest securely but loosely in your fingers. This also prevents the ball from rolling out of your hand when you toss it, so there's less spin on it and it's easier to control.

2. **Lower your arm into a comfortable position directly in front of you, as shown in Figure 11-2.**

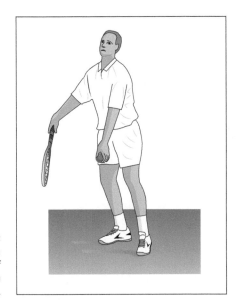

FIGURE 11-2:
Get the ball down and in front of you as you prepare to toss.

3. **Raise your arm in front of your body using your shoulder (see Figure 11-3A), and let go of the ball when your arm is fully extended above your head (see Figure 11-3B).**

    Don't just flick the ball or pop it up into the air from somewhere around your midsection. Flicking the ball up leads to accuracy problems. Raise your arm with a relaxed motion until it's fully extended, gently letting the ball go.

TIP

Don't chase an errant toss. There's no rule that after you toss the ball you have to hit it. If it's not in the spot you want, catch it and start your motion again. In fact, you can start over as many times as you like. Your opponent may get frustrated, but there's nothing they can do about it. If it happens frequently or you sense your opponent starting to stew, calling out "Sorry" when you catch the toss is generally appreciated.

Rotating your shoulders in the backswing

As you toss the ball with your nondominant hand to serve, your upper body rotates toward the back fence. For some players, it's actually easier to turn the shoulders ahead of making the toss. But if you break the components up so they don't flow into each other — toss the ball up and then turn the shoulders — the serve becomes disjointed. What usually ends up happening is you'll toss the ball and skip the shoulder turn, which turns the serve into an all-arm swing.

A

B

This coiling of the shoulders helps establish a smooth rhythm and add more power to the shot. At the same time, it also naturally helps your hitting arm get your racquet behind you and into the backswing. As you raise your hitting hand and elbow, the racquet face should drop down so the racquet looks practically upside down. This is the traditional "back-scratcher" position that gets you ready to unwind and hit a serve. You can see the back-scratcher position in Figure 11-4.

As a beginner, you may actually feel the racquet touch your back. But once you get more comfortable with the motion, the racquet should pass quickly through this position. Your face looks up, and your serving elbow points straight up.

As you get into the back-scratcher position, you should feel most of your weight on your back leg as it readies to transfer to your front leg when you bring the racquet face up to contact during the next phase of swing.

MAC SAYS

If you look at pictures of the world's best servers, you'll see that they often rotate so much that their chests are practically facing the back fence as they get ready to swing at the ball. But then, that's why they're pros. A little rotation will go a long way for you, and you can add more as you improve your serve.

FIGURE 11-4:
Getting into the
back-scratcher
position.

TIP

When you're just becoming familiar with the serve, you may find it easier and more natural to begin the service motion with your racquet already in the back-scratcher position. Then all you have to do is toss the ball and swing at it. Try it if you really have trouble with the timing and placement of your backswing and toss.

Uncoiling and swinging up to contact

As the racquet moves out of the back-scratcher position on the way to hitting the ball, your shoulders rotate back toward the net, and the nondominant arm drops down out of the way before it eventually tucks into the stomach. Follow these tips to send the ball well on its way into the other court:

>> **Reach up and out.** Even though you make contact with the ball above the level of the net on the serve, you still need to swing up at the ball. The quality of your toss really counts here. If you made a good toss, you should feel like the ball is almost, but not quite, beyond your reach. You should really be going up and after it, not waiting for it, hurrying to hit it before it drops too low, or swatting at it. You can see in Figure 11-5 how you fully stretch and move forward at the moment of contact.

FIGURE 11-5:
Reaching up
and out for
your serve.

>> **Accelerate through the swing.** The speed of your swing determines the amount of power you generate. You have time to accelerate, so don't rush it. Make your backswing slowly and add acceleration as you come out of the back-scratcher position. Don't swing as hard as you can. You might hit a few really good serves, but more likely, many, many more faults. Start swinging at about 50 percent of your natural, full-swing speed and gradually add arm speed. Swing for control, not for power, to develop a reliable serve.

>> **Keep your chin up.** More than any stroke, when you hit a serve you want to see your handiwork. And prematurely pulling your head down to see the shot pulls your upper body with it and is a sure way to put that serve in the net. Watch the ball from the moment you begin your toss and keep your head up after impact. Your follow-through will bring your head forward and down, so you can pick up the ball again with your eyes.

Keeping a loose arm and a fluid motion

Ideally, the serve should be one continuous loop. When the racquet starts moving, it never stops, gradually building momentum into contact. A smooth service motion is almost balletic. However, it does take time to develop. Integrating all the different pieces of the serve takes serious muscle memory. It's ok if you start with a little bit of choppiness as you work on refining your technique.

WARNING

One of the most fundamental mistakes that beginners make that causes hitches in their serve is swinging with a locked, stiff arm, in a kind of windmill motion. Your arm, elbow, and wrist should all be loose as you swing. See for yourself: Take a firm squeeze on the handle. Immediately you'll notice the added tension running through your forearm. Take a few shadow swings. Notice how stiff and forced it feels in motion. Now, take a very loose grip on the handle — so loose that it may feel as though the racquet might fly out of your hand when you swing. Again, try a few shadow serves. I bet the racquet makes a much more distinct *whoosh* sound as it flies through the contact zone, and with less effort.

Allowing your arm to naturally decelerate

TIP

As you make contact with the ball your hitting arm should be fully extended. Your hitting shoulder is now tilted above the level of your nondominant shoulder. They've practically switched positions from where they were during the toss to the contact point. That's a good sign that you're hitting up on the ball. (Compare Figures 11-4 and 11-5 to see what I mean.) *Shoulder over shoulder* is a serving cue often used to hammer home this concept.

Figure 11-5 also shows how the left arm tucks into the stomach. This puts the brakes on the shoulder rotation and allows the hitting arm to pick up more speed. If you're using the continental grip, this is where your forearm needs to *pronate* (turn or rotate) in order to square up the racquet face with the back of the ball. For many beginners, this is the most complicated aspect of using the continental grip. If you use more of an eastern to semi-western forehand grip, it does this for you without any adjustment. Again, this type of grip is fine to start with if pronating feels too unnatural. But learning to pronate is worth it because it makes a huge difference in the quality of your serve.

TIP

You can consciously think about the wrist snap, but don't force it. Overdoing it usually just leads to more errant serves and can eventually bother your wrist. It should feel like a natural extension of your service motion. If your wrist is weak or your timing suspect, just concentrate on keeping your wrist loose rather than locked into a single position at the moment of contact. Think of your wrist as the flipper in a pinball machine; you can really affect the path of the ball with very little effort.

After the ball leaves your racquet, you need to follow through. As with all your other strokes, your serve isn't complete (not to mention effective) until you follow through. Don't try to abruptly stop your hitting arm. That's a recipe for pain. Allow the arm to gradually slow and come down across the body, essentially replacing your nondominant arm, which moves out of the way.

Figure 11-6 illustrates the across-the-body path of the follow-through that you should use on your typical flat serve.

FIGURE 11-6: The service follow-through goes across your body (A), carrying you into the court (B).

(a)   (b)

Your follow-through carries you forward into the court. If you executed the fundamentals of your toss and swing, the sheer momentum created by your service motion will drive you into the court.

REMEMBER

Where you end up after you serve is a telltale sign of the quality of your toss. If your toss doesn't bring you into the court, you aren't tossing the ball far enough forward. Most recreational players slip into the habit of playing it safe, tossing the ball straight up or even slightly behind them, where they don't really have to go up after it. Sure you can get away with this "safe" technique, but it's a sure sign that you aren't using your reach, body weight, or shoulder rotation to full benefit.

Hitting the Three Types of Serves

Just like groundstrokes, you can use different spins to vary your serves. This allows you to mix up the speeds and trajectories of your serves. Not only does it make you a more well-rounded player, but it gives you options to keep your opponents guessing.

Flat

The serve I describe in the serving sequence is essentially a flat serve (see Figure 11-7). Flat serves don't have very much spin, allowing them to travel faster through the air with good accuracy. You can grab the early edge in a point with a strong flat serve. If you place it well, you can get aces with it, even if you don't have a lot of power.

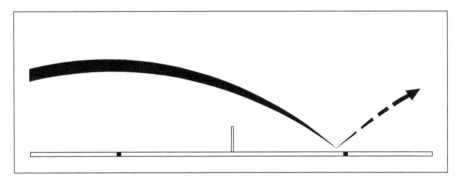

FIGURE 11-7: The arc of a good flat serve.

But the flat serve hit with any kind of authority is also a low-percentage shot. On a great day, you may put 65 percent to 70 percent of your flat first serves into play. That's a great first-serve percentage. But that percentage on your second serve means that you'll hit way too many double faults. That's why it's primarily used on first serves.

If you use a flat serve to hit second serves, you'll resort to slowing your racquet down and hitting with less power. You'll end up "patty-caking" the ball, using gravity to bring it down safely in the service box. That's okay if you're a beginner, because your first commandment is "Thou shalt get the ball in play." But as you develop your game, the limitations of hitting weak, flat second serves will become clear. That's where adding spin to the serve becomes a valuable asset.

Slice

When your slice serves bounce, they swerve away from the receiver in the same direction as the spin. (The right-handed server's slice always swerves to the right of the receiver.) The added spin slows the serve down, which helps get it into the service box, making it more dependable than a flat serve. The skidding nature of a slice is particularly effective on faster surfaces, such as the grass courts of Wimbledon.

In order to get slice on the ball, you need to meet a different part of the ball than you do on the flat serve, and with your racquet head at a different angle. You'll also need to adopt a continental grip. It's extremely difficult to muster the wrist action needed for an effective slice serve without using the continental grip.

TIP

To create slice on your serve, vary your point of impact on the ball in the following ways:

>> **Make contact with the outside edge of the upper half of the ball.** Your strings should meet the ball at an angle and brush around it, as if you were trying to peel the felt off the side of the ball.

>> **Flick your wrist forward to add a little zip to your spin.** Hitting with a relaxed wrist will give you sufficient spin, but a little flick, or "snap," really increases the spin.

Slice serves are tough to return because the ball stays low and swerves away, while flat serves bounce higher and travel in a straight line. If you just stick your racquet directly in the path of a flat serve, you'll usually make contact. As you gain experience with slice serves, you'll be able to anticipate how the ball curves.

Left-handed players love the slice serve — it naturally swerves away from the right-handed receiver's backhand. Southpaws, like my brother John, often hit and use slice serves more effectively than righties.

TIP

Slice serves are especially effective on fast hard courts and indoors because the ball stays low and squirts away from the receiver. If you play often on such courts, you'd be wise to mix in slices on both first and second serves.

Topspin

Topspin serves are valuable because, when you put forward spin on the ball, it's in an extra hurry to land again. The momentum of the ball brings it down into the court faster. This allows you to swing as hard as you would on a flat serve, yet use the spin to bring the ball safely down into the service box. The serve has higher net clearance and more margin for error. This makes topspin serves much more reliable than flat ones and the preferred choice on second serves.

When a topspin serve (or any topspin shot) lands, it leaps up and accelerates. That's why it's often referred to as a "kick" serve. This action can catch the receiver by surprise and also force them to hit the ball from an uncomfortably high position if the shot has a lot of topspin.

The swinging motion needed in a topspin serve often causes the ball to have a little twist right after it bounces, but it doesn't have nearly the same curve as a slice. The amount of spin that you apply will determine whether your topspin serve is a nice, safe serve or a weapon.

TIP

To hit a topspin serve, vary your service motion in the following ways:

>> **If you can, use the continental grip.** Some players even find it more conducive to hit a topspin serve holding the racquet with nearly an eastern backhand grip. (Chapter 7 covers all the essential grips.) This closes the racquet face a little more, which helps when brushing up the back of the ball.

>> **Your toss should be at the same height as for your flat serve, but located almost directly overhead or above your hitting shoulder.** You may see some professionals toss the ball well behind their heads to get extra spin on their kick serves, but you don't need that degree of difficulty. It's also an invitation for arm and back problems.

>> **Allow the ball to drop a little farther than you would on a flat serve before you make contact, because you can't create topspin with a fully extended racquet.** The face has to be angled slightly to brush over the top of the ball. Instead of swinging the racquet head toward the net as you would on a flat serve, the motion is more toward the right net post.

>> **Make contact with the lower-left portion of the ball and brush up through to the upper-right portion.** If the back of the ball were a clockface, you would be hitting it at 7 o'clock and brushing up to 1 o'clock. (Lefties would have a 5-to-11-o'clock motion). Your strings should meet the ball at an angle and brush forward over it, as if you were trying to peel the felt off the top of the ball.

>> **Your racquet should finish closer to the right or dominant side of your body than with your flat serve, because you exaggerate the wrist action up and to the right in producing topspin.**

TIP

Topspin is especially pronounced on slower, grittier courts like clay or slow hard courts. If you play on those courts, developing a good topspin serve will pay off. Just like the slice, you should work in a solid kicker as both a first- and second-serve option.

Chapter **12**

Completing the Arsenal: Lobs, Overheads, and Drop Shots

The Fabulous Four — the serve, forehand, backhand, and volley — are the foundations of your game. But because tennis is a game of motion and adjustments, three important variations on the Fab Four exist: the lob, overhead, and drop shot. These three strokes are situational, meaning that you use them less often than the fundamental strokes, depending on how you (and your opponent) play. You may play an entire match without using any of them, or you may end up using one or more of them during every point. Carlos Alcaraz, a world number one and multiple-time Grand Slam champ from Spain, has a drop shot that has become one of the biggest weapons in the sport. Knowing when and how to make use of these strokes can add a lot of fun — and success — to your game.

Loving the Lob: An Underappreciated Asset

The *lob*, quite simply, is a ball hit high in the air. Compared to booming serves and monster forehands, the lob often looks like a meek, defensive, softly hit shot. But the lob is a very useful, even sneaky, shot that can really hurt your opponent, especially one who insists on attacking the net.

The key features of a good lob include the following:

>> **Height:** A lob that doesn't get high enough gives your opponent the chance to win the point with an easy-to-hit winner called an *overhead*. Well, the pros make it easy, but for juniors and developing players it actually can be a challenging shot. (You can read more about the overhead later in this chapter.) And hitting the lob with the right amount of height makes it even more daunting.

>> **Depth:** You want the lob to be deep enough that, if your opponent is at the net, it goes over their head. Ideally, the lob should bounce near your opponent's baseline. But the first rule is to keep the ball in play, especially when your opponent is positioned back near the baseline and you're throwing up a lob just to stay in the point.

TIP

You call on the lob under the following circumstances:

>> **When your opponent hits a shot that pulls you way off the court.** You can buy yourself time to get back into a good position by putting up a very high lob.

>> **When your opponent's shot comes at you so quickly that you don't have time to hit a groundstroke.** Scooping or blocking up a lob takes less time than a full-fledged groundstroke.

>> **When your opponent is at the net prepared to hit a volley.** The closer your opponent comes to the net, the better your chances are of lobbing over them successfully. If you hit your lob deep enough on those occasions, your opponent may get caught flat-footed at the net, with no chance of running down the shot. Even if they do, they'll be in a mad scramble to return the shot, and you'll have taken control of the point.

>> **When you want to change the pace of play.** Changing the pace during a rally with a lob can really throw off your opponent. Say that you're exchanging hard, fast groundstrokes, running from side-to-side. Suddenly, you

throw in a high lob that floats deep across the court, giving your opponent ages to figure out what to do with the next shot. This is sometimes referred to as *taking pace off the ball.* Breaking up the rhythm of the point like this and giving your opponent more time to go through all their hitting options can draw an error born of impatience or confusion. Errors like that can really drive opponents mad.

MAC SAYS

A player who hits naturally high groundstrokes that are essentially deep lobs is often labeled a *moonballer* or *pusher.* Parents of juniors say it all the time, and it's never given as a compliment. That's because their kids often lose to these steady and crafty players. The truth is, there's nothing underhanded or devious about the playing style. Never underestimate anyone who is skilled at consistently getting the ball back in play. Developing players who have a knack for hitting moonballs generally go on to become solid all-around players because they have good control over the ball.

The lob comes in two basic flavors: offensive and defensive.

Offensive lobs

The offensive lob is an aggressive stroke that's meant to either end the point with a winner or force your opponent to hit a really difficult overhead. Either scenario puts you in charge. The technique of the offensive lob is very similar to a topspin groundstroke (see Chapters 7, 8, and 9). The biggest difference is that you aim higher over the net with a more exaggerated lifting motion, using a little extra topspin to bring the ball back down in the court.

TIP

Follow these steps to get your offensive lob airborne and working to your advantage:

1. **Bring your racquet back well below the level of the incoming ball.**

    Drop the head of the racquet during your backswing, with the head as close to the ground as it will go without forcing the issue (see Figure 12-1). This helps you brush up the back of the ball more severely than you would on a topspin drive ground stroke.

2. **Lean back slightly as you swing (see Figure 12-2).**

    This allows you to transfer more of your weight up into the shot, rather than forward. It also angles your chest up more toward the sky — your intended target — and encourages a more vertical swing path.

FIGURE 12-1:
Keep your
racquet way
down, closer to
the court.

FIGURE 12-2:
Your racquet
should point
upward as you hit
the ball, giving
the ball height.

3. **Follow through, keeping the ball on the strings with a nice long stroke that finishes above your shoulders (see Figure 12-3).**

   Make sure you accelerate the racquet as you would on a topspin drive. Slowing down the racquet as if you're guiding the ball leads to short lobs and easy overheads for your opponents. Trust that the extra spin you're putting on the ball will bring it down into the court.

FIGURE 12-3: You must follow through with your lob as you do with all your shots.

Defensive lobs

The defensive lob is used to buy time when you're in trouble, change the pace of a rally, or lift the ball over the head of a net-hugging opponent. From a stroke production standpoint, it has a lot in common with a slice groundstroke (see Chapters 7, 8, and 9). Because it travels with underspin, it's slower through the air than a topspin lob. It also slows down and checks up after the bounce. So, if it does get over your opponent's head, it's easier to track down. You may not win the point outright with a defensive lob, but it can turn the tide in your favor.

Follow these tips to improve the quality of your defensive lobs:

>> **Scoop under the ball, with the hitting surface of the racquet open, or nearly facing upward (refer to Figure 12-2).** The angle of the racquet face when it meets the ball determines the direction of the shot. To produce very high shots, the racquet comes up from under the ball, with the face almost parallel to the ground. The prime difference between this and a slice ground-stroke is the more open face and low-to-high swing path.

>> **Follow through, keeping the ball on the strings with a nice long stroke that finishes above your shoulders (refer to Figure 12-3).** Under calm practice conditions, you should feel almost like you're lifting the ball up into the air with the racquet face. Don't just pop the ball up from underneath. Prolonging the point of contact always adds control to your shots.

TIP

Your opponent's incoming shot will often dictate the type of lob you can hit in response. Lobs that are hit off hard shots rarely need help from any kind of a swing on your part. The pace of a hard shot bouncing off the open face of your racquet is usually enough to send back a good, high, deep lob. On the other hand, if your opponent's shot is medium-paced, with a high bounce, you have more time to produce a full swing. That's a better opportunity to beat them with a more aggressive, offensive lob.

The Overhead: Smashing Success

The overhead, the most nuclear shot in tennis, is a powerful antidote to the sneaky little lob (which you can read about in the preceding section). The stroke shares similar characteristics to the serve, except for a few notable differences:

>> It's generally hit from close to the net or the midcourt rather than from behind the baseline.

>> Instead of the service boxes, your target area is your opponent's entire side of the court.

>> Instead of hitting a self-toss, you try to hit the ball as it descends rapidly from well above your head (hence, the name).

It's this last part that can cause developing players to dread the overhead. Timing contact off an opponent's lob — the typical setup for an overhead — can be tricky. If it's just a split second off, you can easily shank the ball off your frame. And nothing is more embarrassing than duffing an "easy" overhead. But if you understand and apply the proper technique, with a little practice, the overhead can become a trusty weapon.

You use the overhead, also called the *smash*, during the course of a point to hit balls that come to you from over your head — like a low-flying lob. When you hit an overhead, you can take advantage of court positioning near the net and a high contact point to put the power into the shot so that the ball goes slamming down into the opponent's court at top speed, hopefully leaving them helpless to return it. When you hit an overhead, you can finish the point with one decisive blow. If you have a good overhead, attempting to lob becomes a very risky proposition for most of your opponents.

Outfielder footwork: Backpedal, side-shuffle, or crossover step

Just like any stroke, tracking the lob to hit an overhead takes good footwork. The more efficiently you get in position, the better you set yourself up for a winning result. Many players are comfortable running side-to-side or forward to hit a shot, but are less sure moving backward. But it's the critical first step (no pun intended) in hitting a good smash.

TIP

When you see that the ball is achieving the height you need and it's falling in a position that sets you up well for the overhead, start with these steps:

1. **Adjust your grip to your service grip.**

   I suggest using the continental grip if possible. (Chapter 7 tells you all about the various grips.)

2. **In one motion, pivot your body so that your shoulders, chest, and feet are facing the side fence as you take a large step back with your dominant leg.**

   A common beginner mistake is to face the net and retreat by backpedaling to position yourself underneath the ball. This is a real no-no. Not only is it slower footwork, but it also doesn't keep you as balanced.

   Instead, if after turning sideways toward the fence the ball appears that it will still be too deep to hit an overhead, take a crossover step — your front foot crossing over just in front or to the side of your back foot — and then step back and plant again with your dominant foot. At this point, you may still have to take a few more small shuffle steps to get into the perfect position.

This is the type of footwork outfielders use to track down and catch deep flyballs hit over their heads. It's also similar to when a quarterback takes a snap from center and drops back to pass. Making sure you have the proper spacing is key: It keeps the ball in front of your body and allows you to transfer weight forward into the shot.

Taking an abbreviated backswing

As mentioned earlier, overhead technique has similarities to the serve. Instead of a full motion, though, the racquet travels a much shorter distance. It doesn't drop down or perform a loop behind your body. With the overhead, less is more.

As you move back to get in position, bring the racquet handle directly up to just outside your dominant ear. The end of the handle should be above the hitting shoulder and even with the ear. When you're starting out, it's often a good idea to also have the racquet in the back-scratcher position (see Figure 12-4). Although this will shorten the swing and lessen the power, it makes it easier to make clean and well-timed contact.

FIGURE 12-4: Spot the ball like a good outfielder.

© John Wiley & Sons, Inc.

Tracking the ball with your nondominant arm and hand

Your nondominant arm serves a couple of important functions during the overhead:

>> **Fully extending the arm and pointing at the ball helps track it during flight and guide you to the proper hitting position.**

>> **Just like on the serve, it helps rotate the upper body and raise your nondominant shoulder slightly above your hitting shoulder (refer to Figure 12-4).** This promotes the upward "shoulder-over-shoulder" swing that encourages full extension and good power at contact.

WARNING

If your opponent hits a really terrific, high lob that lands near your baseline, you must be very confident in your stroke to hit the overhead. Hitting one from that far back is similar to serving a ball, although you have the advantage of returning it anywhere into your opponent's court, not just the service box. If your overhead is still a work in progress, let the lob bounce and then get in position and hit a groundstroke.

To bounce or not to bounce

Whenever your opponent hits a lob, you have an immediate, important decision to make: whether to hit the ball while it's in the air (on the fly) or after it bounces.

Playing the bounce

TIP

Hitting the overhead is always easier if you let the ball bounce first. This removes much of the difficulty of timing the overhead out of the air. The higher the lob and the more vertical the trajectory, the better off you are allowing it to bounce before hitting the overhead, especially if the extreme height of the lob allows your opponent to recover to a neutral position on the court.

Playing the ball in the air

Hitting the overhead out of the air is harder than letting it bounce. But it does have its advantages. The lower the *trajectory* (arc) of the lob, the more likely it is that you should hit it on the fly, provided that you can reach it. Otherwise, if it's hit hard enough to land near your baseline, letting the ball bounce will put you in a very defensive position and most likely lose you the point. Those lower lobs also don't give your opponent as much time to recover back to the center of the court, and taking the ball right out of the air can give you more of the court to hit into. Just take aim at the open space and smash the ball away.

Contact point: Out in front and above the hitting shoulder

As with just about every shot, you want to make contact with the ball in front of your body on an overhead. This gives you a better chance to find the sweet spot on your racquet and transfer your weight into the shot. A common mistake is for players to make contact with the ball when it's directly above them or, worse, a little behind them. That turns what should be an attractive opportunity to hit an offensive shot into a risky proposition.

TECHNICAL STUFF

If you want to be technical, contact with the ball should not be directly over your head. That would be a mistake because your body would get in the way and you wouldn't have a smooth, full swing. Your hitting shoulder is actually the proper spot. However, *overshoulder* just doesn't have the same ring to it.

Follow these steps to make sure your contact point on the overhead results in a smashing success:

1. **Time your swing so you make contact with the ball at the peak of your reach, slightly in front and to the right of your head (see Figure 12-5).**

   Even though you make contact above the net, you still need to hit up and make contact with the back of the ball. If you try to hit down on top of the ball to bring it into court, you'll most likely just put it into the net.

2. **Snap, or pronate, your wrist and forearm forward at the moment of contact to help drive the ball with authority toward your target.**

   This helps square the racquet face with the back of the ball. If this motion doesn't feel natural, work up to it slowly as you become more familiar with the shot.

3. **Follow through across your body, allowing the racquet to gradually decelerate (see Figure 12-6).**

   Following through also gets you in a good position, moving forward into the court, to follow up your shot, if necessary.

WARNING

Remember to keep your head and chin up until the ball leaves the racquet strings. Pulling your head down — and your upper body with it — to see where the ball is going is a sure way to see the ball land in the net. Even though the smash is a hard-hit shot, you'll still have time to track it. Besides, if you keep your head up and hit it well, there's a good chance all you'll see is the ball slamming into the back fence.

FIGURE 12-5:
You should be
fully extended
when you make
contact with
the ball.

FIGURE 12-6:
Follow through to
the bitter end.

TIP

Practice taking overheads on the bounce to become familiar with the stroke. Have your partner hit high, defensive lobs that land between the net and your service line. As you become confident with the shot, overheads hit closer to the net become a piece of cake.

The backhand overhead: Necessity meets invention

A savvy opponent will often try to lob over your backhand side when you're at the net to prevent you from employing your standard overhead. This strategy is especially true in doubles because lofting a lob over the net player's backhand side off a weak serve is a smart tactic.

The good news is that you usually have plenty of time to get under a defensive lob, taking it with your standard overhead. However, there are occasions when the lob must be hit with a backhand overhead — an athletic, advanced shot that calls for a little improvisation.

The backhand overhead is a very relaxed, flowing stroke that benefits from a brisk, forward flick of the wrist at the moment of contact. Your racquet head travels through the stroke like the flipper in a pinball machine, but at an unfamiliar angle beginning near your nondominant shoulder blade.

Follow these steps to hit the backhand overhead:

1. **When you see the lob coming over your backhand side, in one motion turn your body so that your shoulders, chest, and feet are facing the side fence, and take a step back with your nondominant leg.**

   Use your usual backhand volley grip, preferably the continental. Keep your feet spread about the width of your shoulders.

2. **Bring the racquet back over your nondominant shoulder, with the grip very close to the top of your shoulder, and your hitting elbow tilted up in the direction of the ball (see Figure 12-7).**

3. **Time your swing so that you meet the ball with your arm fully extended (see Figure 12-8).**

   Punctuate your overhead by flicking your wrist forward and down, in the direction you want the ball to go, at the moment of contact. If you have trouble using your wrist at first, just complete the swing with a smooth follow-through, down and across your body, to the right.

4. **Follow through, turning your body back toward your opponent, just in case they can return your wicked backhand overhead (see Figure 12-9).**

© John Wiley & Sons, Inc.

© John Wiley & Sons, Inc.

FIGURE 12-9:
The overhead
ends as you
follow through.

© John Wiley & Sons, Inc.

The Drop Shot: Sneaky and Satisfying

The *drop shot* is a soft and gentle shot, designed to barely clear the net. You can hit it with the forehand, backhand, or volley. In fact, the technique to hit a good drop shot has a lot in common with the volley.

If a groundstroke winner is a point-ending fist bump, the drop shot is a winking emoji. This is the softest shot in tennis, emphasizing placement over power. You use the drop shot to just *feather* or *drop* the ball short into your opponent's court so softly that they have little or no chance of getting to the shot before it bounces twice.

If you hit a good drop shot, you feel like a magician using a wand instead of a racquet. It's an ideal finishing touch for your repertoire of strokes.

WARNING

The drop shot can be a *low-percentage shot,* meaning that the success rate is low unless it's well executed at the right time. Hit the shot too gently, and it won't get over the net. Don't hit it gently enough or with enough disguise, and your opponent may run up and smack the ball for a winner. So, although it can be an effective shot, you don't want to abuse it.

Prime-time drop shot opportunities

The drop shot is designed to end points outright or within the next couple of strokes. But if you have a talent for hitting it, the drop shot is a versatile tool that you can use in three additional ways:

>> **To test — or stress — your opponent's mobility:** Players who don't move very well often have trouble reaching even mediocre or poor drop shots. If your opponent misses your drop shot, you've discovered valuable information about their quickness.

>> **To change the pace and nature of a point:** Throw in a drop shot, and the entire nature of an ordinary rally changes (as well as both of your positions on the court) because the ball just clears the net and lands in an unusual position on the court.

>> **To draw your opponent to the net.** Many players avoid the net. The drop shot makes them come up and play from it. So, you're taking them out of their comfort zone. (See Chapter 13 for more on using your drop shot as part of your strategy.)

Consider the following important factors (in addition to your confidence in the shot) to determine when to use a drop shot:

>> **Your opponent's position:** Use your drop shot when your opponent is really off-balance, pulled off to one side of the court or well behind their own baseline.

>> **Your own position:** Keep this handy little rule in mind: When hitting a drop shot, try to be standing closer to your service line than your baseline. A soft drop shot hit from way back in your own court not only is that much more difficult to execute successfully but also travels slowly and gives your opponent lots of time to move forward and make a play. The pros make it look easy, but the farther you are from the net, the more difficult it is to execute an effective drop shot.

>> **Preparation time:** Never rush a drop shot. The shot is too tricky to attempt unless you see the opportunity to use it and have enough time to execute it.

Drop shot technique

You can hit drop shots with the forehand or backhand. You can even "drop" a volley if your timing and *touch* (your ability to play softer and delicate shots) are good

enough. Most drop shots are played off the backhand side, for two important reasons:

>> **Disguising a drop shot on the backhand side is easier than on the
forehand side, especially with a one-handed backhand.** That's primarily
because you hit the drop shot with slice or underspin, which is much more
common on the backhand side.

>> **The grip change needed to hit the drop shot is generally more elaborate
on the forehand.** If you use a semi-western or full western grip, even more so
(see Chapter 7 for more on grips). It takes smooth handling to make the grip
change and do it in a subtle fashion so as not to tip your hand to your
opponent that you're about to hit a drop shot.

To hit a drop shot, follow these steps:

1. **Take the racquet back as though you're planning on executing a typical
    groundstroke or volley.**

    See Chapters 8 and 9 for the details on hitting forehand and backhand
    groundstrokes. Chapter 10 tells you about the volley.

2. **If you aren't already using it, change to the continental grip as the
    racquet starts forward toward contact.**

    Disguise is key on the drop shot. An obvious grip change, especially on the
    forehand, can ruin the surprise.

3. **Turn your racquet face so it's slightly open, and brush the strings
    underneath the very bottom of the ball, as lightly as you can.**

    You want to cup under the ball as you would on a volley, only here you slow
    down the racquet as it comes to contact. Think of it this way: Instead of
    clobbering the ball, you want to catch it momentarily on the strings.

TIP

    Release most of the pressure on the grip of the racquet. The tighter you hold
    the racquet, the more resistance it offers the ball, which translates to the ball
    coming off the strings with more energy and pace. A soft, relaxed grip helps
    absorb the pace of the incoming shot, which allows you to return it gently
    over the net.

When you hit a good drop shot, the ball floats just over the net, bounces, and dies
in its tracks before your opponent can reach it. At the same time, you can close in
on the net, heading right for the ball. That way, even if your opponent does manage to reach your drop shot, all they can do is try to flip it back over the net. And
you'll be there to end the point with an easy volley.

Chapter **13**

Winning Strategies and Tactics

Okay, I want you to think for a moment about how tennis resembles chess. Don't worry, I'm not going to bore you with the genius of the Queen's Gambit or the Sicilian Defense. It's just that a good tennis player can use the court like a chessboard to move an opponent around and win points through various stroke combinations. (Doing so requires that you have a good command of your shots; to implement your strategies, your shots have to go where you want them to go.)

One of the most satisfying and challenging aspects of tennis is the chesslike stroke combinations you can use to improve your results. Implementing the basic strategies I suggest in this chapter will help you maximize the efficiency of your game — and give your opponents fits.

Serving Up a Storm

The first tactical decision you make about your serve happens before you start the match. If you win the coin toss or spin of the racquet, you can choose from among four choices regarding the serve. (See Chapter 5 for more information on the spin of the racquet.) Most of the time, the winner elects to serve. The loser usually picks which side to take for the first game.

TIP

Confident servers choose to serve first because if you win, or *hold* your service games, as you're expected to do, you have a one-game lead every time your opponent serves in the set. That can put a lot of pressure on your opponent, especially in the late stages of a set, when you lead by, say, 5-4 or 6-5. If your opponent can't hold serve then, you've won the set.

You can choose to receive — not a bad move against a player with a weak serve — and take advantage of an opponent's pre-match jitters to win the game, or *break serve*. If you break serve at least once and hold your own serve the rest of the way, you'll win the set. You may also choose to receive if you want to try to break serve before your opponent is fully warmed up.

TIP

I suggest choosing to serve, because it puts you in greater control of the match at the start. Then concentrate extra hard on establishing your serve as a force to be reckoned with.

Service placement: Wide, body, and T

You can serve up a storm in many different ways, not just by blowing the ball by your opponent for an ace. In Figure 13-1, I show you the three targets you can aim to hit during your serve.

Now take a closer look at each of those serves, assuming that the server and returner are both right-handers:

>> **Serve A:** This is the serve up the T. It's called that because you're trying to hit the cross section of the center and service lines, which form a T on the court. It takes the shortest route of the three serves, and it also travels over the lowest part of the net. Hit well enough, it could produce an ace. It also goes to the backhand side of the returner, which is the weaker side for most players.

>> **Serve B:** This is the body serve. Hit either flat or with spin, it flies right toward the body of the returner. (Chapter 11 tells you all about flat and spin serves.) When this serve is placed correctly and has enough pace or spin, it can "jam" an opponent, leaving them no room to swing and no clear-cut return option.

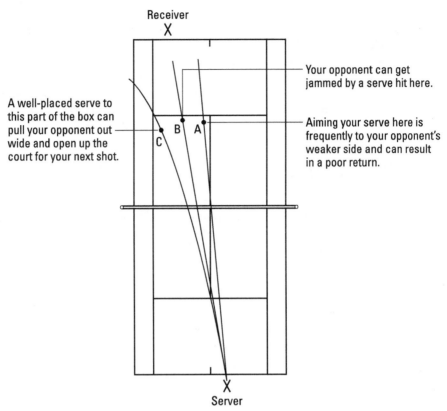

Receiver
X

A well-placed serve to this part of the box can pull your opponent out wide and open up the court for your next shot.

B A
C

Your opponent can get jammed by a serve hit here.

Aiming your serve here is frequently to your opponent's weaker side and can result in a poor return.

FIGURE 13-1: Targeting the best places to serve.

X
Server

© John Wiley & Sons, Inc.

>> **Serve C:** This is the wide serve. It takes the longest route, but if you hit it wide enough, it's tough to return. But beware: You're serving to the forehand side of the returner, which is usually the stronger side. It also travels over a higher part of the net, which can make it more challenging.

This serve poses two other potential dangers. It opens up the court for both the down-the-line and sharp crosscourt-angle returns, making you scramble to make your next shot.

TIP

If you want to play conservative points based on rallies, with the ball staying near the center of the court, serve down the middle or T. If you want to take chances by opening up the court, serve wide to either side, tempting your opponent to return the ball down the line.

These tactics apply to both your first and second serves, with one big asterisk. Serve A, hit hard and flat, is strictly a first-serve option because it's a lower-percentage shot; try it on a lot of second serves, and you may end up hitting a lot of double faults.

WARNING

In an effort to protect their backhands, many players line up in a return position that really opens up the forehand side to your serve. Players with powerful forehand returns really love this tactic as well. They basically dare you to try to get a serve past their forehand. Don't get sucked into that ploy —unless you have so much open court on that side that you can consistently win points by going there with your serve. Otherwise, you should still pepper in serves to all parts of the service box to keep your opponent off-balance.

Using serve-plus-one tactics

Although missing your first serve still leaves you with a second serve, don't waste your first-serve opportunities by going for unrealistically powerful or angled serves. Hit the majority of your first serves at no more than 80 percent of your maximum racquet speed, and less if you can't control the ball by swinging that hard. Strive for accuracy and consistency and add power as your serve becomes more reliable.

When you consistently get your first serve into play, you put a lot of pressure on the other player. The options that you have keep your opponent off-balance and guessing. They also allow you to start the point on your terms. This is where some of that chess strategy comes into play.

For instance, say you hit a solid serve down the T to your opponent's weaker backhand. You can expect a so-so return most likely hit down the middle. If you take a step or two to your left after hitting the serve, you'll be in a great position to hit your forehand. You can then drive another solid shot at your opponent's backhand corner and be in prime position to dictate the point.

If you get a chance to watch pro players, this is something they try to do all the time. It's called *serve-plus-one tactics* — you're hitting the serve and setting up the next shot. It doesn't mean you've got the entire point figured out, but you'll be clearer on how you want to start it. And that can lead to better execution on those first few shots.

REMEMBER

When you have to hit a second serve, your paramount goal is getting the ball into play. But that conservative approach also allows your opponent to return the serve more aggressively. That's why it's a good idea to strive to put at least 60 percent of your first serves into play, even if you must hit with less than your full power or put some spin on the ball.

Keep the score in mind when you're serving. If you're ahead, 40-love, it's okay to try to hit a blazing, flat serve down the middle for an ace. But if you're behind 30-40, missing a low-percentage, hard first serve puts you under a lot of pressure to hit a good second serve. The specter of the double fault looms larger at break point and other potentially decisive moments in a match. So, on those pressure points, like 30-40, go for a solid first serve that's hit with a little spin to increase your chances of landing it in the box.

TIP

Vary the placement of your first serve to keep your opponent honest. If you've won two consecutive points by serving flat balls to the outside corner of the service box, hit your next first serve down the middle, with a little spin. Think of yourself as a pitcher mixing up their pitches to keep hitters off-balance. Avoid falling into a predictable pattern.

However, always keep hammering away at places where you're winning most of your first serves. Failure breeds frustration, and a frustrated player is much more likely to sink even deeper into a funk than to pull out of it.

Getting a kick out of second serves

Having to step up and hit a second serve, especially on a key point, is one of the most challenging situations in tennis. A second serve can be especially nerve-racking for beginners, who aren't completely comfortable when hitting safe, spin serves. (You can read more about spin serves in Chapter 11.) Developing even a modest spin serve does wonders for your confidence and will go a long way toward help avoiding those dreaded second-serve *yips* (poor service execution caused by nerves and a lack of confidence).

TIP

Hit your second serve to the place where you feel most comfortable and confident, no matter where your opponent lines up or how you'd like to play the rest of the point. You can take those other factors into consideration as your game improves.

It's okay if your second serve is just a patty-cake shot, hit without spin. You can only work with the tools you have. Concentrate on getting the ball nice and deep into the service court, even if it travels through the air more like a lob than a hard, flat serve. The deeper you put the ball, the more the serve will limit your opponent's offensive options.

Strive to use spin on your second serve, if at all possible. Balls hit with spin travel in a higher arc than flat ones do, which makes it easier for them to clear the net. The more spin you use, the larger your margin of safety. This spin factor becomes important when you hit angled serves toward the sideline, where the net is highest. The topspin, or *kick*, serve is generally the most consistent and effective option on a second serve for more advanced players. In fact, many will sprinkle it in on first serves for a change of pace.

REMEMBER

When you hit second serves, don't think ahead to the rest of the point. And don't gawk at your second serve either, biting your nails as you wait to see whether it lands in or out. Just assume that the serve will be good, and get ready to jump on any opportunity presented by the return.

Returning Serve

A reliable, confident return of serve is a terrific weapon that can strike a blow at the heart of your opponent's ability to perform the most fundamental challenge: holding serve.

TIP

If you use different grips for your forehand and backhand, you have a decision to make in terms of which grip you hold the racquet with when waiting to return. For many players, the backhand is the tougher shot, and they prefer starting with the backhand grip and then switching to the forehand if necessary. Other players, especially those with two-handed backhands, like to hold the racquet with a forehand grip in their dominant hand, and the backhand grip for their nondominant hand. That way, they're ready and waiting to hit the return with their preferred stroke, but a subtle grip change as they take the racquet back can produce a solid backhand return. Either method can work. Experiment with both to see which produces the most consistent and desirable results.

Setting up shop to return: In tight or back behind the baseline

As the returner, you can set up anywhere you like, at any time you want, as long as you don't distract the server.

Where you line up to receive should be determined by the quality of your opponent's serve and the serving pattern that emerges as you play. If your opponent's serve is a puffball, stand 3 or 4 feet inside the baseline. You want to step into the ball and hit it firmly, not run up and scoop it off the ground.

TIP

Lining up with your feet parallel with the sideline may seem logical and is an acceptable practice. However, some players return better by lining up with their feet pointing toward the server, even if this stance puts them at an angle to the sideline. Again, some trial and error should determine what works best for you.

If your opponent has a strong serve, stand with your feet just behind the baseline. Against a really strong server, you may even want to take several steps back from the baseline. You'll see many pro players take this tactic to extremes by standing close to the back fence when returning. Keep in mind that the farther back you go, the easier it is for your opponent to hit effective wide serves to either side of the service box. So, if you repeatedly get burned by wide serves because of a deep return position, you'll need to adjust by taking a few steps forward.

If you feel confident in both your forehand and backhand returns, you can line up just about in the middle of the receiving court — perhaps a shade more toward the singles sideline. However, if you want to limit the amount of returns one stroke faces, line up at least 2 feet farther over, toward your weaker return side. By "overplaying" to one side, you make your weakness harder to get at. You can go farther, even quite a bit farther, if you need to. This does leave openings for your opponents, so make the necessary adjustments if they're able to take advantage.

TIP

Because of the difference between first and second serves, you can usually take a few steps forward from your first-serve receiving position to take a second serve. But for all serves, keep the following things in mind:

>> **Cover the server's best serve.** As your opponent's serving pattern emerges, you'll discover which ones are their favorite. You'll want to adjust your positioning accordingly. For instance, wide serves (refer to Figure 13-1) can hurt you if you line up too close to the middle of the receiving box. If you're consistently being stretched to the maximum to get your racquet on the ball, chances are, it has as much to do with your positioning as with your opponent's serve.

>> **Get ready.** Don't just stand there, racquet dangling at your side, as your opponent gets ready to deliver. Keep your feet spread about the same width as your shoulders and keep them moving as you wait to return, shuffling or lightly shifting your weight from one foot to the other. Hold your racquet just as you do for your groundstrokes, with both hands on the racquet frame, at about waist level, and bend your knees.

>> **Get your weight moving forward.** As your opponent tosses the ball up to serve, take a small hop forward (called a *split-step*). This will better prepare you to spring into action to track down the serve. This doesn't mean you have to step into the shot — sometimes you won't have the time. But standing flat-footed makes you slow to react.

>> **Get aggressive.** You just won't win many points if you don't move forward to meet the serve with confidence. Think of yourself as a cat ready to pounce on a fuzzy yellow ball. A weak serve is a ball you can really attack.

Seizing the initiative with your return

If you're facing a really strong serve, less is more. Cut down or even eliminate the backswing on your return. Just block the ball back by turning your shoulders and reaching out to meet the ball with the face of your racquet. The same holds true if you're returning the serve from well inside the baseline — the closer you stand in, the shorter the backswing.

Strive to get good depth on your service return. If you can hit your returns close to your opponent's baseline, you've leveled the playing field. And if your opponent has a weak serve that you can play from well inside the baseline, a solid, deep return tips the scales in your favor.

First serve back, second serve attack

TIP

An old tennis adage is that when you're returning serve, don't throw your opponent roses (short for *return of serve errors*). You want to make it as difficult for the server as possible by getting as many returns in play as possible. When returning a first serve, simply try to get it back in play. Hitting it deep down the middle is never a bad result. If you can, try to get your return to your opponent's weaker side. If you accomplish that, you automatically shift the advantage in the ensuing rally to your side.

Returning a second serve is an opportunity to put an opponent on their heels. If your opponent hits a weak serve to your backhand, run around it and belt back a forehand. If you're in the minority whose backhand is better, then by all means expose it to the server when you line up to receive by protecting your forehand side, and let it rip.

TIP

The safest return on a wide serve is the crosscourt shot. It travels across the lowest part of the net, and you also have about 30 percent more of the court available than you do when you try to return down the line.

Going down the line, over the highest part of the net, is slightly more risky, but if you feel confident and your opponent's weaker side lies there, go for it. When the serve comes at you down the middle, you'll be able to return it over the lowest part of the net and still get it pretty close to either corner, which is the trade-off for the server who tries to make an ace down the center stripe.

REMEMBER

If the serve is the most important shot in the game — especially at the higher levels — then it stands to reason that having a dependable return of serve is a real difference-maker. Yet, many players overlook it in practice. If you take the time to develop this crucial asset, your return can be every bit as much of a weapon as your opponent's serve.

Riding Your Groundstroke to Victory

No matter what kind of baseline game you ultimately play, keep this in mind: The player who is farther inside the court almost always has the advantage. So, even when you're rallying with your groundstrokes, try to move into your court as much as your opponents' shots allow.

The farther in you get, the more you'll be able to hit your own shots deep, driving your opponent even farther back. Working your way into the court also allows you to hit more and more sharply angled shots. When you're rallying, you want to be the puppeteer, not the puppet.

WARNING

Don't force the issue of hitting from inside the court if it means playing the ball from a very low bounce or getting stuck in no-man's land between the baseline and the service lines.

Managing errors: Grinding down opponents

It's the simplest strategy in tennis: Don't take many risks, and let your opponent pile up the errors. Players who adopt this style of consistent play are often maligned as "pushers," because they don't do much more than push the ball back in play. But outside of the highest levels of the game, it's arguably the most successful strategy. If you can keep the ball in play longer than your opponent can, you win the point. Do that on the majority of points, and you win the match.

Playing to your strong side

When your forehand is a weapon, you can position yourself closer to the backhand side of the court. That means leaving a good portion of the court on your forehand side open, in effect daring your opponent to try to sneak a good shot past your greatest strength.

To play to your forehand, move over after you serve, or return, until you're about three-quarters of the way to the sideline. If your opponent makes a great shot that you can't reach with the forehand, so be it. Otherwise, you can now hit the shot you want, a penetrating forehand.

Use your strong side to implement strategy. It's typically the forehand, but if your backhand is your bigger weapon, then certainly lean on that stroke. If you can hit a few good shots crosscourt, driving your opponent back, follow them up with a down-the-line shot. If it's a really good one hit deep to the corner that has your opponent scrambling just to return it, you have an ideal chance to follow it to the net to end the point.

Placing your shots

Crosscourt shots are very useful for setting your opponent up. Down-the-line shots are good choices to end a point, because a shot hit down the line has less distance to travel. That makes it easier to hit winners down the line, or to force your opponent to scramble and rush the return, which could coax an error out of them.

You can also use your shots to pin an opponent in either corner. On the crosscourt side, you can move your opponent farther over, stroke after stroke, by increasing your crosscourt angle. This strategy opens up the court for the down-the-line shot. If you have a good down-the-line shot, you can trouble most opponents by pinning them in their own backhand corners. Because most players have weaker backhands than forehands, they may not be able to hurt you at all after you move them into the backhand corner.

Lastly, you can vary the depth of your shots. Hitting the ball deep into your opponent's court is always good policy. The deeper they are, the less options they have to hit a shot that can give you trouble. But hitting short in the court can also be useful because it tests their ability to move forward and hit tricky shots from well inside the baseline.

Picking on an opponent's weakness

Instead of doing what you do best, sometimes playing smart tennis is doing what your opponent likes least. For instance, say you really like to smack your crosscourt forehand, and you get a lot of mileage out of it winning matches. However, on this day, so does your opponent. In fact, theirs is just a little bit better. That's a losing proposition.

Instead, you'd be better off discovering the shortcomings of your opponent's game. Often, especially when players are just starting out, it's the backhand. Simply peppering a lot of shots at your opponent's backhand side can be enough to draw a lot of errors. But at the higher levels, this isn't always the case. That's when you have to put your chess master hat back on and strategize.

Maybe your opponent has solid groundstrokes but has zero confidence in their volleys. Well, drawing them to net would be more profitable than engaging in long baseline exchanges. Or maybe those groundstrokes are super consistent, but not when they're forced to hit a passing shot. In that case, getting to net would be a smart tactic, even if volleying isn't your favorite thing to do.

Playing keep-away, not catch

When you rally with your playing partner, you hit the ball pretty much right to them so they can easily return it. It's almost like a game of catch. Playing points or a match is more like a game of keep-away. You want to place your shots so your opponent is forced to move, which makes returning them more challenging. Your first priority is to get the ball over the net. After that, you need it to land inside the lines. But as you develop, the basic strategy to employ is to hit the ball where your opponent is not.

Netting Profits with Your Volley

When you approach net, the closer you are to the net, the easier it is to create an angle with your volley. Under those circumstances, you should almost always hit the volley crosscourt. You're in such a commanding position at the net that any sharply angled crosscourt volley is a pretty safe bet. And the closer you are to the net, the safer the bet.

TIP

If net play becomes a regular part of your strategy, you often have to hit volleys from less-than-ideal positions. When you're closer to the service line than the net and not well set up to play the volley with plenty of time, use your first volley to set up a subsequent volley from a more advantageous position. Figure 13-2 shows how this scenario plays out.

In Figure 13-2, the server hits a hard first serve down the middle to the returner's forehand. Following the serve to the net, the server intercepts the return and hits a safe first volley to the opponent's backhand side. The returner then goes for a crosscourt passing shot, which the server, moving forward, knocks off for a volley winner to the returner's forehand corner.

When you're starting out, a good rule of thumb when it comes to directing volleys is to play the opposites. For instance, if your approach shot is deep in the court and forces your opponent to hit the return shot from behind the baseline, hit your next volley shorter in the court. If the approach shot draws your opponent well inside the baseline, hit your next volley deep. Or, if your opponent hits a passing shot down the line, hit your volley crosscourt. You get the picture. Not only does this take some of the guesswork out of volleying, but it implements that game of keep-away with your opponent.

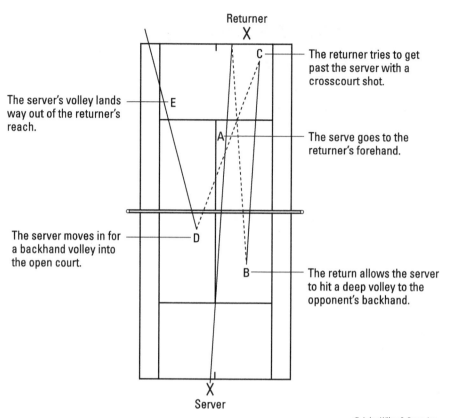

Returner
X

The returner tries to get past the server with a crosscourt shot.

The server's volley lands way out of the returner's reach. — E

The serve goes to the returner's forehand. — A

The server moves in for a backhand volley into the open court. — D

The return allows the server to hit a deep volley to the opponent's backhand. — B

FIGURE 13-2:
Getting your opponent into position to make the most of a second volley opportunity.

X
Server

TIP

The serve-and-volley strategy is the most basic attacking strategy of them all. It used to be a staple on the fast grass courts at Wimbledon, but it has become much less prominent in the modern pro game. It's still an effective play, but now it's used more as a changeup tactic to catch opponents off-guard. Even before serving, the serve-and-volley player is committed to rushing to the net behind the serve and trying to win the point with a volley. Although you need good skills and athleticism to play serve-and-volley tennis, even beginners can get a lot out of the intimidation factor when they charge the net after they serve. Returners are often so distracted by the onrushing server that they blow the shot.

If you follow the path of the server in Figure 13-2, you see that the second volley was hit from considerably closer to the net than the first one. Closing on the net is a great idea unless the first volley you hit is so tentative or poorly placed that it leaves you vulnerable to the lob or easy passing shot. But when you hit a good, penetrating volley, keep moving forward behind it.

Passing Shots

The passing shot is your primary tool against an opponent at net. In a passing shot, you note your opponent's position at the net, and then you fire a shot to either side that ideally whizzes right past them. Obviously, to achieve this, your passing shot must be very accurate.

Although your passing shots must be more accurate than your typical ground-strokes because of the privileged position that your opponent holds at the net, you have this big consolation: Your passing shot doesn't have to be hit deep into the other court. There's nobody back there! All you have to do is get the ball by your opponent. And getting the ball by your opponent can come in different forms, which I cover in the following sections.

Hard drives

If your opponent sets up shop at net, you can try to nail a shot right past them. You're basically going for an outright winner with one swing of the racquet. You want to pick a spot that they're not, and try to hit the ball so it crosses just above the net. Again, depth is not a priority. This way, if your opponent does get their racquet on the ball, it's still a challenging volley. If it's too high, they have a much better chance of putting the volley away.

TIP

These are the best times to hit your passing shot crosscourt:

>> **When you're near the middle of the court:** If you're at or behind the baseline within 3 feet of the centerline to either side, your choice is a toss-up. Chances are, your opponent will lean toward protecting the line (the side you're closer to), because your route to a winner is shorter and faster there. That, combined with the low height of the net at the center, makes going crosscourt worthwhile.

>> **When your opponent is overplaying toward the sideline:** They want to protect the sideline from your down-the-line shot, but they end up opening up the court for a crosscourt attempt.

>> **When doing so forces your opponent to hit the volley with their weaker stroke:** This one is a real trade-off, but it can elicit errors from players who have a significantly weaker volleying side.

WARNING

Don't try to hit crosscourt passing shots when you're stretched and running in the direction opposite from where your shot would go. The degree of difficulty is high, and only very skilled players can pull it off. Instead, fire up a lob and then get back into position near the center of the court.

Your down-the-line passing shots come in very handy in the following situations:

>> **When you have time:** Your down-the-line shot needs to hug the line, so having the time to execute your stroke really helps you thread the needle.

>> **When you're closer to your own service line than the baseline:** Don't get fancy and try to outfox an opponent when you're in such a good position to drive the ball through the obvious, open hole.

>> **When the down-the-line shot is on your opponent's weaker volleying side:** Exploiting your opponent's weakness is a sure way to force an error.

Down-the-line shots are riskier because of the height of the net. But they also get to where they're going more quickly, and they're easier to make in some typical defensive situations. Your high school geometry comes in handy in tennis — the shortest distance between two points on the court is still a straight down-the-line shot.

Two-shot combos

Sometimes the quality of your opponent's approach shot puts you in a defensive position that doesn't afford you an opportunity to hit an offensive passing shot. Under those circumstances, you're better off hitting a safer, neutralizing shot that forces your opponent to hit a volley, and then go for the clean passing shot on the next ball. Like a boxer, you're using a one-two combination to deliver the knockout shot.

Here are a few setup options:

>> **Dip the ball at their feet.** Volleying from below the level of the net is tough. If you can hit the first ball so that your opponent must volley up and over the net, it'll usually be a neutral or defensive shot. Then you'll be in better position to hit the ball by them on the next shot.

>> **Hit down the middle.** This is a useful setup shot for a couple of reasons. First, it gives you the most margin for error, so you're more likely to stay in the point. Second, if your opponent volleys from the middle of the court, they're forced to create all the angle on the shot. It's easy to overcook it and send the volley wide. Often, they'll just volley it right back down the center, giving you another chance to hit the passing shot.

>> **Go after their weaker volley.** Rinse, lather, repeat. When in doubt force your opponent to hit a volley with their weaker side. If doing so doesn't force an error, there's a good chance you'll at least see another ball.

Lobs

When your opponents are at net, the most room you have to pass them is above their heads. Your lob has a great hidden virtue beyond merely winning points. It also keeps an attacking opponent from continually crowding the net. So, you have a better chance to make good passing shots because of the threat posed by your lob. Even if you prefer to hit passing shots, hit a few lobs early in a match to establish your willingness to use it.

TIP

The lob is especially valuable when a bright sun makes it hard for your opponent to look up, watch, and hit the ball with the overhead. Lobbing into the sun is the oldest trick in the book. And don't feel bad about it — your opponent will gladly do the same.

Unlike a hard-hit passing shot, the direction of the lob is not that important. As long as it gets over your opponent's head and lands inside the lines, mission accomplished. If you have the time, try to lob to your opponent's backhand side. That makes it more difficult for them to set up for the overhead. If possible, hit your lob crosscourt as well, because you have more court space to land the ball, and it can make your opponent lose track of their position on the court.

TIP

One of the deadliest ways to use your lob is in a combination with your drop shot. It's particularly devilish against players who don't like to move forward or play at the net. Throw in a drop shot when you're in a good position — such as several feet inside the baseline — and force your opponent to scramble in to retrieve it. If they do manage to scoop it over the net, immediately throw up a lob on the next shot. They'll have to slam on the brakes, gather their momentum, and then burn back to the baseline to track down the lob. They'll feel like a yo-yo.

Winning Ways for Doubles

The first step toward developing a winning doubles game is recognizing that it isn't just a kind of tag-team singles. (I discuss the fundamental differences between singles and doubles in Chapter 1; Chapter 5 highlights the serving mechanics used in doubles.)

If you watch good doubles, you quickly notice that they move as one. They move forward toward the net together, and they move back together. They change sides of the court at the same time. When a shot goes up the middle, they call "Yours" or "Mine" to indicate who should take a particular shot. The key to success in doubles is playing and communicating as a team.

Lining up to receive serve

Although you can line up any way you want in doubles, most teams line up one player at the baseline and the other at the net, whether they're serving or receiving — although it's much more common these days for both returning players to start the point back on the baseline (I explain why in a little bit).

In the traditional one-up, one-back formation on the serving team, the server is the back player. On serves to the deuce court, the net player on the serving team lines up 2 or 3 feet from the net, about 4 feet from the left sideline boundary. On serves to the ad court, the net player lines up the same distance from the net and the right sideline. This enables the net player to guard against a down-the-line service return and to still block off a substantial part of the rest of the court.

The net player on the returning team lines up just inside the service line. By standing a little farther back from the net, the returning team net player has a little more time to react to shots from the serving team when a point starts. From this position, the net player can also serve as a linesperson for their partner and help call whether the serve is in or out.

If you're not confident at the net, or you're playing a team with really good serves, you can line up with both players back. This positioning makes more sense for the returning team, which is on the defensive to begin with at the start of the point. And it has become popular in today's game, where players feel much more comfortable hitting groundstrokes over volleys.

But when the returning team lines up two back, the net player on the serving team becomes the fox in the henhouse, prowling the net area with impunity. Playing two back on the serving team is unwise and highly irregular, because the returner can place the service return anywhere, with no fear of the opponent's net player.

Seizing the advantage at the net

The team that takes control of the net usually wins in doubles. Controlling the net is an advantage because you pressure your opponents to hit the ball into tighter spaces. At the net, you can hit sharply angled volleys for winners. You can also intimidate your opponents into making errors with your presence, if not your expertise. Those are powerful reasons to take control of the net, if you have the moxie and skill to volley.

However, beginners are often uncomfortable with hitting volleys, especially on the move, so they stay back, and if the ball is kept in play, they have a crosscourt rally with the returner. It's also common to see players at all levels stay back when facing opponents with strong returns of serve. And some players just have more confidence, and success, driving groundstrokes in crosscourt exchanges. That's where having an active net player really helps a team, because they can get involved by intercepting one of those groundstrokes and seizing the advantage in the point.

Poaching

Just by being up in the traditional position, the net player on the serving team puts a lot of pressure on the returner to hit crosscourt. With just a bit of confidence and quick first step, the alert net player can take advantage of any ball that isn't hit at enough of an angle by intercepting it. This maneuver is called *poaching.*

Poaching is one of the most basic and productive tactics in doubles. The most common form of poaching occurs when the net player on the serving team intercepts the service return.

TIP

Natural poachers can really help their partners hold serve, feasting on service returns like sharks at feeding time. But always remember that the net player on the serving team must also guard the sideline. Players are demoralized when they go to make an interception and the other team's back player hits the ball behind them, down the line, for a winner. The key to successful poaching is remaining still until the returner has committed to the crosscourt shot. Then, even if the returner makes a great crosscourt shot out of reach of the poacher, no real damage is done, because your partner is there to return it.

The net player on the returning team fulfills a similar function, forcing the server to hit their second shot, whether it's a groundstroke or a volley, crosscourt. Just as the net player on the serving team can poach, the returning team's net player can also move over to intercept the shot of the server, hitting it into the open court for a winner or forcing the net player on the serving team to make a difficult reflex volley.

TIP

One of the best defenses against an eager net player is the lob return. When you use your lob return, you neutralize the serving team's net player and cause the serving team to change sides of the court, throwing them off-balance. If you're really on your toes, you and your partner can then move forward to take the offensive from the net position, taking full advantage of the other team's change of position. However, this strategy is less effective if the net player on the serving team lines up a little farther back from the net, ready to hit the overhead if you hit all but the best of lobs.

Playing the percentages

TIP

With four players on the court, hitting excellent angled shots or moving the ball around well in baseline rallies isn't as effective as it is in singles. The court is much smaller in doubles, and that fact dictates following different strategies for success:

>> **Hit down the middle.** As the saying goes, the middle is the riddle. Hitting down the middle can cause confusion for the other team. They may freeze, each player thinking that the other one will play the next shot. As a rule, the player who made the previous shot has the right-of-way, so to speak, if the next shot is within reach. But even experienced teams — the kind that communicate a lot — can be caught in this split.

If you successfully keep the ball in play down the middle, you can often catch your opponents off-guard, leaning that way. That opens up chances to hit an angled shot to the doubles alleys. Use the middle of the court to open up possibilities on the wings.

>> **Get a high percentage of your first serves in.** Because the returner needs to make a good crosscourt shot to avoid the net player on the serving team, keeping your opponent under pressure and off-balance with good first serves is a great advantage, even if that means taking a little speed off the serves to get more of them in play.

>> **Use the lob to mix it up.** When you hit a good lob over two players at the net, they both have to turn to retreat before the nearest one plays the ball. When you hit a good lob over the net player in a one-up, one-back situation, the other team has to change courts as the back player retrieves the lob. The more you can force the other team to change sides, the more effectively you can disrupt their teamwork.

>> **Hit at the net player.** If an opponent playing from the back hits a poor, short lob or a high, floating groundstroke, return the ball between the net player and the back player or hit it at the feet of the net player.

Outfoxing a Lefty

MAC SAYS

Lefties are a real pain in the neck for us righties. Trust me, I know. I have two left-handed brothers, and they taught me early how I had to change my game to have good results against them. But because both John and Mark are southpaws, I also ended up with a big advantage when I went out to play on the pro tour. I had a lot of experience against lefties.

Left-handed players enjoy certain natural advantages. The biggest one is that, for reasons nobody can really explain, lefty spin serves are especially deadly. Lefties also serve more comfortably in the ad court, while righties naturally prefer the deuce court. With most of the key break points contested in the ad court, lefties enjoy a slight advantage over righties, provided they can exploit it.

On the other hand (no pun intended), the most powerful and natural shot that most righties have, the crosscourt forehand, goes to a lefty's backhand. Advantage, righties. But that is nullified somewhat by the fact that lefties are more comfortable playing righties. It's a numbers game, really — lefties play many more righties, so they play their natural games, where the righty often has to adjust.

TIP

Keep these simple tactics in mind when facing a lefty:

>> **Use your crosscourt forehand.** Unless your opponent has a terrific backhand, or you have a shaky forehand, this bread-and-butter shot can really level the playing field.

>> **Protect the wide side of the ad court during the serve.** Lefties love to go for angled, spin serves in the ad court. If you're a righty, that's also your backhand side. Make sure that you cover the wide angle, even at the expense of giving up the centerline — or T — of the service box. If your opponent can hit aces or unreturnable serves there consistently, so be it.

>> **Serve wide in the deuce court.** If you're playing a righty, serving out wide in the deuce court means challenging their favored forehand. It's not something you want to do consistently. That's probably why righties don't often develop the same kind of swing serve out wide in the deuce court that lefties have in the ad court. But that wide serve is at the lefty's backhand. Unless they've got a really good one, it should make up the majority of your serves to the deuce court.

3

Taking Your Game to the Next Level

Nothing can compare with the thrill of using your racquet to make the ball go where you want it to go. Gaining this kind of control over your game takes practice, conditioning, and often a few lessons. I take the pain out of these game-building activities in this part. I also tell you about places where you can put your hard work to good use in tournaments and at other venues. And just in case you experience a few aches and pains while honing your game, I dedicate one chapter in this part to describing a few common tennis injuries — and how to avoid them.

Chapter **14**

Enjoying Your Amateur Status

When you start to feel comfortable with your game, you should investigate the many opportunities to play at different venues and with different opponents. If you stick to playing with the same people at the same place, you'll never get the full experience that tennis has to offer. You won't improve as quickly, either. Plus, you'll probably get bored with the game.

In this chapter, I tell you about different locations you can play tennis, organizations you can join to find competition, and other ways to make the most of your time on the courts.

Finding Places to Pick Up a Game

When looking for a place to play that suits your ambitions, your temperament, and even your pocketbook, you have lots of choices.

Public parks

Many cities and towns operate public tennis courts. The overwhelming majority of these are hard courts, because hard courts require little maintenance. However, in some parts of the world, many public facilities feature clay courts. (See Chapter 2 for more information on hard and clay courts.)

WARNING

Although you can wear any kind of athletic sneakers you like on a hard court, you must wear smooth-soled, all-court tennis sneakers on clay to keep from digging up and ruining the courts. Many running shoes, cross-trainers, and other types of recreational shoes have unacceptable types of soles. If you show up at clay courts with inappropriate shoes, the facility may not allow you to play.

Some of these public facilities offer services and amenities that rival those offered by tennis clubs — from private lessons and clinics given by certified pros to snack bars and pro shops where you can buy shoes and racquets. Some public courts even equip their courts with lights so you can play at night. You see this feature more often in the south or out west, where year-round play is more prevalent. But even in the northeast, in my neck of the woods, playing tennis can be a beautiful thing on a soft summer night.

Although you can play for free at lots of public courts, you often have to pay a nominal fee (ranging from $5 to $20 per hour) at a dedicated public tennis facility. If your local public courts charge a fee for use, check to see whether you can pay one lump membership fee for the whole playing season or if they have some other kind of discount — such as reduced lesson fees — for town residents.

Public tennis facilities are a terrific deal. One of the great things about them is that they often stage tournaments in which you can play. Most public facilities will even find playing partners for you. They can introduce you to an entire tennis culture and broaden your horizons as a player by making it easy to play with a great variety of partners.

Most public facilities have attendants on duty, and the heavily used ones, like the complex in New York's Central Park where I regularly practiced during my early years on tour, have strict sign-up policies to prevent the local cell of tennis die-hards from hogging up all the courts for hours on end. Fortunately I had an "in" who helped manage the courts and hooked me up with extra court time. People were constantly asking me if I needed a game, because most had to wait for hours to get a court.

For people who can play only outside of traditional working hours, when the courts are in peak demand, many facilities have reservation systems, which allow you to book well in advance. This is now often done through smartphone apps and websites.

When you play at a public facility that has no attendant or sign-up procedure, the general rule is that you and your partner(s) have use of the court for one hour (on a first come, first served basis). Some facilities permit more time if you're play-ing doubles. If you get to your local public courts and find them filled, feel free to ask the players how much longer they plan to use the court. But don't march right up and interrupt their game — wait for them to finish the current game before asking.

TIP

If you plan to play a lot at unattended public facilities, throwing an old broom and even a squeegee into the trunk of your car is a good idea. The broom is good for getting rid of debris such as fallen leaves. With a squeegee, the kind you clean your car windows with, you can play soon after a summer shower. If you squeegee the puddles where water collects on a hard court, the remaining water dries in just minutes under the sun. At many public courts, large brooms and squeegees are available to players.

WARNING

At many public facilities, the courts are so crowded that you're only allowed to use a maximum of three balls on the court. This cuts down the number of interrup-tions that occur when balls being used on one court go rolling or flying onto oth-ers. When you play a match of any kind, you never use more than three balls. But for practice, many players use a basketful of balls to cut down on time spent col-lecting them. Make sure that you know the policy at the courts before you go out to practice with more than three balls.

Tennis clubs

You can find dedicated tennis clubs scattered all over the United States. These clubs require some form of membership to use their facilities. The simplest ones have one-room clubhouses and a handful of courts. In some ways, these small clubs offer the best of both worlds: the intimacy and court access of a private club, combined with the low-cost and "just tennis" atmosphere you usually find at public tennis facilities.

These tennis clubs are very different from full-blown, fancy country clubs. They're run by tennis nuts, for tennis nuts. Most of them don't have swimming pools, golf courses, snack bars, or any of those other higher-priced amenities. They're like tennis co-ops, in which a group of like-minded people get together and pool their resources to play tennis under the best conditions possible.

But these clubs are private, and depending on the size and enthusiasm of the local tennis culture, they may have long waiting lists for membership. To become a member, you may have to be nominated by other, current members. In other words, you gotta know somebody to get in. Others operate on a yearly first come, first served basis.

The initiation fees and dues at most small tennis clubs can range from several hundred to a few thousand dollars a year. The fees cover the cost of operating the club and keeping the courts and clubhouse in good shape. They may also go toward paying for a teaching pro who gives lessons and handles the club's operations.

The courts at tennis clubs are usually well maintained, the level of play among the members can be high, and the calendar is often chock-full of events, like member or member-guest doubles tournaments. Bragging rights can be fierce, and it's common for members to recruit ringers like ex-pros or high-level collegiate players in order to win the title.

If you develop a real passion for tennis and live in an urban or suburban area, you'll inevitably find out about these small tennis clubs as you become part of the tennis culture. As you get to know some of the members from your weekly doubles game, you can inquire about membership.

You can also play tennis at more elaborate country clubs. Most of these clubs offer golf and tennis, often with the emphasis on golf. But some are dedicated tennis clubs. These clubs usually offer all kinds of amenities, from lavish dining rooms that serve great food to swimming pools and gyms for working out after your tennis game.

Sure, some people join country clubs with a greater interest in clinching business deals over lunch than working on their backhands. That's the stereotype projected in movies. But the reality is usually that a lot of good tennis players belong to these clubs. Hey, when you have a comfortable lifestyle, you can afford to take a lot more lessons and spend more hours on the court.

THE WEST SIDE STORY

The West Side Tennis Club, in Forest Hills, New York, is a grand old tennis club with an important history. Besides offering beautiful grass courts, clay courts, and a regal, Tudor-style clubhouse, the West Side Tennis Club also happens to offer a stadium that seats 12,000. The U.S. Open was played at this stadium until 1977, by which time the tournament had grown so big that it was moved down the road to the specially built National Tennis Center. The stadium still houses occasional professional exhibitions and has become a premier concert venue for live music.

If you become a member at a typical country club, you'll usually be able to play plenty of great tennis, with a variety of partners. But membership sometimes isn't just a matter of writing a check. Country clubs are social organisms, not commercial ones. In other words, they like to have control over the people who join. In order to join most country clubs, no matter how much money you have, you usually have to go through a nomination and screening process. Active members of the club nominate you, the membership committee looks at your résumé, and then — if you're lucky — you get to write a big fat check to get into the club.

Look into the tennis program at any club you're thinking about joining. Often, tennis is a very weak stepsister to golf. Country clubs that take their tennis seriously usually have at least one "club pro" who gives lessons, pro shops that offer racquet-stringing services, and a range of activities from partner matchup services to tournaments.

TIP

Even if you don't join a country club, a member may ask you to play at one from time to time. Country clubs often adhere to a dress code — even restricting attire to white shirts, and white shorts or skirts. Many of them insist that you wear a shirt with a collar. (Sounds starchy, doesn't it?) Make sure that you know the dress code when you're invited to play at a country club. Bring new balls along and play with them, as a little thank-you gesture.

Fitness facilities

Indoor clubs sprang up all over the United States in the 1970s, when tennis was booming. Such clubs are also popular in Canada, England, France, and Germany. These indoor clubs provide tennis enthusiasts with places to play even during the cold months of the year. Over the years, many of these clubs evolved into "full-service" facilities, offering squash, racquetball, basketball, and gym facilities, in addition to tennis. You can hit the weights or take a Peloton class before working on your serve. Most fitness facilities are commercial ventures, not social ones. So, you don't have to worry too much about waiting lists or knowing the right people in order to get in — you just plonk down your membership dues, and you're in business.

These clubs typically have much bigger footprints than a tennis-only club. Due to the size and various programs offered, these clubs are often fairly pricey — they usually charge initiation and membership fees ranging from a few hundred dollars to a few thousand dollars. In addition, members must pay for court time. During the winter months, the fees can be as high as $40 or $50 per hour during prime time.

Resorts

Most resorts, including ski resorts, either offer tennis on-site or have an arrangement for access to courts nearby. In addition, numerous travel companies cater specifically to tennis players, offering full-service tennis vacations. These packages come complete with unlimited court time, special lessons packages, and spa treatments to soothe those sore muscles after a full day of the game.

As a resort activity, tennis ranks right up there. You can get a good workout in just an hour on a tennis court, and it doesn't have to cut into the other activities you and your family may have in mind for the day.

REMEMBER

If you decide to take a plane ride to a resort where you plan to play tennis, remember that most U.S.-based airlines allow you to bring your racquet on board as a piece of carry-on luggage. If you must check your racquet as baggage, a padded carrying case can save your frames some abuse.

Joining the U.S. Tennis Association

The United States Tennis Association (USTA) is the governing body of tennis in the United States. It consists of 17 geographical sections. In each of those sections, volunteer USTA members assume the daily, grassroots job of getting people together to play by offering tournaments, a ranking system, league play, and programs for beginners. Read on for the details and then contact the USTA directly for its current offerings in your area. You can contact the USTA through its website (www.usta.com) or through its smartphone app (available in your phone's app store).

Many countries have their own national tennis associations that sponsor programs similar to the USTA's offerings. Just goes to show you that tennis really does have global appeal.

Player ratings

Quantifying just how good you are at tennis can be difficult. You may play exceptionally well against your best friend, but then your neighbor may clean your clock every time you play, and their neighbor may crush them with ease when they play. So, just how good are you?

The USTA came up with its official National Tennis Rating Program (NTRP), which is one of the standards for describing skill levels in various players. The NTRP rates players on a scale from 1.0 (stone-cold beginner) to 7.0 (world-class touring pro). A player's rating can fall in between two numbers, such as 3.5 or 4.5. This creates 12 rating levels in total.

You don't just choose your own NTRP rating. To get one, you must complete a self-rating questionnaire at `https://tennislink.usta.com` or through the TennisLink app. This is the entry-level rating all players need if they want to play in USTA leagues. After compiling enough wins and losses, you'll earn a more accurate *computer rating* — also sometimes referred to as a *year-end rating*. Depending on your results, you'll typically either stay at your self-rating or get bumped up or down 0.5 rating points.

You have to be a member of the USTA to take part and get a rating. A membership currently costs $44 annually for an adult and junior membership (under the age of 19) is available at no cost.

When you meet another tennis player at a barbecue, it isn't rude to simply ask, "Do you have an NTRP rating?" If the player has one, the answer will be just as simple. "Why, yes, I'm a 3.5." The NTRP ratings really cut to the chase on ability. They eliminate a lot of hemming and hawing and long-winded descriptions about how you play.

Of course, many players — particularly many advanced ones — don't bother to establish their ratings. They play where they play, they know what they know, and they have plenty of regular partners. And even when a potential partner is familiar with the NTRP rating, there's no guarantee of honesty. The ratings haven't eliminated the role of ego in such things, even if the facts don't agree.

MAC SAYS

All you can be honest about is your own game. And I urge you to take that course, instead of trying to impress — or sandbag — a potential playing partner with an inflated or deflated rating. Neither you nor your partner knows the real level of your respective games until you start hitting balls. That's why it's important to be open-minded, flexible, and sensitive when you play with a new partner. Having a sense of humor really helps, too.

USTA League and tournament play

The USTA League is the country's largest recreational competitive tennis league. It combines serious recreational competition with many of the social aspects that make tennis fun. You test yourself as an individual in singles or doubles competition, and you get to share the glory of a win — or the disappointment of a loss — with teammates.

Having teammates means built-in practice partners and, in many cases, new friends who you would never have met if it weren't for your common interest in tennis. Instead of going to a tournament in an unfamiliar place all by yourself, your USTA League team can all jam into somebody's minivan, turn up the radio, and head out for that big road game. Afterward, you can all celebrate or commiserate with your favorite adult beverage.

The best thing about USTA League play is that anyone can either find a team to play on, with the help of the USTA, or form one from scratch. You only have to meet the following criteria to play in a USTA League:

>> You must meet the league's age requirement.

>> You must be a member of the USTA.

>> You must hold an NTRP rating.

The USTA League offers programs for various age groups for 2.5 through 5.0 level. Players must play at or above their rating level, but never below. A 4.5 player can play in a 5.0 league, but a higher-rated player cannot play down, just as a 50-year-old can play in a 40+ league, but a 35-year-old is not eligible.

Some doubles leagues use a format in which the doubles team's combined rating must be equal to or less than a certain number. For instance, a 9.0 mixed-doubles league team can consist of a 4.0 male and a 5.0 female, or they can each be rated 4.5. This opens the league up to a wider range of players.

In order to join a team, you need to create a profile on the TennisLink page (https://tennislink.usta.com). All that takes is your USTA membership number. There currently is a $33 registration fee for each team you join. On your profile page, you'll see your most recent match results, as well as team rosters, schedules, and league standings.

WARNING

If you convince a 5.0 friend to self-rate as a 4.5 to slip into your league lineup, they may get tarred and feathered by your aggrieved opponents. And if that doesn't happen, the USTA keeps computerized records that, among other things, can identify ringers and disqualify them. In fact, your entire team can be disqualified for such shenanigans.

In local league play, the match format can vary depending on the league. For instance, many follow a five-match format: two singles and three doubles. But in the 5.0-and-under league, it's a three-match format: one singles and two doubles matches. You need the minimum number of players on the roster to form a league team. The team that wins the most matches wins the contest.

A typical league season lasts from 6 to 15 weeks. In some areas, a team may play as few as three matches or as many as a dozen, depending on how many rival teams are within reasonable distance. The home team captain submits the results of each league match online at TennisLink or through the TennisLink app.

Depending on the size of the league, the season can culminate with a series of local, regional, and sectional playoffs. The teams that win its section at their level, go on to compete against the other section winners in a national championship held in October at various sites around the country.

USTA-sanctioned tournaments

USTA-sanctioned tournaments are at the top of the recreational, competitive pyramid. The majority of sanctioned events are restricted to certain age groups. In junior tennis, players must be 12 and under, 14 and under, 16 and under, or 18 and under to play in the appropriate events. I played my first tournament at the age of 6, in a 10 and Under event. Adult tournaments are also often categorized by age, NTRP rating, or both.

ENTRY-LEVEL TEAM TENNIS WITH THE USTA

The USTA offers Junior Team Tennis (JTT) for kids ranging in age from 5 to 18. Kids new to the game compete in singles, doubles, and mixed doubles against other coed teams. The emphasis is on fun, fitness, and the social benefits of tennis rather than sheer competition. The expectations are kept to a minimum: You need to be able to serve, maintain a rally, and know how to keep score. It's a program for developing players who are ready to test their strokes against others, and who want to be part of the tennis culture without diving headlong into the serious competition of junior tournaments.

In addition to any other sanctioned events, each USTA section has sectional championships in various age groups. The size, makeup, and enthusiasm of the section determine how many and what kinds of events it offers. Large sections offer many sanctioned events, in most age divisions. Smaller sections may have just a few events all year.

The best players in the sections often qualify for national rankings, and they can play in national-level tournaments that generate the ultimate in amateur status: a national ranking. But being a good player in a relatively weak or sparsely populated section won't automatically qualify you for a national ranking or a place in a national-level tournament. Strong sections, serving tennis-mad states like California, Florida, Georgia, and the Carolinas, produce the most nationally ranked players.

The tournaments at the very top of the USTA pyramid are the various national amateur championships, held in various age groups. And towering above that pyramid is the U.S. Open, which began as the USTA's national championships but evolved into a competition open to qualified comers from all nations, pro and otherwise.

WARNING

Playing at the sectional and national level can be time-consuming and costly. An entry fee for a sanctioned tournament can range from about $50 to $80, which often buys you nothing more than the privilege of losing in the first round. You also have to consider the expense and time to get to and from tournaments that may not be close to your home.

Earning your prized ranking spurs

If you play enough sanctioned events in your section, and win enough matches, you may grab a prized sectional ranking and someday brag to your grandchildren that you were once a highly ranked player. The number of ranked players in any division in any section depends on how many players compete in the sanctioned tournaments and how much usable data exists to make meaningful rankings.

Sectional rankings also determine whether you qualify to take part in national-level tournaments, in which you can earn a national ranking. Your national ranking, if you get one, is determined by your sectional ranking and your performance in national-level sanctioned events.

MAC SAYS

Now every ranking and result can be found on your phone, but I used to nervously await the mail at ranking time, anxious to know my final ranking for the year. I think the ranking system is the single greatest cause of gray hair among tennis players.

Entering sanctioned tournaments

In order to play in sanctioned tournaments, you must be a member of the USTA. When you join, the USTA automatically lists you as a member in your section. The tournament schedule for your section and the regulations and procedures that you must follow to compete in them can be found on the USTA website.

REMEMBER

The details of tournament entry and play may vary from one section to another, but you can find all the information on the USTA website.

Keep these tips in mind to make your entry into USTA-sanctioned tournaments as smooth as possible:

>> **Submit your entry fee in early.** If your payment arrives after the deadline, you may not get to play.

>> **Contact the event coordinator to find out your start time for your first-round match.** Nowadays, this is typically done through text or email.

>> **Arrive early and check in.** If possible, plan to arrive at the event up to one hour before your scheduled start time. Some events require registration on the day before the event starts, so make sure that you know the procedure. Have your USTA membership number handy, just in case you need it.

>> **Bring a can of new balls suitable for the court surface on which the tournament is being played.** Most tournaments provide balls for matches, but play it safe.

>> **Report your scores to the tournament director when you win a match.** Reporting your scores is your responsibility. Do this as soon as possible after you win to avoid any potential confusion. When you report your score, try to get the name and contact info of your next opponent, if necessary.

>> **Be prepared to play in the consolation events.** Many tournaments hold such events for early-round losers. Besides having fun, you can improve your competitive talents and get a little more bang for your buck.

Creating a Universal Tennis Rating Profile

Created in 2008, Universal Tennis Rating (UTR) is the newer ratings kid on the block. It uses a more elaborate 1.00 to 16.50 scale based on a unique algorithm that's intended to give a more accurate reflection of a player's skill level. It starts at the rank of beginner and goes all the way up to top-ranked touring pro.

The website's database tracks match results and players in more than 200 countries across a wide array of sanctioned competitions. Aspects like rating differential between opponents, expected outcome, and match format are factored into the rating. It isn't based solely on wins and losses. Lose a tight match to a higher-rated opponent, and your rating could actually go up. The rating is derived from up to 30 of your most recent matches over the preceding 12 months. There are ratings for both singles and doubles.

The UTR is not only more comprehensive, but cuts across gender, age, and playing federations from around the world for a more global rating. Similar to a golf handicap, it's designed to make it easier to compete against players from all parts of the game who are truly at your level. It has become increasingly popular with junior players, and having an up-to-date rating is more or less essential if you're interested in playing in college.

The rating is free, and all it takes is a few completed matches to get one. You just need to create an account on the UTR website (www.utrsports.net) or app. There is also a member program that offers fuller ratings, discounted entry fees into UTR events, advanced analytics, and gear and apparel deals; as of this writing, membership costs $12 per month or $120 per year.

UTR doesn't have the sections and local infrastructure of the USTA, so its calendar of events isn't as widespread or plentiful. That said, UTR does sponsor and run tournaments throughout the year, especially for rising juniors. It also sponsors the UTR Pro Series, which consists of small-prize-money events held around the world for professionals ranked outside the top 200. Because entry into its tournaments is based on a player's rating — not rankings, age group, or section — UTR matches are often quite competitive.

A more relaxed format for developing players is the UTR Flex Leagues. These are essentially mini-leagues in which you commit to play four matches over a five-week span. It consists of four to ten players or doubles teams of similar playing levels in the same general geographic location organized through the UTR website or app.

Unlike typical leagues with host sites and designated times, Flex Leagues have players connect with each other and arrange matches at their own preferred locations and times. You could play at a nearby public park or at the club of one of the players. Court fees are determined accordingly.

Completed matches count toward your rating, league standings, and possible playoff qualification. Flex Leagues run every six weeks, so if life intrudes on your tennis, there will be another opportunity around the corner. It's a more flexible format and a great way to compete and improve while growing your tennis network.

MAC SAYS

The UTR has become very influential, for better or worse. On the one hand, it has created more opportunities for players to find and compete against other players of similar ability. On the other hand, it has created added stress because players are quite protective of their rating. It's particularly problematic in the juniors. I've seen kids walk off the court at 3-0 in the first set to avoid having a result that could drop their rating.

Getting into Unsanctioned Organized Competition

Organized tennis competition exists in many forms. Many informal, competitive events take place outside the jurisdictions of the USTA and UTR, the two most popular governing bodies of tennis and promoters of sanctioned tournaments. Chances are, the annual tournament at your local park isn't affiliated with either.

Playing in unsanctioned tournaments

Unsanctioned tournaments don't count toward any official rankings. The important practical difference is that a sanctioned tournament usually attracts the very best players in the area, and entry is not open to all.

You don't need any special license to hold a tournament. Unsanctioned tournaments occur anywhere that there are tennis courts, from clubs to public parks to commercial or municipal tennis facilities. Even the USTA puts on many small local tournaments because relatively few of the thousands of players out there in Tennisland are good enough, or committed enough, to play for official rankings in typical sanctioned tournaments.

Unsanctioned tournaments can be either closed or open. A closed tournament is restricted to invited players. The annual club championships held at most tennis clubs are closed, because you have to be a member of the club to play in them. Tournaments held in parks and at public tennis facilities usually are open to all comers willing to pay a nominal entry fee to help cover the cost of staging the tournament, and the price of the trophies. Usually, there is a deadline date for entering a tournament, and if you don't sign up for a popular one in time, you may not get into the draw.

The tournament is run by a tournament director, either a volunteer tennis fan or an employee where the tournament is held. Most local tournaments seed players, although it's an inexact science to say the least. You never know when a new face in town or an entrant from a neighboring city will turn out to be a ringer, capable of beating the top seeds in your local event.

Tournaments are played within a specified time frame, often over the course of one or a few weekends and potentially the week in between them. It's easy to schedule the opening round(s) and the semifinals and finals, but what happens in-between depends on the tournament director, the needs of the players, and the weather. No hard-and-fast rules apply to unsanctioned events; they can be run as informally or as tightly as the tournament director wants.

Scaling the local tennis ladder

The name of this form of competition comes from the physical entity used to keep track of the competition, which is usually a paddle-shaped board, featuring a vertical row of hooks. The hooks hold the individual name tags of the people on the ladder, with the top-ranked player occupying the top hook and the weakest player on the very bottom. In most cases, this has given way to a digital app or something similar, but the name has stuck.

The ladder is a challenge-style competition. The idea is to get to the top of the ladder by challenging (the easy part) and beating (the hard part) all the players ranked above you. You move your name up (yes!) or down (bummer) as you win or lose matches.

Unlike a tournament, ladder competition doesn't have to be played in a specific, short time frame. The ladder competition can go on all summer, or even year-round at an indoor club. But players on the ladder usually have to accept challenges within a reasonable amount of time, so they can't duck the competition. Conversely, lower-ranked players can't continually issue challenges to better players day after day, hoping eventually to score an upset. And there are usually rules in place stipulating how many spots up the ladder a player can issue a challenge.

Playing in school

Almost all high schools and colleges have tennis teams. You make the team by trying out. If you've had a highly successful junior career, you may even get recruited to play in college. School teams require a commitment of time, because you have frequent team practices and regularly scheduled matches against other schools in either a spring or fall season.

Most high school team matches consist of five matches or courts — three singles and two doubles. The scoring format is often best-of-three sets. However, for the sake of time, many substitute a 10-point tiebreaker for the third set. And yes, you do get a varsity letter if you play on the team.

Most college competitions consist of nine matches: six singles and three doubles. The doubles matches are played first in a single tiebreak set format. The team winning at least two of the three doubles matches receives one overall point (this is called the doubles point). Then the six singles matches are played, each counting for one point. The singles matches are best-of-three tiebreak sets. If a third set is necessary, it's usually a ten-point tiebreaker. Both singles and doubles use no-ad scoring. (You can read more about no-ad scoring and tiebreak sets in Chapter 4.) The school that gets to four total points first wins the overall team match.

DRAWING UP YOUR OWN EVENT

Some people aren't lucky enough to live in areas offering lots of opportunities to compete in organized events. Still others may not be willing or able to tap into the programs and events that do exist. If that's the case for you, keep in mind that you can create your own event. For instance, if the local school courts have a regular cast of players, suggest starting an annual tournament.

You can put on a tournament with any multiple of two players, but it's the most fun if you have at least eight players. If you have an odd number of players, fill the draw with

(continued)

(continued)

byes until you have 16 or 32 players and award the byes to your seeds. (You can read more about seeds and byes in Chapter 19.)

You can really raise the level of everyone's interest if you charge a modest entry fee and use the money to buy balls, drawsheets, and a little — or humongous — trophy to award the winner. You may be surprised by how many players come out of the wood-work, eager to play, when word gets around that a tournament is taking place.

Turning to tennis apps

If you go to the App Store (Apple) or Google Play (Android) and type **tennis** in the search bar, you'll find a slew of apps. Many cover the ins and outs of the profes-sional game, but an increasing number cater to the recreational player, and more are being added all the time.

In addition to the big ones, like USTA and UTR, there are apps with simple soft-ware designed to help players find and organize games in their local areas. They're generally free and used in areas to set up small tournaments or mixers, book court time at nearby courts, or organize local ladders. They're essentially a way for players to form their own "clubs" without having to join an actual club.

Chapter **15**

Practice: The "P" Word

N ot all dirty words have four letters. In sports, one of them has a whopping eight. That word is *practice*. No getting around it — to improve for actual play, you must put in your practice time. Remember: nothing worth doing comes easily. But that doesn't mean it can't also be fun. In this chapter, I show you the drills you need to improve your skills.

Off-Court Solo Practice

For beginners, I recommend three different kinds of solo practice that don't even require the use of a tennis court. Work frequently on these "appetizers" of your game to jump-start your development.

Mirror, mirror, on the ball

If you have a full-length mirror at home, you can practice most of your strokes without even having to get out of your pj's.

You'd be surprised at how mirror practice can help you understand stroking mechanics and refresh your memory about the fundamentals of your strokes when you have few opportunities to play.

Practice your forehand before a mirror by following these steps:

1. **Face the mirror square on, and assume the ready position.**

   Hold the racquet using your forehand grip, and cradle the throat of the racquet with your other hand. Your feet should be parallel to each other, pointing toward the mirror, and spaced about shoulder-width apart. (You can read more about the forehand grips, ready position, and stroking mechanics in Chapter 7.)

2. **Pivoting on your dominant foot, step toward an imaginary ball hit to your forehand side.**

   At the same time, turn your shoulders to your forehand side, letting the racquet go with your nondominant hand and bringing it back into a comfortable backswing position.

3. **Look in the mirror. Make sure that your nondominant foot is at about a 45-degree angle to the mirror and roughly parallel with your rear foot.**

4. **Check the position of your backswing, making sure that the racquet isn't more than a few inches above the level of your waist.**

5. **Make sure that you haven't over-rotated.**

   If you can see your nondominant shoulder blade in the mirror, or if you've drawn the racquet so far back that the racquet face is behind you in the mirror, you've exaggerated the rotation of your backswing.

6. **Begin your forward stroke, using your shoulders to help bring the racquet around.**

   Stop the racquet at the imaginary point of contact. Make sure to shift your weight to your forward leg.

7. **Check the face of your racquet.**

   If the hitting surface is tilted up (open) or down (closed) to a noticeable degree, turn your wrist until the hitting surface is perpendicular to the ground, or square to the ball. (You can read more about the importance of meeting the ball with a square, or flat, face in Chapter 7.)

8. **Look at your chest in the mirror.**

   It should be almost square with the mirror, approaching the way it was when you assumed the ready position in Step 1. If your chest is exactly square to the mirror or turned a few inches to the left of square, you over-rotated or mistimed your stroke.

9. **Continue the stroke, with the racquet traveling upward until the conclusion of the follow-through.**

The grip of the racquet should be about even with your left shoulder, with the head pointing up at about a 45-degree angle. Your chest should be turned slightly to the left of square to the mirror, with your arm blocking your view of it. Your feet should be in about the same position as they were when you completed your backswing, but with your right heel off the ground due to the transfer of your weight and your forward momentum.

You can adapt mirror practice to all your strokes, checking each aspect of the shot against the mirror and the mechanics described in the appropriate chapters of this book.

Shadow tennis

Shadow tennis is playing your strokes without using a ball. It helps you develop the physical discipline required to prepare good shots, hit solid strokes, and get back in position to continue the point.

In shadow tennis, you play all your strokes in any sequence or combination you choose. Following is a nice, logical sequence for a shadow tennis point based on a typical real point. Memorize the sequence and then have at it:

1. **Prepare and hit an imaginary serve.**

Imagine that you're really putting the ball in play.

2. **Hit six groundstrokes: three backhands and then three forehands.**

Make sure that you bounce back to the ready position after each imaginary shot, just as you do in a real game. Get down to the ball and follow through on your strokes.

3. **Move forward to hit an approach shot.**

Concentrate on having your feet in motion constantly between strokes, lightly bouncing on the balls of your feet or shifting your weight from one foot to the other, just as you would when you're actually playing.

4. **Hit two volleys — one backhand and one forehand.**

Focus on really stepping into the ball and punching it.

5. **Finish the point with an overhead.**

Remember to turn sideways to the net early. Boom! You've just won Shadow Wimbledon!

WARNING

Give yourself plenty of room when you play shadow tennis. If you practice indoors, put lots of distance between yourself and the flat-screen TV or the family pooch, because you don't want to smack either when you get carried away trying to reach a backhand or leap high to smash an overhead!

Beating your (racquet) head against the wall

Hitting the ball against a wall, garage door, or any smooth surface helps you develop steady, smooth strokes and stamina.

Many public facilities have special walls set aside for this purpose — called *backboards.* A backboard is usually dark green in color and has a horizontal line painted on it at about the same height as the net. Some backboards even have a rectangle, like a strike zone, painted just above net level so that you can practice hitting at a target.

Start the drill by standing 15 feet from the backboard. Hit soft shots that make contact with the backboard between 4 and 5 feet above the ground. Let the ball bounce after it comes back off the wall and hit your shot.

REMEMBER

You want to do more than just block back the ball. You want to have enough time to hit a nice, smooth, full stroke. The harder you hit the ball, the less time you have to make your next shot, which gives you an even better workout. However, don't hit the ball so hard that you don't have enough time to properly set up for the next stroke.

As you get the hang of it, move back 3 feet at a time. You need to add more power as you move back to ensure that the ball bounces back to you.

Don't back off so far that you're forced to lunge forward to hit every shot. Save those nifty moves for real playing on the court. If you fine-tune your racquet speed and your distance from the wall properly, you can hit ten times as many nice, smooth shots against a wall as you do on a tennis court in the same amount of time.

You can also improve your volley stroke and your reflexes by playing volleys off the wall. Start 6 or 8 feet from the wall, with gentle shots. Don't expect to hit more than two or three shots successfully, because it's hard to control the ball. The backboard is very good at this game!

A wall is also an excellent place to practice your serve. This time, use the same 39-foot distance that a proper court has between the net and the baseline. Draw a box about 3 feet square at least 4 feet above the ground with a piece of chalk if the backboard doesn't have such a target. Aim for the target and hit 20 serves, keeping track of how often you hit the box.

Hitting with a ball machine

If you're looking for a playing partner who is always available, is never late, and rarely — if ever — misses a shot, then you'll want to look into getting a ball machine. These gadgets come in various shapes and sizes and cost anywhere from about $600 for a stripped-down ball launcher up to $1,500 or more for a highly sophisticated pseudo drill instructor. They can house more than a case of balls (at 72 balls per case), so you'll do a lot of hitting before stopping to reload. And many have rechargeable batteries, eliminating the need for a nearby power source.

As opposed to a wall, a ball machine is like having an automated coach feed you balls exactly where you want them. And unlike wondering whether you just hit a good shot, you get to see where it lands in the court. Pretty much every ball machine allows you to scale the speed and location of the feeds to suit your ability level. Some of the high-end models even have accompanying apps that let you design your own customized drills. It not only improves your strokes, but makes for an exhausting workout as well.

A ball machine definitely falls into the luxury item category, but if you get serious about your tennis, it's the best way to ensure you can always work on your game.

Starting Small with Mini-Tennis

In standard tennis, you hit your groundstrokes from the baseline; in mini-tennis, you position yourself at the service line and play from there, keeping the balls inside the service boxes on each side of the net. If you lack strength, fitness, or athletic experience, mini-tennis allows you to concentrate on your strokes (instead of getting to the ball).

To play, you and your partner stand at the intersection of the centerline and the service line on either side of the court. One person taps a ball into play, and the two of you exchange backhands and forehands or even volleys.

Mini-tennis makes keeping the ball in play easier, because the ball doesn't have very far to travel to cross the net. You can work on things like polishing your footwork, improving control, and hitting nice, smooth strokes.

You don't have to be very strong, or very fit, to play mini-tennis. But if you keep the ball in play, you can get a surprisingly good workout.

MAC SAYS

Even though you don't have to hit with full strokes when playing mini-tennis, I still recommend it. This makes the exercise more difficult, but also more beneficial. In fact, we force juniors at our academy to perform it with full strokes because it teaches them better control of the racquet face and the ball. You'd be surprised how many players can rally reasonably well from the baseline using full strokes but can't do the same from the midcourt. Learning how to slow down the racquet and control the ball is an important step in a player's development.

Developing Skills with Practice Routines

When improving your game is a priority and you have the time and ambition to make tennis a regular part of your life, practice as often as you can. I recommend up to three times a week if you can swing it.

MAC SAYS

Don't play or practice if you're not having fun. All devoted tennis players occasionally get burned out. When that happens, take a few days off and put the racquets down. Play another sport or even give your body a complete break from activity. If you start to miss playing, that's a good thing.

A solid one-hour session

If you want, you can dispense with the traditional warm-up (see Chapter 7) before a practice session because you won't be hitting volleys, overheads, or serves until a good 20 minutes into the practice. By that time, you should be well warmed up from hitting a lot of groundstrokes.

Grab a training partner and follow the steps in this basic, one-hour routine to maximize your practice time and spice it up with a little competition:

1. **Hit five minutes of mini-tennis, as described earlier in this chapter.**

   This is a good warm-up, even if you stretched and loosened up earlier.

2. **Hit ten minutes of forehand practice — first crosscourt shots for five minutes and then switching to down-the-line shots for five minutes.**

You want to develop command over your shots to develop the accuracy and consistency of your strokes. Start with both players just inside the baseline on either side of the court. If the ball inadvertently goes in the wrong direction, run over and catch it, instead of letting it go or hitting it.

After every stroke, each of you should shuffle back at least a few steps toward the middle of the court. Don't get lazy and take up positions where you don't have to move.

If you're both right-handed or both left-handed, your down-the-line shot will go to the other player's opposite shot (forehand to backhand, or vice versa). That's fine because when you move to Step 3 in this routine, the player hitting the backhands gets the forehands they missed.

3. **Do ten minutes of backhands, starting with crosscourt shots for five minutes and then switching to down-the-line shots for five minutes.**

4. **Hit ten minutes of volley practice.**

Your practice partner hits groundstrokes to you at the net, and vice versa. Each of you hits volleys for only five minutes.

To maximize your time and practice your accuracy, the player at the net should try to hit the ball back to either the forehand or backhand for the first two and a half minutes, and then change to the other side for the same amount of time.

To get the most out of volley practice, don't station yourself right on top of the net. Start at least 3 feet back from the net and move back as your skill level improves, until you can practice your volleys just like advanced players do, from just inside the T intersection of the service box.

The farther back you stand, the more different and difficult volleys you hit. It's also where you often have to hit a lot of volleys over the course of a match. When you stand right up at the net, the ball is either within your reach or past you before you can react and get your racquet on it. Besides, when you're right on top of the net, blocking a volley back any old way is just too easy.

5. **Hit five minutes of overhead and lob practice.**

Take up your position at the net and try to hit your overheads back to your practice partner at the baseline. Your partner should try to return your overhead shot with a lob that you can hit again. Hit 20 overheads and then change positions.

6. **Do ten minutes of serving and returning practice.**

   Take up typical serving and returning positions in the deuce court, with one of you hitting serves and the other trying to make good returns. After two and a half minutes, change to the ad court and do the same. Change the role of server and receiver after five minutes and repeat. If there's an area to steal a little extra time, the serve is a good choice. It's that important of a shot.

7. **Enjoy ten minutes of playing time.**

   Play a 12-point tiebreaker to put a little into your practice sessions. (See Chapter 4 for more information on how to play a tiebreaker.)

Improving accuracy

Using targets can really improve your accuracy, and it almost always helps you focus. Something about trying to knock over a ball can or a tiny traffic cone beats trying to place a shot to an unmarked area of the court.

REMEMBER

Hitting a target is a real sharpshooter's trick. You don't have to actually hit a target to improve your game. Just having one to aim at and seeing how close your shots come to it can help.

Honing serves

To work on your serve, use three ball cans. Set one up just inside the lines at each corner of the service box, and one just inside the service line, halfway between the corners. Those are the three targets for the wide, T, and body serves (see Chapter 13). You and your partner can take ten serves each, seeing whether you can knock any or all of the cans over. Make sure you take turns serving in both the deuce and ad sides of the court.

You can also take turns allowing the returner to choose the placement of the can, if they want to work on a particular return of serve. While one of you is madly trying to hit the can, the returner has a great opportunity to zero in on and hone their service returns.

Sharpening groundstrokes

A welcome mat (you know, the kind you can find at just about any hardware store or garden center) makes a good target for your groundstrokes.

Place the mat in a corner of the court, on either the forehand or backhand side on your side of the court. When you start hitting at targets, place them at least 2 feet inside the lines — even farther inside if you find yourself hitting too many balls beyond the line. Then, as your game improves, move the targets farther back, but never closer than within 6 inches of the line.

Rally until your partner hits the mat, and count each successful shot as a point. After they hit the target ten times (or close enough), switch the mat to their side of the court so you can practice. Or, better yet, if you both have mats — or whatever targets you choose — play a game to see who's the first to hit it a set number of times. Set some stakes with the winner getting a fresh can of balls or a post-practice beverage of their choice.

Drilling Away at Success

Drills are set stroking routines based on repetition, often performed in rapid fashion. You don't necessarily need to make a certain shot in a drill, and you almost never try to win points or count them when you do. The point of many drills is to keep the drill going, like a perpetual motion machine. Doing that takes skill, discipline, and stamina, which are three critical traits you're trying to develop through practice. That's why drills are so popular.

If you ever end up attending a tennis camp or signing up for a clinic at a local club, chances are, you'll do lots of drills. That's because many drills are designed so that one or two teaching pros, the "feeders" in a drill, can keep up to six or eight players constantly moving and hitting. They hit balls to you from hoppers the size of shopping carts and bark a few quick technique pointers while you chase after their feeds.

You can get a taste of the drill experience without the help of a pro. All you need are your regular practice partner and a bucket of balls.

The crosscourt and down-the-line drill

This two-player drill develops variety in the placement of your groundstrokes. It also works on your ability to change the direction of the ball, an important skill to develop. In this drill, one player hits all shots crosscourt, and the other player hits all shots down the line.

To start, take up positions at either baseline, at about the center hash mark. Feed the first ball to your partner, who returns it to you crosscourt. Then hit your shot down the line. This is changing the direction of the ball. Don't worry if you hit the shots at poor angles. Just do your best and make every effort to keep the ball in play.

If you can keep the ball in play and place it pretty effectively, both of you run from one corner of the court to the other until one of you misses. Then change roles, so you're hitting crosscourt and your partner is hitting down the line.

The scramble drill

This drill, which uses one feeder and one "scrambler," develops quickness, the ability to change directions, and stamina. You can make this drill as demanding or as gentle as you like, so it's suitable for players of most ages and skill levels.

To start, take the bucket of balls and set it up 2 or 3 feet from the net, in the center of the court. You start as the feeder. Your partner, the scrambler, should get ready, standing at the center hash mark of the baseline in the opposite court. Take a ball from the hopper and hit it to your partner's backhand side. As soon as you've done so, take another ball and hit it to their forehand side.

As the feeder, you must feed balls quickly but not so fast that the scrambler can't possibly get to them. The scrambler's job is to hit good shots on the run. It's important not to compromise good form just to get the ball in play because this could reinforce bad habits.

After you use up all the balls in your hopper, switch places — it's your turn to suck wind.

The high-low drill

This drill improves your overhead and volley, in addition to showing you the value of coming up to the net. It is physically demanding and takes a certain measure of skill, so if you're not in good shape or still getting comfortable at net, work your way up to the high-low drill:

1. **Take up a position at the center hash mark on the baseline, with three balls in your possession.**

   Your partner should be across the net in the forecourt, straddling the center-line, halfway between the net and the service line.

2. **Feed your partner a lob.**

3. **Your partner hits an overhead to your forehand side.**

   Your partner shouldn't try for a winner; you want to practice form by keeping the ball in play.

4. **You hit a groundstroke, trying to keep the ball low over the net.**

   Don't end the drill with a passing shot. Make your partner come to the net to volley.

5. **Your partner hits a volley back to you.**

6. **You hit another lob.**

   Try to back up your partner to get the most exercise value out of this drill.

7. **Repeat Steps 3 through 6.**

As soon as the ball is no longer in play, even if you didn't complete Steps 1 through 6, begin the drill again immediately by hitting a lob with the next ball. Don't forget to change positions after your partner gets tired!

Dink doubles

Dink doubles familiarizes four players of any age or skill level with the importance and frequency of angled play in doubles. Dink doubles resembles mini-tennis, which is to say it's a lot of fun!

To start, each of the four players lines up at the middle of the service line in one of the four service boxes. One player starts the drill by hitting a soft shot into either of the other team's service boxes. The two teams then keep the point alive in the service boxes, until someone hits the ball long of the service boxes or into the net. This compels you to use lots of touch, angles, and patience to win points. You can even set a rule that players have to let the ball bounce, which forces you to play with extra smarts and finesse.

Change sides periodically in this drill, so all players get accustomed to playing in the different service courts.

The all-advance doubles drill

Net play is very important in doubles, and this four-player drill gives excellent practice hitting volleys at all different heights and from many different angles. You can also do this drill with two players, or even three. The drill always helps sharpen your volley from different positions.

To start, all four players should be at the baseline, positioned in the courts they customarily occupy as returners. (See Chapter 5 to read about all the rules surrounding doubles play.) Any of the players can start the point by drop-hitting a ball with a groundstroke deep to either player on the other side of the net; the receiving player then returns it anywhere near the baseline. As soon as the next ball is hit, all four players must advance to the net, playing any ball that comes their way. The hitters can put the ball anywhere they want. The idea is for all four players to get to the net and end the point with a rapid, close-quarters exchange of volleys.

In this drill, play all the balls you can reach, even if they may be sailing deep or wide. You want each player to hit as many volleys as possible.

Dingles

Dingles is a four-player game that is a mash-up of both singles and doubles. Two doubles teams start the point on opposite baselines, positioned as though they're receiving serve. A point begins when both players on one side each feed a ball to their crosscourt opponents and engage in two simultaneous crosscourt singles points using half the court including the doubles alleys. With no serves or returns and less court to cover, extended rallies are common. You have to be both steady and creative to win the rally.

When one point ends, the players playing that point yell "Dingles!" and the remaining ball is played out as a doubles point between all four players using the entire court. You always have to be on your toes because you never know when one rally will end and everyone is involved. A team needs to win both rallies to secure the point. Play to a set score and then switch partners. You get to hit a lot of balls, and the combination of both singles and doubles allows players to work on their full arsenal of shots.

Chapter **16**

Physical Conditioning for Tennis

ennis players come in all shapes and sizes. Some of them are rail thin, with arms hardly thicker than sticks, and they can hit supersonic serves. Others are short and stocky, with muscular legs that enable them to run around the court for hours without seeming to tire. Despite the differences in their outward appearances, these players share the trait of being physically fit.

Tennis success requires a combination of strength, elasticity, and endurance. The stronger you are, the more power you can generate into your shots. The more flexible you are, the better you can stretch and change directions. And the more you have left in the tank late in a close third set on a hot day, the better your chance of winning the match.

You don't have to be ripped to have fun and play good tennis. You can just go out and hit back and forth at whatever pace feels comfortable and improve your conditioning as you play more frequently and more intensely.

MAC SAYS

But I urge you to work on your conditioning for a few important reasons:

» **Injury prevention:** A little injury goes a long way toward ruining your tennis. Trust me — I had my second shoulder surgery shortly before writing the first edition of this book. It brought my professional playing days to a grinding halt.

And I had been pretty good about taking care of myself throughout my career! Injuries can take a lot more out of you than what you need to put in to avoid them. That means that the more fit and careful you are about avoiding injuries, the fewer you will suffer.

>> **Elevated performance:** It's not 100 percent guaranteed, but improving your strength and conditioning in the gym generally results in improved play on the court. You move faster and more easily, have greater stamina, and can hit the ball with more force. Plenty of players use tennis as a way to get into better shape, but if you want to perform up to your best, working out off the court will greatly benefit your game.

>> **Overall satisfaction:** Getting into shape makes you feel better, and it even makes you sleep better. It's good for your health.

In this chapter, I show you how to care for and strengthen your body to avoid injuries and play at your best.

Stretching Your Game to New Heights

When you stretch, you loosen up the muscles that you need to play tennis. Over time, stretching increases and maintains the elasticity of your muscles, which enables you to do things like change directions quickly or lunge for shots.

REMEMBER

Always stretch before you play tennis, preferably for several minutes before you go out on the court for your warm-up. This becomes increasingly important as you get older and more susceptible to injuries. (See Chapter 7 for a suggested warm-up program.) Cooldown stretching is also a good habit to get into — your muscles are already loose, limber, and primed for deep stretches. It also can help lessen next-day muscle tightness following a vigorous match or workout.

You can do the same basic stretches for warming up or cooling down, but as you become a crack fitness expert, you'll substitute or add some of your own.

Getting the most out of your stretches

TIP

You can tell that you're stretching correctly when you feel the mild "burn" of your muscles expanding beyond their present comfort level. Follow these additional tips to get the most out of your warm-up and cooldown stretches:

>> **Warm up first.** Stretching a cold muscle isn't a great idea — it can lead to a quick strain or tear. Whenever possible, do some light aerobic activity — ride a stationary bike, walk or run on a treadmill, jump rope, jog around the court — for a few minutes to stimulate blood flow and raise your core body temperature. This is also a good time to use a foam roller to work on any chronic sore areas.

>> **Breathe deeply.** As you begin your stretch, take a nice deep breath. Exhale slowly and then breathe through the rest of your stretch.

>> **Move slowly.** Don't rush through the stretches. Hold each stretch for the recommended time, if possible.

>> **Avoid bouncing or jerky movements.** Smooth stretching allows you to accurately gauge whether you've stretched too far or just enough.

>> **Don't "stretch" it.** A stretch shouldn't hurt, and the mild burning sensation in the muscle being stretched should not be painful.

>> **Know your limits.** Your age and physical characteristics determine the right degree of stretching for you. Don't try to imitate anyone else or meet some preset goal.

>> **Do your stretches in sets of three.** Repeat each stretch at least three times for each muscle or muscle group you're working.

>> **Pace your stretches.** Allow 5 to 10 seconds of recovery time between each stretch, and from 10 and 30 seconds recovery time between each set of stretches. The recovery time allows your muscles to relax again, and the next time you stretch the muscles, they expand more willingly. Hold each stretch for 15 to 20 seconds, really focusing your energy on the muscle being stretched.

Don't prolong your stretch, and don't try to increase the burn you feel. When you feel a mild burn, you're getting maximum benefit from the stretch. Increasing the stretch won't increase the benefit, and it could lead to injury. A stretch is a mild, gentle, but firm exercise, not a torture session.

Mobilizing the neck

Begin your stretching session by loosening up your neck and upper shoulder muscles by gently but firmly tilting your head all the way to the right and then all the way to the left a few times, holding the maximum comfortable tilt for 15 to 20 seconds. Then move your head in a circular, clockwise motion for about 20 seconds. Try it, and you'll feel and hear lots of stuff moving and clicking and loosening up.

Loosening the shoulders and arms

Use this stretch to prepare your shoulders for serving. Pick up your racquet and follow these steps:

1. **Grasp the middle of the racquet grip with your right hand.**

2. **Touch your back with the racquet.**

   Your right arm should be fully bent, with your forearm close to your right ear and the racquet flat against your back.

3. **Grasp the head of the racquet at its tip with your left hand.**

   Your left hand should be close to the small of your back, at about waist level.

4. **Gently pull down on the racquet so your right elbow points straight up.**

5. **Holding the racquet firmly with your left hand, pull with your right hand until you feel your right shoulder and the area below your left arm being stretched.**

6. **Hold the stretch for 20 seconds.**

7. **Repeat, changing arms.**

The overhead stretch, which you see in Figure 16-1, prepares your arms, shoulders, and trunk for the serve and overhead action. Follow these steps to get the most out of your overhead stretch:

1. **Stand with your arms extended straight up.**

2. **Cross your wrists.**

   It doesn't matter which wrist is in front.

3. **Put your palms together.**

   You can lace your fingers together lightly if it's more comfortable.

4. **Stretch your arms slightly backward, and as high up as you can.**

   You should feel the burn in your shoulders and upper arms.

5. **After you feel the burn, gently bend a few inches to your left, until you feel the burn extending down the right side of your body. Hold this position for about 10 seconds.**

6. **Bend back the other way, to your right, until you feel the burn extending down the left side of your body. Hold this position for another 10 seconds.**

7. **Gently lower your arms and wait 10 to 20 seconds before repeating Steps 1 through 6.**

You can extend this stretch to 30 seconds because you're working both sides of your body alternately. But don't try to force more of a burn. Stay within your comfort zone.

Opening up the hips and lower back

You have to lie down to get the most benefit from the hip-twist stretch, which you see in Figure 16-2, but it's well worth getting your shorts a little dusty. It helps to find a patch of grass, soft flooring, or exercise mat to provide some cushioning for this movement. Follow these steps to really limber up those back and hip muscles with the hip-twist stretch:

1. **Lie on your back.**

Your knees should be bent with your feet flat on the ground.

2. **Extend both your left and right arms.**

Your arms stabilize your upper body in this position, allowing you to get the maximum benefit in your lower back and hips.

3. **Place your right ankle just outside your left knee.**

   The position resembles the one you may use seated in a chair, scrolling through your social media feed.

4. **Use your right leg to pull your left leg toward the floor, across your body, until you feel the burn, and hold for 20 seconds.**

   Keep your upper body flat against the ground. Don't try to drag your right leg down to the floor. Just maintain a noticeable but comfortable burn.

5. **Relax for 5 to 10 seconds.**

6. **Reverse the starting position of your legs and repeat Steps 1 through 5.**

FIGURE 16-2:
The hip-twist stretch opens up the lower back.

Elongating the calves

The calf stretch, which you see in Figure 16-3, works on your calf muscles and your Achilles tendon — the thick, cordlike tendon immediately above your heel. You want to take special care of the calf, because as you age, it becomes much more susceptible to injury. Find yourself a wall or sturdy object and follow these steps to stretch your calves before you play:

1. **Take a position between 2 and 3 feet from a wall or fence.**

   You need something solid to lean against when you do this stretch.

2. **Extend your arms to about shoulder height and place your palms against the wall or fence directly in front of you.**

3. **Move your right foot straight back between 2 and 3 feet, and bend your left knee slightly, (see Figure 16-3A).**

Your toes should point straight ahead.

4. **Keeping your right knee straight with your heel on the floor, bend your left knee deeper and lean your trunk forward, toward the wall (see Figure 16-3B).**

Don't arch your back; keep it straight.

WARNING

Don't push the wall or fence like you want to knock it over. You're using the wall only to lean against, supporting and balancing your upper body while you stretch your calf muscles.

5. **Hold the stretch for 20 seconds.**

6. **Change the position of your legs, so the left one extends behind you, and repeat Steps 1 through 5.**

TIP

If you have the time, repeat this stretch on each side with one key difference: Bend your back knee slightly, toward the ground, and lift your heel 2 inches off the floor. This gets more stretch into your lower calf and Achilles tendon.

FIGURE 16-3:
The calf stretch helps prevent calf injuries which become more frequent with age.

(a) (b)

© John Wiley & Sons, Inc.

Warming up the hammies

Your hamstrings are the main muscles in the backs of your upper legs. A "pulled" hamstring is one of the more painful injuries you can sustain in tennis. Keep them in good shape with the hamstring stretch, which you see in Figure 16-4.

FIGURE 16-4:
Warming up with the hamstring stretch.

To do the hamstring stretch, follow these steps:

1. **Sit on the ground with both legs straight out in front of you, toes pointing up.**

2. **Bend your left knee to bring your lower leg toward your body (see Figure 16-4).**

   The bottom of your left foot rests on the inside of your right knee. Your legs essentially form a reverse figure four.

3. **With your back straight, reach forward with both hands toward your right foot, keeping your right knee as straight as possible.**

   The burn will be immediate and unmistakable.

4. **Hold the position for 20 seconds and then relax.**

5. **After 5 or 10 seconds, change the position of your legs and stretch your left hamstring.**

Activating the quads

The quadriceps muscles are the big guns of your legs. They provide you with most of your power, especially when pushing off and changing direction. They're the muscles right above your knees in each leg, and they extend all the way up to your hip bone.

The stork quadriceps stretch, which you see in Figure 16-5, is an easy, effective stretch for this muscle group. (The name comes from the common position assumed by a stork when it wants to stretch its quads.) Follow these steps to do the stork quadriceps stretch:

1. **Stand with your feet together.**

2. **Raise your right foot behind you, toward your buttocks, and grasp your foot with your right hand.**

   If you need to, hold on to a chair or wall for balance.

3. **Gently but firmly pull your foot toward your butt.**

   Keep your back straight and your butt tucked in, and point the knee of the leg being stretched toward the ground as you do this.

4. **Hold for 20 seconds and then relax.**

5. **Change legs so you're grasping your left leg, and repeat Steps 1 through 4.**

FIGURE 16-5:
The stork quadriceps stretch hits the quads and tests your balance.

© John Wiley & Sons, Inc.

Bulletproofing Your Body: Getting Stronger and Protecting Against Injuries

Not long ago, the idea of regular weightlifting was frowned upon in a racquet sport like tennis. The thinking was, you didn't want to really bulk up because it would limit your range of motion and slow you down. So, players were more wiry and focused primarily on speed and endurance. And it's true — you don't want bulging muscles like the Hulk. However, the top players now pack on long, lean muscles that make them more powerful and athletic. It not only helps from a performance standpoint, but also helps steel the body for the rigors of the game.

REMEMBER

If you lack strength in certain critical areas, you can get stronger with the help of dumbbells, barbells, and other free weights. They help build muscle mass and are more functional for tennis players than machines.

Free weights aren't ones that you get at no charge — they're any kind of weight that you can pick up and move around, that aren't attached to a fixed object or machine. The most basic free weight is your body.

For the purposes of this book, I'll focus on training with dumbbells. They're highly versatile — you can use them to load almost any movement — and available at any fitness facility. Dumbbells are usually about 12 inches long, with permanent or adjustable weights on either end. Fixed-weight dumbbells come in a variety of weights, starting at about 1 pound. They also allow you to train unilaterally — each arm or leg working independently. Tennis players tend to overuse their dominant side; dumbbells help strengthen the off-side and correct any muscular imbalances.

If you're a beginner, I suggest starting out with very light dumbbells — only use poundage you can comfortably and safely lift. Add weight in small increments as you get stronger. If you have experience working out from playing other sports or frequenting the gym, then feel free to use weights that will adequately challenge the targeted muscles.

REMEMBER

Try to do all weight and strength exercises in sets of three, each set consisting of 10 to 15 repetitions. Your recovery interval in these exercises, especially the ones involving free weights, should be longer. Give yourself at least 30 seconds between each set, and allow at least a minute after each exercise before you move on to another exercise.

Safeguarding the shoulder

The serve and overhead actions make shoulder strength especially important in tennis. The upright row is a good exercise for building strength in your shoulders:

1. **Stand with your knees slightly bent.**

    Hold the dumbbells at arm's length on either side.

2. **Turn your arms slightly, so your palms face inward and your elbows face out at your sides.**

3. **Slowly raise the dumbbells to your chest, keeping your elbows higher than your wrists.**

    Don't arch your back; focus on making your shoulders do all the work.

4. **Slowly lower the dumbbells to the starting position.**

5. **Repeat 10 to 15 reps for a total of three sets, taking a 20-second break between sets.**

MAC SAYS

Resistance bands are convenient and relatively inexpensive workout aids that can help you build strength or loosen up before playing. Made of stretchy, tough rubber, they generally come in a loop or with a handle at each end. Varying lengths and thicknesses provide different levels of resistance. They're extremely lightweight, so you can toss them in your bag and have them handy whenever you want a quick workout or to wake up your muscles before hitting the courts. You see them all over pro tour training rooms and practice courts.

Enhancing upper arms, forearms, and wrists

The best way to strengthen the large muscle in the front of your upper arm, called the biceps, is with the dumbbell curl. This exercise also increases the strength in your forearm and wrist. Follow these steps:

1. **Stand holding the dumbbells with your arms fully extended at both sides.**

2. **Turn your palms upward.**

3. **Slowly raise the dumbbells by folding up your arms at the elbow, until the weights reach shoulder height.**

    Keep your upper arms against your sides, which forces your biceps to do most of the work and get most of the benefit.

4. **Slowly lower the dumbbells the same way.**

5. **Repeat 10 to 15 reps for a total of three sets.**

Your triceps is the other major muscle in your upper arm. It's at the back of your upper arm, opposite your biceps. The triceps extension is similar to the shoulder stretch exercise described earlier in this chapter, except that you do it with a dumbbell instead of a racquet. Use it to tone and strengthen your triceps, following these steps:

1. **Hold your dumbbell in your right hand.**

2. **Raise your right arm and lower the dumbbell behind your back, with your arm fully bent.**

   Your right elbow should be pointing up, and your upper arm should be close to your right ear.

3. **Grasp your right arm just below the elbow with your left arm.**

   This keeps you from cheating the exercise by moving your right arm.

4. **Slowly raise the dumbbell until your right arm is fully extended overhead.**

   Don't work with a heavier weight than you can handle — you don't want to drop it on your head.

5. **Slowly lower the dumbbell back to the starting position.**

6. **Repeat 10 to 15 reps for a total of three sets.**

You can do a variation of this exercise with two hands, holding one end of a dumbbell with two hands and raising and lowering it behind your head. You can work with more weight when doing the two-handed triceps extension, but be careful — you can easily lose control of the dumbbell, or bang your head with it, if you use too much weight.

Your wrist can play a major role in your tennis strokes, especially when you hit spin serves or topspin groundstrokes. Most wrist exercises have the added benefit of working your forearms. Try doing wrist curls with a 1-pound dumbbell, following these steps:

1. **Sit down, resting your right forearm on your right thigh.**

   Your right wrist and hand should extend out over your knee, unsupported, holding the dumbbell or an object of similar size, shape, and weight.

2. **Turn your arm so the palm of your hand faces up.**

   Hold the dumbbell firmly.

3. **Gently roll your wrist as far up as you can.**

4. **Lower the dumbbell to the starting position.**

5. **Repeat 10 to 15 reps for a total of three sets.**

You can vary this exercise by working your wrist from side-to-side. Just alter Step 2, turning your forearm so your thumb faces up. Then move the dumbbell from left to right, as far as you can stretch.

Developing powerful legs

Legs usually require less work than other parts of the tennis body, simply because you use your legs enough every day to keep them in pretty good shape. However, if you want to play up your leg strength, try leg lunges using dumbbells:

1. **Holding your dumbbells in your hands, stand with your arms extended at your sides.**

2. **Take a comfortable step forward with your right leg, bending both knees.**

   Your left knee should come to within 2 or 3 inches of the ground without actually touching it. Don't let your right knee track out much farther than your toes. Keep your arms and dumbbells at your sides, moving them as little as possible.

3. **Briskly step back up into the ready position.**

4. **Repeat immediately, this time stepping forward with your left leg.**

5. **Repeat 10 to 15 reps for each leg for a total of three sets per leg.**

WARNING

Leg lunges can tire you quickly. To stay within your safety and comfort zones, adjust the amount of weight you use, the depth of your lunges, and the pace at which you repeat them.

The tuck jump is another excellent leg exercise that also improves your stomach muscles. But it's strictly for fit players. To do the tuck jump you stand with your feet spread at a comfortable distance, arms at your sides. Then jump with both legs at once, trying to tuck your knees into your chest. Land softly with bent knees to absorb the impact. Reset as quickly as possible and repeat the jump 10 to 15 reps for a total of three sets.

Stabilizing the core

Sit-ups are one of the best ways to firm up your abdominal (stomach) muscles, or "abs." Traditional sit-ups have fallen out of favor in recent years for putting too much strain on the lower back. Crunches are a less risky option being used to work the abs instead.

Crunch-type exercises, many stretches, and even free-weight routines are performed sitting or lying down. If at all possible, buy a lightweight exercise mat to increase your comfort when working out.

Follow these steps to do a basic crunch:

1. **Lie flat on your back with your knees bent and the soles of your shoes touching the ground.**

2. **Place your hands behind your head, with your arms and elbows pointing away from your body on either side.**

   This is the same position you may prefer for taking a nap.

3. **Curl your upper body, including your head and shoulders, up from the floor, until you feel a strong contraction in your abdominal muscles.**

   Make sure that you don't pull your head or shoulders forward with your arms. Just support your head with your hands and focus on doing the exercise with your body. At full crunch, your shoulder blades should be about 3 inches off the ground.

4. **Slowly lower your upper body back to the floor.**

5. **Rest for 5 to 10 seconds and then repeat 10 to 15 times for a total of three sets.**

The crossover crunch exercises your *obliques*, the muscles responsible for trunk rotation. These muscles serve a subtle but important role in many tennis shots, most of which begin with a rotation of your shoulders and body — hence, your trunk. Stand up for a moment and turn your shoulders in either direction. Feel the tension in your sides? That's your trunk. Build up strength in these muscles with the crossover crunch, following these steps:

1. **Lie flat on your back with your knees bent and the soles of your feet on the ground.**

2. **Place your hands behind your head, arms and elbows pointing away from your body on either side.**

3. **Lift your right leg and place the ankle on your left knee.**

   This is similar to the position you may use when you're sitting in a chair and scrolling on your phone, but you're lying down.

4. **Lift and curl your upper body to the right.**

   Imagine that you're trying to touch your left elbow to your right knee. It's too far away, of course, but that's the idea. Don't pull your head and shoulders with your hands — your hands are there only to support your head while your trunk does the work.

5. **Slowly return to the start position, keeping your right leg in place.**

6. **Repeat 10 to 15 times and then change the positions of the legs to work the oblique muscles on the right side of your body; do a total of three sets per side.**

MAC SAYS

If you don't like crunches, planks are a simple, pretty much risk-free alternative that is great for your core. Lie facing the floor with your forearms and toes supporting your weight. Your elbows should be beneath your shoulders and your body should form a straight line from your head to your feet. Hold that position for a set time or until your form breaks. Try to keep your midsection and backside from sagging or lifting up.

Bolstering upper and lower back

Backs, as you may know, can be very tricky. You can really build up your back strength with an exercise out of the crunch family — the Superman. Just follow these steps:

1. **Lie flat on your stomach.**

2. **Extend your arms straight in front of you.**

   Your legs should be straight.

3. **Lift both arms and legs simultaneously.**

   You should look like Superman, flying. Concentrate on squeezing your shoulder blades together — like you're trying to crack a walnut between them — to work the upper back.

4. **Hold for 1 to 5 seconds.**

WARNING

This exercise is highly effective and focused, and it's almost impossible to sustain for longer than 5 seconds. Don't attempt it — you don't want to strain your back. But as you build up strength, you can intensify the movement by holding light weights in your hands.

5. Return gently to the start position.

6. Repeat 10 to 15 reps for a total of three sets.

You can vary this exercise by lifting just the right arm and left leg, and then the left arm and right leg. It's equally effective either way.

The simple toe touch also provides great exercise for your lower back. Stand straight, with your arms extended at your sides. Bend slowly at the waist — and I mean that just like it's spelled, *s-l-o-w-l-y*, with your knees locked, trying to touch your toes with your fingers. Don't strain yourself if you don't get there. You should also feel a stretch in your hamstrings. Slowly straighten up. Later on, you can incorporate dumbbells, which turns the exercise into more of a stiff-legged dead lift.

Quickness Drills: Building Speed and Endurance

Quickness drills help your tennis in two critical ways: They improve your ability to track down your opponent's shots, and they improve your fitness. The following drills help you develop your quickness and the endurance to take advantage of it. Do each drill in this section, or do one drill three times, as often as possible.

Running the lines

This drill improves your breathing, your footwork, and your ability to change directions moving forward as well as backward. You perform it without your racquet or balls, touching all the lines on one side of the court, by following these steps:

1. Line up outside the doubles alley, facing the court, about 3 feet from the net post.

2. Sprint forward and touch the nearest line.

   The first line you touch is the singles sideline, which is pretty close.

3. Backpedal (run backward) to a position outside the doubles line, 3 feet closer to the baseline than the place you started from.

4. Sprint forward at a slight angle toward the baseline and touch the next line, the centerline.

5. **Backpedal again, until you're outside of the doubles line again, a few feet closer to the baseline than your previous starting position.**

   From now on, repeat Step 5 after touching every line. You work your way closer to the baseline as you go.

6. **Sprint forward and touch the next line, the far singles sideline.**

7. **Sprint forward and touch the far doubles sideline.**

   Remember to repeat Step 5 right after touching every line.

8. **Sprint forward and touch the far singles sideline again.**

   You touched this line before, but this time, you touch the line at a point closer to the baseline because you're working your way down the court.

9. **Sprint forward and touch the area about 3 feet into the court from the centerline.**

10. **Sprint forward and touch the near singles sideline again.**

    This concludes the drill. At the end, you should be standing — panting — at the corner of the court. You've made a forward and back zigzag pattern, from near the net post to the baseline.

Do this drill with a partner, each of you completing the drill on one side of the court. You can also time yourself with a stopwatch and keep track of your performance as you repeat the drill.

Five-ball pickup drill

The five-ball pickup drill builds your leg strength and improves your ability to change directions and your hand-eye coordination. Use your racquet and five balls (they can even be old dead balls) in this drill.

Count out your five balls and follow these steps to experience the benefits and test your mettle:

1. **Position the five balls in the places you see in Figure 16-6.**

2. **Place your racquet just outside the centerline at the baseline on the same side of the court.**

   The object in this drill is to run and pick up each ball, one at a time, returning it and placing it on the face of the racquet as fast as possible.

3. **Pick up the balls in the order in which they're numbered in Figure 16-6 and place them on your racquet.**

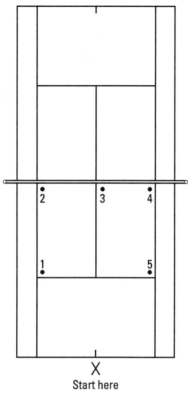

FIGURE 16-6:
The five-ball
pickup drill.

X
Start here

© John Wiley & Sons, Inc.

If you really want to test your stamina, immediately repeat the drill in reverse order, taking the balls from the racquet face and replacing them in their original positions.

MK Drill

The MK Drill was devised by Mark Kovacs, a high-performance coach and former colleague when I worked in player development at the United States Tennis Association (USTA), and the technical editor for this book. While researching his PhD in exercise physiology, Mark created this on-court test to evaluate tennis-specific endurance. It's a series of sprints with specific rest times based on the amount of work performed. Mark has since used it with many of his athletes to track and test their progress. Fair warning — it's a lung-buster. But if you make it a regular part of your training regimen, it will yield great results.

All you need is a tennis court and a stopwatch. If a court is unavailable, two markers 12 yards (36 feet) apart — the distance between two doubles lines — will do just fine.

Begin just behind the doubles sideline and facing the other doubles sideline on the same side of the court. Hit start on the timer and sprint across to the other doubles sideline, and then sprint back. This constitutes one repetition.

The repetitions are performed in a ladder format. This means you add one repetition with each round. After each round, you take an increasing amount of rest. The series of sprints increases up to six repetitions in a round. Then you work back down the ladder — starting from six repetitions — until performing a single repetition, which ends the drill. As the number of sprints performed decreases, so does the rest time (see the following chart).

Reps	Rest Time (seconds)
1	15
2	30
3	45
4	60
5	90
6	120
6	120
5	90
4	60
3	45
2	30
1	—

REMEMBER

The MK Drill works best if you use a stopwatch that's capable of monitoring laps. This allows you to keep an overall running time while tracking your splits of each round and differentiate between work and rest intervals. Pretty much any fitness watch or smartphone has this functionality.

All told, you'll be doing 42 sprints back and forth from one doubles sideline to the other. With the rest period fixed at 11:45, total time will depend on how fast you perform those 42 repetitions. According to Mark, a good target time for a competitive adult player would be under 17 minutes. Don't worry if you come in over that mark. Whatever your time, now you've got something to beat!

Eating Right and Fueling Your Body for Competition

Now that I'm a creature of the broadcast booth with my playing days long behind me, my diet isn't nearly as strict as it used to be. Certain foods that I tried to avoid — pizza, french fries slathered in ketchup, and desserts — sometimes find their way onto my plate now that I'm retired. But as much as I like all kinds of rich foods, I did have to eat right to make the most of my tennis career. You know what? It wasn't so bad, and you can come up with a very healthy diet that helps improve your fitness without ever having to go near bean sprouts, tofu, or radish shakes.

REMEMBER

If you're looking to get fit, it's best to limit fatty and high-calorie foods, including fried foods, which tend to be both. Or, if you can't resist that order of cheese fries, share it.

Carbohydrates, which include grains, vegetables, and fruit, are the best source of energy and nutrition when you play a lot of tennis. Your body can digest carbohydrates more easily and quickly than high-protein foods like red meat, and because of that, they give you quick energy.

WARNING

Carbohydrates aren't a free ride. If you eat a diet high in carbohydrates but don't get enough exercise, you don't burn up the fuel and it gets attached to your body as fat. Also keep this in mind: If you douse that plate of spaghetti in a cream-based sauce, like Alfredo sauce, you add a lot of hard-to-digest fat to an otherwise good source of quick power and energy. It takes much longer for your body to digest such meals, which keeps you from realizing the advantage of carbohydrates.

TIP

The following dietary tips should steer you in the right direction when it comes to food. (*Hint:* That direction is not toward the potato chip aisle at your local market.)

>> **Moderate your intake.** The less you eat, the less weight you're likely to gain. You'd be surprised how much less most people can eat when it comes to portion size and still feel satisfied afterward. Part of eating large portions is pure habit, and some restaurants thrive on feeding that habit.

>> **Think lean.** If you like animal-based protein — in other words, meat — stick with the leaner, lighter choices like chicken, turkey, or fish, which have fewer calories and less fat.

- » **Use mustard as a substitute for mayonnaise.** Mustard spices up a sandwich without nearly the same amount of calories as mayo.

- » **Eat lots of fruits and veggies.** If you have to snack between meals, go for a banana or apple rather than a candy bar.

- » **Don't drink your calories.** Regular sodas, sports drinks, and juices are often loaded with added sugars. If you're reaching for a soft drink, opt for flavored seltzers or diet sodas. Same goes for fancy coffee and tea drinks. The pump of simple syrup and dollop of whipped cream turns a low-calorie beverage into a waistline killer.

  Until recently, it was believed that caffeinated drinks like coffee dehydrate you. That myth has been dispelled, but caffeinated drinks can make you pee more frequently, which may force you to plead for an unplanned and embarrassing bathroom break in the third set of a tournament match.

- » **Drink plenty of water.** The current recommendation from the National Academy of Medicine is a daily fluid intake of about 13 cups for men and 9 cups for women. And if you're going to be sweating away on a tennis court, you'd be wise to bump up those numbers a bit.

TIP

Eat a light meal two hours before you play. My own favorite pre-match meal was a salad with an oil-and-vinegar-based dressing (no creamy ranch or blue cheese, please!), a piece of grilled chicken with rice, and a piece of fresh fruit. When I had bread with the meal, I didn't use butter (too much fat). Okay, maybe a *little* butter.

IN THIS CHAPTER

» **Finding out about the most common injuries in tennis**

» **Preventing tennis injuries**

» **Treating injuries**

» **Coping with routine aches and pains**

» **Dealing with the mental part of the game**

Chapter **17**

Handling the Physical and Mental Challenges of Tennis

Tennis is not a sport with a very high risk of injury — say, like football or skiing. Most tennis injuries are nagging little ones, like sprains, pulled muscles, and blisters, that can be taken care of with a little medication and TLC. But other injuries warrant a visit to a doctor.

In this chapter, I take you on a tour of the injury "hot spots" of the tennis body. I also look at some ways to prevent injuries and methods for treating your aches and pains. I also tackle some of the mental hurdles that tennis presents. You're all alone out there, so it can be an emotionally bruising sport at times. I explain the best ways to handle these challenges and how to prevent them from diminishing your joy on the court.

The Little Aches and Pains

With any luck, you won't ever experience a tennis-related injury that requires medical care. But you'll almost certainly have to deal with the smaller, mostly annoying injuries that are a part of every athletic life.

People at the extreme ends of the tennis playing spectrum — those who play often, like three times a week or more, and those who play only occasionally — are especially vulnerable to little aches and pains. If you fit into either one of these categories, make sure to read every word of "Keeping Injuries at Bay," later in this chapter.

Blisters

Although blisters are in the "aches and pains" category of injury, they can be just as debilitating to your game than far more serious injuries and ailments. Every year on the pro tour, blisters cause several players to quit during matches or default the match before it's played.

Friction is the main cause of blisters. For example, if you haven't swung a racquet for a long time, your fingers and palms may develop blisters due to the excessive friction that they aren't used to. Even if you play regularly, your feet and hands can blister during a long match that produces more friction on your feet and hands than you're used to.

New or excessively worn shoes are a major course of excessive friction on your feet. If your shoes are new, make sure to wear athletic performance socks that are in good condition (no holes). If your shoes are worn out to the point that you blister after play, you need to buck up, set sentimentality aside, and buy some new shoes. (Chapter 3 gives you some ideas about what to look for in a tennis shoe.) And if you use a racquet with the wrong size grip, that may also be a source of blistering on your hands.

If you're lucky enough never to have had a blister, you need to know that tenderness or redness at points of friction — such as palms or toes — is the early warning sign of a blister paying you a visit. Putting on an adhesive bandage or a cushioning pad of some kind may allow you to play on in greater comfort, and it may even send the blister packing. However, an adhesive bandage often just forestalls the inevitable.

WOULD YOU LIKE A HAMBURGER WITH THAT?

Harold Solomon, a tough baseliner who won 22 tour singles titles in the '70s and '80s, habitually drank pickle juice before matches. He swore it helped prevent cramps. At the time, people thought he was just another eccentric in a sport full of them. However, Harold may have been on to something — pickle juice is loaded with sodium, an important electrolyte that helps you stay hydrated and stave off cramps. It's also vinegary, which has been shown effective in dealing with cramps. It's no wonder pickle juice is now sold in convenient packaging — no need to strain it from the jar — and marketed as a sports drink. You may even see touring pros swigging it during long, difficult matches. As for the taste, let's just say it's no Gatorade.

To prevent blisters, keep the following tips in mind:

>> **Play in moderation until you toughen up the skin at the friction points in your racquet hand and feet.** If you think that your skin may be soft and vulnerable to friction, play for only about 20 minutes and see how you're holding up before you continue. Gradually work up to a full hour of play.

>> **Coat the friction points of your feet and hands with preventive rubs.** There are any number of anti-blister sticks and balms that can be rubbed on hot spots to help prevent chafing. If you prefer old-school, low-tech options, applying petroleum jelly to the area and sprinkling talcum powder in shoes also helps. This advice comes in especially handy the first few times you wear new shoes.

>> **Wear absorbent, moisture-wicking socks that provide good cushioning in the heel and forefoot.** If you're already dealing with a blister problem, small, foam rubber donuts and various cushioning pads available at drugstores or online can provide additional protection against friction.

Cramps

Cramps are a loathsome minor injury that can become extremely uncomfortable. I've had my whole body cramp up after an exhausting match, causing me to literally scream in agony. That probably won't happen to you, but cramps, in addition to causing discomfort, may make it impossible for you to continue playing right in the middle of a match. Any part of your body may cramp, including your hands or lower back. But the most common cramps occur in your calf or thigh muscles.

Dehydration can cause cramps. Once upon a time, people thought that you weren't supposed to drink too much water during a match, because it bloated you and cut down your athletic efficiency. Once upon a time, they also treated headaches by applying leeches to your eyebrows. Although you should never drink so much water that you feel bloated, proper hydration is the most basic preventive measure against cramps. You can read more about hydrating yourself later in this chapter.

You can't do much about cramps except rest, lightly massage the area, and drink enough water and electrolytes. Your body needs time to overcome the condition that causes cramps, so if you have a serious bout of cramps in a match, chances are, you'll have to call it quits.

Pulled muscles

You can easily pull a muscle through overexertion, especially in your legs or arm when serving. When you feel anything out of the ordinary, especially irritation, take a little pressure off by hitting the ball or running with less power and energy. But if and when you actually feel pain, stop immediately.

Often, you won't know how seriously you've pulled a muscle until after you cool down. You may cool down enough to tell whether you pulled a muscle in about an hour, but I recommend that you stop for the day and see how you feel the following morning. If you feel pain, consult a doctor.

You can help prevent pulled muscles by warming up properly, which you can read about in Chapter 7.

Shin splints

If you feel mild pain and tightness on and around your shin bone, you may have shin splints. This condition is more than an injury, and it isn't threatening, but it sure is uncomfortable. And if you don't take it easy, it could develop into a stress fracture.

You get shin splints from overuse of your calf muscles, usually from playing for extended periods on an unforgiving or uneven surface. Players with flat feet or high arches may also be more susceptible to shin splints.

Wearing well-cushioned shoes and cushioned socks, or even two pairs of socks, reduces your chance of developing shin splints.

The only effective treatment for shin splints is rest, although taking over-the-counter nonsteroidal anti-inflammatories (NSAIDs), such as ibuprofen, may lessen the discomfort. Gentle stretching and light walking may also speed recovery.

Tennis toe

You do a lot of lunging in tennis, and you change directions frequently. In the process, you may jam your big toes against the front of your shoes. Wearing ill-fitting shoes greatly increases the chances. (Chapter 3 has more details on picking out the right shoes). These acrobatics can lead to *tennis toe,* an unpleasant condition in which the skin under your toenail turns black and the tip of the toe becomes tender. Usually, tennis toe is more uncomfortable than it is painful and more unsightly than it is dangerous. The feet I've seen in pro locker rooms have not been a pretty sight, believe me.

Aggressive movers are the most susceptible to tennis toe. Pushing off in the opposite direction and making sudden stops, or stepping into the ball with a pronounced action, may cause tennis toe.

To prevent tennis toe, make sure that your shoe is roomy enough to spread your toes somewhat while still holding your foot firmly in place. If the shoe sags — you can feel it hang off your foot when in motion — that can be an issue. Adding extra layers of socks can give you a better fit in roomy shoes and add cushioning.

You can't do much about tennis toe except put your feet up — preferably where nobody can see your toe. Tennis toe will eventually go away as your nail grows out or falls off and your toe recovers from the pressure.

Be vigilant when it comes to cleaning and drying your feet, especially between your toes. I unfortunately can say this from experience: If you don't give proper attention to that area, you run the risk of forming a nasty fungus, often called *athlete's foot,* and it's all kinds of awful.

Sunburn

Sunburn can produce dizziness, nausea, and severe headaches, but it mostly just stings and can be painful to play through. And in the long run, constant sun exposure without protection can cause skin cancer, something many former touring pros can attest to.

Always use sunblock when you play under a bright, overhead sun, even if it doesn't feel too hot. Use a spray or lotion with a minimum of SPF 30. Apply the sunblock to your face, your ears, the back of your neck, and to the exposed portions of your arms and legs.

A hat can also protect you from sunburn, with the added benefit of keeping the sun out of your eyes. Hall of Famer Ivan Lendl would sometimes wear a Legionnaire cap during blistering hot days at the Australian Open. The cap provides coverage to the back of the neck as well — you still see some ball kids and spectators wearing it in the stands on sunny days — but it doesn't score points in the fashion department.

Hats should be considered an added layer of defense and should never stand in for applying sunblock to your face.

If you get sunburned, don't peel the flaking skin. Let the scorched skin peel and flake off naturally. You can buy various lotions to alleviate the suffering and keep your parched skin moisturized.

Bad Injuries Can Happen to Good Players

Most sports create stress on specific parts of the body, the parts that you use most often or strenuously. In tennis, those areas can vary because of circumstantial factors like the surface of the court you play on, your playing style, or your equipment.

For example, if you play on hard courts, the pounding can do a number on your knees, ankles, and lower back. If you play a lot on clay, a soft, slow surface on which you may hit many more balls in a typical workout, you're more susceptible to arm and shoulder problems like tendinitis (which I talk about later in this chapter). If you play with a stiff racquet, or one in which the strings have lost their bounce, or with dead balls, your arm absorbs more punishment, and you can end up with a sore shoulder or tennis elbow (which I talk about a little later in this chapter).

In addition, the way you hit the ball can prevent or lead to injury. If you cultivate good stroke fundamentals, different parts of your body all contribute to make power smoothly and easily, without putting too much stress on any part of your anatomy. If you ignore the fundamentals, parts of your body like the arm and shoulder become overworked, and an injury is in the making. (You can read more about stroking fundamentals in Chapter 7.)

Unfortunately, regardless of precaution, these types of difficult injuries can still rear their ugly heads, especially if you're an avid player. Warming up properly and strengthening these vulnerable areas are the best ways to safeguard against getting seriously hurt. However, if you do feel the symptoms of any of these injuries, stop play immediately and consult a doctor.

The rotator cuff

The rotator cuff, shown in X-ray vision in Figure 17-1, is the area where your upper arm meets your shoulder. It's made up of four tiny muscles and their tendons that help stabilize the shoulder joint. When people speak of rotator cuff injuries, they're really talking about tears in these tendons that connect your shoulder and arm. (*Tendons* are tough tissues that unite muscles and transfer energy during athletic activity.)

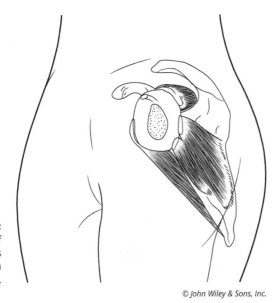

FIGURE 17-1: The rotator cuff and the muscles that join your arm to your shoulder.

A partial tear to a tendon in your rotator cuff may cause you some vague pain in the area of your shoulder, but you may be able to use your arm in a normal range of motion. But if you completely tear a tendon, you usually struggle to raise your arm up from your side. Activities like driving a car, brushing your hair, and even sleeping can be agonizing. Depending on the severity, it could require surgery.

Sports like tennis that can overwork the shoulder with lots of overhead movement are prime candidates for rotator cuff injuries. Older players are particularly susceptible because those small muscles weaken and the connective tissue loses elasticity with age. Serves and overheads, in particular, can strain the rotator cuff, so always make sure to adequately warm up both of these strokes before playing. And for lasting healthy shoulders, follow the warm-up routine I show you in Chapter 7 and the stretching and strengthening protocols described in Chapter 16 to defend yourself against rotator cuff injuries.

Tennis elbow

This injury is so common among tennis players that it takes its name from the sport, but the condition is officially known as *lateral epicondylitis.*

Overuse of the muscles and tendons in your racquet arm causes tennis elbow. The muscles of the forearm that bend the wrist back, called the *extensors,* begin at the *lateral epicondyle,* with a common tendon attachment (see Figure 17-2). Most experts believe that tennis elbow is created when small tears or inflammation occur in the tendon. Although the tears begin to heal naturally, continued use prevents them from fully healing or getting a sufficient blood supply. And because you use your wrist and forearm in many daily activities outside the tennis court, it's an injury that can linger for quite some time.

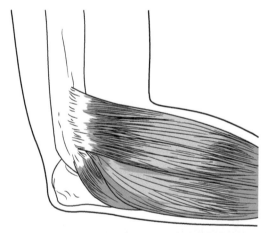

FIGURE 17-2: What Superman sees when he looks at the human elbow.

© John Wiley & Sons, Inc.

You can easily identify tennis elbow by the tenderness and pain it causes at the outside bump on the elbow of your racquet arm. If the condition is serious enough, simple lifting activities, like reaching into the fridge for a carton of milk, can be very painful.

Tennis elbow can creep up from general overuse, but it commonly results from improper form. Faulty mechanics can cause added stress to the elbow, which degenerates over time. For instance, players who frequently hit their backhands late in the stroke's forward motion make themselves more susceptible to tennis elbow, especially if they hit one-handed backhands without the help and support of the other hand. (See Chapter 9 for more on how to hit the backhand correctly.)

Tennis elbow can also be a compensation injury for shortcomings above or below the joint. If the hitting shoulder or wrist has weakness or poor range of motion during a stroke, the elbow may be forced to take up the slack. The added burden causes overload and inflames the tendon. Identifying and working on those trouble spots can do wonders for your elbow.

If you want to play through tennis elbow, various supportive sleeves, kinesio tape, wraps, and braces may help alleviate a minor case of it. However, don't continue to play with the aid of these devices unless your doctor gives you the okay. Even if you do get the go-ahead, keep in mind that repeated use will delay the healing process. Truly ridding yourself of tennis elbow may call for physical therapy and a dedicated training protocol.

Ultimately, the best thing you can do is improve the technique on your swing (which is why tennis elbow is an infrequent injury for professional players). One thing I like to do with players is have them really slow down their swing and troubleshoot for any glaring red flags. Often, players have difficulty controlling their racquets in slow-motion when their form is off. Even if it's just hitting the ball against a wall or off of slow feeds from a coach, it's a good way to analyze the stroke and refine it.

Troublesome joints

In addition to the major injuries I cover in the previous two sections, overexerting yourself on the tennis court can cause minor but irritating aches and pains. They may not prevent you from playing, but they're just bothersome enough to affect your game. Worst of all, what starts out as an annoyance can become a chronic issue if you don't give it the proper attention.

Most of the time, these injuries can be handled by limiting play and some basic remedies. However, if you ever develop pain or soreness in an area that will not go away, see a medical professional.

Here are the most common offenders to look out for:

>> **Wrist:** Your wrist gets quite a workout in tennis. Whether helping to accelerate the racquet head through contact or holding it steady to block the ball back over the net, it does some heavy lifting. Squeezing the racquet too tightly and the shock from mishitting the ball also add undue stress to your wrist. If they

aren't ready for all these stressors, the wrist's tendons can get irritated (in a condition called *tendinitis*), causing discomfort when you swing the racquet and contact the ball.

>> **Back:** The lower back is a real sore spot for many players. The constant pounding and rotating, especially when playing on hard courts, can really do a number on the lower back. If you have low-back pain, some players find that wearing a neoprene, girdlelike sleeve around the stomach and lower back helps provide support and warmth for the back muscles. Stretching can also help your back muscles stay limber. (See Chapter 16 for some hints on stretches for your back.) And make sure your shoes still have plenty of spring in them and provide enough cushioning. Old shoes plus a hard court can equal a cranky back.

>> **Knees:** Like the lower back, the knees absorb a lot of the shock from the running, abrupt stopping, and changes of direction needed to play tennis. This can lead to a dull soreness in the knee joint, often felt right around the knee-cap (a condition called *patella tendinitis*). Using a sleeve or strap to support the kneecap can often reduce the pain. Again, having well-padded, relatively new shoes can help as well.

>> **Ankles:** Ankle sprains are one of the most common injuries in tennis — even for the pros. Unlike the overuse problems earlier in this list, a sprain is an acute injury that occurs when you twist an ankle unnaturally or when you roll your foot to the outside. Doing so overstretches and tears the ligaments connecting the bones in your ankle. The area around the ankle usually swells up and often gets discolored over time.

Stray balls cause sprained ankles on the tennis court more often than sudden athletic moves. Keep unused balls off the court and call a let if a stray ball rolls onto your court.

A mildly sprained ankle may heal up in a matter of days, creating only minor pain and inconvenience. But a severely sprained ankle may require serious medical attention and even surgery.

Treating Injuries

When you sustain an injury, you first want to determine whether the severity of the injury merits medical attention. Visit your doctor if any of these three conditions apply to you:

RICE NO MORE

When I was a player, we followed the RICE (rest, ice, compress, elevate) formula whenever we had an injury that involved swelling or pain. Most recent research has shown that this protocol may actually delay the recovery process. In fact, RICE's effectiveness was eventually recanted by the doctor who created it.

>> **Swelling or redness occurs during or just after your match and lasts for several days.** If the area is even slightly larger than normal, go have it checked out.

>> **You have bruises not caused by banging into another object.** If you happen to bump into the net-post handle while changing sides (don't laugh — it happens all the time!), you don't have to run to the doctor when a bruise appears.

>> **You experience steady pain that interferes with your ability to play, or your pain doesn't go away after 24 hours.** It doesn't have to be excruciating pain. Mild pain is a warning sign of worse things to come if you don't deal with the problem.

If your injury doesn't fall into any of the preceding categories but you still experience enough discomfort that you want to do something about it, numerous over-the-counter remedies — such as ice packs, heating pads, and nonsteroidal anti-inflammatories (NSAIDs) such as Advil or Aleve — can help. However, I still recommend seeking advice from an experienced trainer, physical therapist, or doctor before embarking on a treatment plan.

Keeping Injuries at Bay

Overall fitness proves the most powerful preventive medicine against injuries. (You can read more about fitness, conditioning, and stretching in Chapter 16.) You're most susceptible to injury when you suddenly put your body through physical stress to which it isn't accustomed. If you only play tennis and you do nothing else to stay in shape, your body will be more vulnerable to the aches, pains, and injuries that can come with playing the sport. If you make fitness training a part of your everyday life, not only will you minimize those dangers, but you can also take time away from tennis and return to the game with less risk of sustaining a serious injury.

Beyond maintaining your overall fitness, you can prevent injuries in a few other simple ways.

>> **Don't overdo it.** If you're new to the game, work your way into frequent play. Give your body time to acclimate to the rigors of the sport. Until your conditioning allows it, take appropriate rest between practice sessions. Make sure you're feeling fresh when you hit the court.

>> **Warm up and cool down.** Don't neglect these integral parts of the workout. Turn to Chapter 7 for a complete description of the warm-up and cooldown process.

>> **Use wraps and braces.** These aids are not substitutes for trying to rehabilitate an injured area. But if you notice tenderness in one of your joints or muscles, you can have the area taped or use a brace to help support it during play. Not only will it temper some of the discomfort, but may prevent the injury from worsening.

Self-applying kinesio tape is tricky, but doable. Just go to YouTube and search for kinesio tape and the body part you're looking to support (for example, "kinesio tape knee"), and you'll find a slew of how-to videos. However, it's difficult to duplicate the job done by experts like trainers and physical therapists. You can get many of the benefits of taping from elasticized sleeves, cuffs, and similar devices that fit over your elbow, wrist, knee, thigh, or ankle.

Sleek, form-fitting spandex shorts that cling to your buttocks and thighs are not just a fashion statement — they can have real value for preventing injury, especially if they're made from elasticized nylon like Lycra with medical-grade compression that simultaneously firms up and keeps your muscles warm.

>> **Orthotics:** Foot, ankle, knee, and even back problems can be caused by your feet and the way you walk and run. If that's the case, the standard insoles in your tennis shoes may not offer enough support. Orthotics are special insoles made from a mold taken of your foot. They correct imbalances in the way you walk and run, reducing your chances of developing foot problems and perhaps even back problems. Affordable options are available online or in athletic shoe stores, but a custom-made pair through a podiatrist can be quite expensive.

>> **Hydration:** Dehydration causes fatigue and cramps. Keeping your tank full of water and electrolytes helps your body avoid these injuries. If you're a big-time sweater, make sure you're taking in enough sodium. Try to drink at least 8 to 12 ounces of a sports drink every 15 to 20 minutes while you play, even if you don't feel thirsty. By the time you feel symptoms of dehydration, it's often too late to recover.

The Game between the Ears

Sure, I'm biased, but I think tennis is the greatest sport in the world. And one of the things I love most about it is the mental part of the game. Not only do you have to exert yourself physically and have the skills to hit the ball well, but you also need to devise strategy and problem-solve. Plan A isn't working? Time for Plan B. Then there's emotional control — not feeling too high when you're winning, staying out of the dumps when you're not. Oh, and don't forget you have to deal with the vibes coming from your opponent.

All this is to say that your brain can play as big a role as your forehand. And having all these thoughts flying around your head can make this part of the game a real challenge — one that many players struggle with, so much so that it zaps their enjoyment and even causes them to put down their racquets. I don't want this to happen to you. Competition will always bring elements of intensity and nerves, but tennis should generally be an enjoyable and relaxed endeavor. Having an understanding of the mental side of the game helps.

Knowing the downsides of an individual sport

If you've ever played team sports such as football, baseball, or basketball, you know the value of having teammates. Not only do you pull on the same rope in the hopes of victory, but you lift each other up when someone is off their game.

For the most part, tennis is not a group effort. Sink or swim, it's all on your shoulders. Some athletes prefer being completely in charge; others find it a heavy burden. It can be tough having only yourself to blame. Playing doubles gives you a partner to carry some of the responsibility, but you're still heavily involved in the outcome.

The truth is, there's simply no getting around this aspect of the sport. You've got to think for yourself and execute your shots. The good news is, the more you play, the more you'll get used to it. And what most players soon come to realize is that this self-reliance is more of a blessing than a curse.

Remembering that nobody's perfect

In the commencement speech he delivered at Dartmouth University in 2024, Roger Federer told the graduating class that over the course of his incredible career, he won only 54 percent of the points he played. That's it. He lost nearly as many points as he won. His message was that even the greatest players, on their greatest days, aren't perfect. The trick is to accept the result, learn from it, and move on to the next point.

In tennis, you will miss shots. You'll even miss easy shots you have no business missing. When you do hit the ball in, you often won't strike it as cleanly or effectively as you intended. That's just part of the game. Don't have unrealistic expectations of yourself. The game doesn't always come naturally, and improvement can take time. If Roger Federer can be content with imperfection, so can you.

Zeroing in on performance instead of outcome: Winning isn't everything

I had a doubles partner in the juniors who remains a super-competitive guy to this day. He always says that if he's going to play something, he's going to try to win. That's why you keep score, right? Well, yes and no. I'm not going to tell you that winning is meaningless. It can give you a sense of accomplishment and validate the work you put in on the practice court. And it certainly feels better than losing.

However, don't let the scoreboard define your experience. Otherwise, unless you win, you'll derive no other pleasure from playing. Instead, pay closer attention to whether you're improving. Use performance goals — higher first-serve percentage, fewer unforced errors — as the barometer for a good day on the court.

Because if you play tennis, you must confront losing. A tournament has only one winner. Throughout my ten years competing on the ATP Tour, in what some would consider a pretty successful career, I won just one singles title, and I had an overall losing record (140-163). That's why the word I use with the juniors and their parents I work with is *resilience.* If you can't handle and bounce back from defeat, tennis can beat you up.

And the truth is, losing isn't all bad. You don't want to make it a habit, but you need to test yourself against better players. If all you do is win against weaker competition, you'll never be forced to expand your skill set. Great players always say they learn more from their losses than they do from their victories.

I have the perfect advice for players who can't deal with the highs and lows of competition. It took me a while, and lots of sleepless nights from my own playing experience to figure it out. Some players find it a bit radical, but it works every time. Ready? Here it is: *Don't do it.* Don't play matches. You can still have a great time on the tennis court without keeping score. Most people who jog don't enter races. Practice your strokes, run some drills, or work on your technique with a pro. I know plenty of players who just like the feeling of cracking a solid groundstroke and getting a great workout. Maybe throw in a few tiebreakers here and there to play some points, but you don't have to do more than that to love the game.

Focusing on what you can control

Here's the situation: You toss the ball up to serve, and just as it reaches its peak — exactly at the point you want to smack it — it hovers right in the path of a blazing sun. Good luck hitting a blind serve.

Or you hit a terrific crosscourt forehand that your opponent has to scramble to return. They don't have time to put a good swing on the ball, barely get their racquet on it, and hit a wounded duck that's floating helplessly toward the net. As poorly hit as it is, the ball has just enough height and oomph to clip the top of the net and dribble over. It bounces twice before you have time to shake your head.

Tennis is full of variables you can't control. For some reason, they always seem to bubble up on big points, too. It's another aspect of the game that tests your composure and emotional stamina. You can blame the universe if you want, but it won't get you anywhere.

Frustrating as these situations are, you have to accept that there's nothing you can do about them — which isn't easy. Being able to let these bad breaks roll off your back is an acquired skill. At the very least, you should take heart that your opponent is also powerless against these same obstacles.

In fact, even when you do everything right — get the racquet back in time, make solid contact, have a smooth follow-through — the shot can still go out or your opponent may hit a return ball that's even better.

I always tell players that they can completely control only three things:

» **Attitude:** An upbeat, positive attitude can overcome a lot of adversity. It will also make you popular with other players, keeping your tennis calendar full.

» **Concentration:** That project at work or your social media feed can wait. Make sure your attention is fixed squarely on the ball and how you're going to hit it.

» **Effort:** This one is nonnegotiable. If you're going to take the time to play, there's really no excuse not to try your best.

IN THIS CHAPTER

» Finding a pro

» Knowing your pro's job

» Taking group lessons

» Getting the most out of a lesson

» Maintaining the right attitude

» Improving your game with websites, apps, and online videos

Chapter **18**

Improving Your Game with Lessons

Tennis challenges you to improve, to hit your strokes and develop your strategy to become a more efficient, effective player. When you improve your game, you don't just become a better player. You also get the satisfaction that comes from mastering a skill.

That's where pros — teaching professionals, not pro players — and tennis lessons come into the picture. When you get serious about your tennis, even if you're just playing for fun, you may want to consider taking tennis lessons.

In this chapter, I tell you what lessons can do for you, how to find a suitable tennis program or pro, and how to make the most from the experience. I also touch on a few other sources of information that can help you improve your game.

Understanding What Lessons Can (Realistically) Do for You

No tennis instructor can turn you from a beginner into Serena Williams or Roger Federer in one hour-long lesson (or even three, for that matter!). However, an instructor can help you improve your game in some very concrete ways, starting with the very first lesson.

Increase your rate of improvement

Most tennis players advance to one playing plateau, spend a fair amount of time there, and then suddenly find themselves jumping up to another plateau. Taking lessons can reduce the time you spend on each plateau, and lessons can make the transition to the next plateau smoother and quicker.

REMEMBER

A tennis instructor can help you improve faster, but you still won't make significant, permanent strides forward unless you put your knowledge of the game into play on-court on a regular basis. The surest way to improve in tennis is repetition — hitting lots of balls, as often as you can.

Break logjams in your game

Left to their own devices, most people develop games full of idiosyncrasies and extraneous stylistic flourishes — just like your buddy with the funny habit of making a windmilling motion with their arm right before tossing the ball to serve.

Many of those touches don't hurt your game. Some may even help you a little bit. But plenty of those twitches and glitches eventually impair your ability to hit a good, clean ball, either in general or with specific shots. As a result, you get stuck at a certain level as a player, even though that level may well be below your natural potential.

A good instructor knows that less is often more. A good instructor not only wants to bring new elements to your game but also wants to get rid of old ones that hold you back, as painlessly as possible.

Finding Strength in Numbers

A group program — often referred to as a *clinic* — makes a lot of sense for beginners. When you first take up the game, you need to master the same fundamentals as everyone else. Your game doesn't have a unique personality, complete with strengths and flaws, that requires the individual attention of a one-on-one lesson.

You hit fewer balls in a group lesson, and you run less. Group lessons can be an advantage for beginners who aren't in great shape or for people who haven't developed enough strength or skill to take advantage of an intensive, hour-long private lesson.

Also, many beginners benefit from watching other beginners, hearing what a group instructor has to say to each student, and watching how others in the group do or don't carry out the instructions of the pro. And just like in a classroom, socializing and learning with other students can be a lot of fun.

Group programs are usually composed of weekly lessons given over a block of time. Typically, you may sign up for a series of 6 to 12 lessons, given on set days and times over a few months or a season.

Prices for a group lesson, which usually lasts for one to two hours, vary depending on the number of players, the facility, and the length of the program. You should expect to pay anywhere from $15 to $70 per lesson, which includes court time and balls. Some beginner programs for juniors and adults are free for the first few lessons. Bring your own racquet and accessories, and be ready to play.

TIP

In order to get the most out of a group lesson, try to get in a class with six or fewer players. More bodies than that on the court really dilutes the lesson. You still may want to take part, either because of the low cost or for the opportunity to meet other people who play tennis, but don't expect much individual attention in large groups.

Try any of the following places when looking for a group lesson:

>> **Your local public courts and clubs:** Most public tennis facilities have teaching pros on hand and offer introductory group lessons.

>> **Municipal programs:** Your town may offer tennis programs through its recreation department. Often, these programs aren't advertised, so don't be bashful about calling or emailing your local parks department and inquiring about their offerings.

>> **The United States Tennis Association (USTA):** The USTA, the organization that runs U.S. tennis, sponsors several beginner programs to get people of all ages to try tennis. (You can read more about the USTA in Chapter 14.) The programs may vary from one USTA section to another, but they usually feature four to eight weeks of basic instruction. Check the USTA's website for programs available in and around your location.

>> **Resorts and dedicated tennis camps:** Taking a vacation at a dedicated tennis camp or resort can provide a great introduction to the game. The programs are moderate to very intensive, but at the best camps they're designed with an excellent sense of a beginner's need.

Hiring a Certified Pro for Private Lessons

The Racquet Sports Professionals Association (RSPA), which was formerly the USPTA, and the Professional Tennis Registry (PTR) are the two giants in the U.S. tennis-teaching industry. Both organizations have one great feature: They conduct elaborate certification programs to make sure that their members are qualified to teach tennis. Both also provide mailings, seminars, and conferences meant to keep their constituents on top of the game, in areas ranging from sports science to actual teaching methodology.

TIP

Certification proves that a pro knows and plays the game well enough to teach. A letter of certification from the RSPA or PTR is as close to a quality guarantee for your pro as you can come.

Most certified pros are affiliated with individual commercial or private tennis facilities. You can start your search for a pro at any of those places.

Some pros teach at private courts in their spare time or have enough students to have their own facility. If the pro you choose isn't affiliated with a commercial or private tennis facility, make sure that they have good access to a court with enough privacy to make the most of your hour without inconveniencing others.

WARNING

Some pros rely on the availability of public courts for their lessons, which can present a host of problems. Most public tennis facilities prohibit independent pros — certified or otherwise — from giving unauthorized lessons on their courts for a variety of reasons, including the distraction that a lesson constitutes for players on adjacent courts. If you take a lesson on a public court from a pro, make sure that you have the right of access. You should also agree on who pays for any court fee.

Word of mouth is a good way to find a good teaching pro. People who had a good lesson experience are usually eager to get their pro more lessons. Some pros advertise on bulletin boards at tennis facilities, but it's a good idea to check them out through references before you commit to taking lessons from them.

TIP

When deciding whether to take lessons from a particular pro, base your hiring decision on the following factors:

>> **Fee:** The fee is the most practical of all the criteria. You pay for most tennis lessons by the hour, especially private, one-on-one lessons. Fees vary widely based on the amount of personal attention, the pro, and your location. On average, you can expect to pay around $50 to $150 for a private lesson with a teaching pro, and anywhere up to $250 for a big-name teacher. Tipping isn't required, but most pros accept tips happily.

Keep in mind that almost all facilities charge a fixed rate for their lessons. There's no bargaining. However, if the pro works remotely at private courts or in a town park, you may be able to negotiate the fee.

>> **Teaching style:** Is the pro in the mold of a Marine drill sergeant? A New Age, "see the ball, be the ball" guru? Not all teaching styles suit all players. Find a pro with a style that seems compatible with your personality.

>> **Background:** Some of the best coaches I know had less-than-brilliant playing careers, and some of the most accomplished players I know have no idea how to teach the game. Playing level — high or low — is often not an accurate barometer of whether someone can coach. How long a pro has worked, for what programs, and the students they taught are much better indicators of whether they're a skilled teacher.

>> **References:** The tennis mavens in your area will usually have the scoop on the best coaches around. If you don't have that resource, you could ask a perspective pro to see them in action. Seeing a pro engaging with their students is the best reference of them all.

>> **Communication skills:** Seek out a pro with an ability to communicate in a relaxed, friendly fashion. You don't want someone who blabbers endlessly about what they did this weekend, but you don't want a stoic, feeding robot either. *Remember:* You're not looking for a new best friend — you're looking for someone who can help your tennis game. A blunt but honest pro can do more for your game than one who flatters you unnecessarily.

This is a two-way street. Feel free to tell a pro what you would like to get out of a lesson, to see whether they feel confident that they can help you. If the pro is a regular fixture at your local courts, you can even ask whether they'll watch you play to see if they can help your game. If you get lucky, the pro may even suggest a brief hit to evaluate you.

CHECKING A PRO'S CERTIFICATION

No law requires you to have a special license or certificate to call yourself a tennis pro. Anybody can set up shop and claim to be a tennis pro.

Most pros who take their jobs seriously belong to either the RSPA or the PTR. If you have any doubts about a pro's qualifications, ask to see their certification. If they're serious about accepting you as a student, they won't be offended by your request.

>> **Goals:** Everyone has different aspirations for their tennis. Are you looking to make the high school or club team? Or is it just a good sweat and a few smiles? Your desires can evolve with your tennis, but knowing that your motivation aligns with a pro's teaching methods and philosophy is a surer path to a positive working relationship.

REMEMBER

You always take a chance when you engage a pro for the first time. No lesson is perfect, but there should be a few aspects about it that you found rewarding. You should either learn at least one new thing in a lesson or get a tip or suggestion that turns on that little light bulb over your head. If you walk off the court completely disappointed after your lesson — it wasn't fun and you didn't learn anything — strongly consider not taking another lesson from that pro.

Taking Your Chances with an Uncertified Pro

You can probably tell from the title of this section that I recommend that you hire a certified pro when you're ready to take a lesson.

MAC SAYS

You have the right to expect pride of craft from someone who is charging you in the neighborhood of $100 per hour for their services. If a pro can't be bothered to take a certification test and participate in the mainstream activities of their professional community, they may not be interested in anything more than your money either.

However, certified pros may be in short supply where you live. Economic realities may also lead you to consider taking lessons from an uncertified pro. You may even strike up a good relationship with a player who seems to help your game, and you may want to repay the kindness.

Your local courts may have a few tennis diehards around who like to help others develop their games, or who don't give lessons often enough to go through the certification process and pay fees to belong to professional organizations. They may even call themselves "pros." Exercise good judgment when you contemplate taking lessons from an uncertified pro.

TIP

Do yourself a favor and do the following before you hire an uncertified pro as your teacher:

>> **Ask the price.** A pro who doesn't belong to the RSPA or PTR should be less expensive. If they charge the going rate for a certified pro, you need to hear a good reason for the price.

>> **Beware the bum's rush.** Think very, very seriously about getting into a paying situation with a self-styled "pro" who seems to have targeted you with flattery and unsolicited commentary on your wonderful game.

>> **Put value on appearances.** Professionals in any field take a certain amount of pride in their appearance and equipment. Opportunists tend to be lazy and oblivious to such issues. For example, don't take a lesson with a "pro" who doesn't have a hopper full of balls.

>> **Observe a lesson.** Uncertified pros almost always teach in public places. Watch the pro give a lesson. If you can't do that, ask to hit with the pro to check out the level of their game.

Maximizing the Efficiency of Your Hour

Ideally, before you show up for your first lesson, your pro should already know something about your game and, therefore, your strengths and weaknesses. If you're going into a lesson blind, come prepared for your lesson with an idea of what you want to accomplish.

For example, you may just want to treat yourself to an hour of intensive play against the pro; that's usually called a *playing lesson*. On the other hand, you may decide that you want to spend 20 minutes each on three specific areas. Don't expect your pro to be a mind reader. Try to communicate as clearly as possible what you'd like to accomplish in your hour.

During the lesson, ask for more information if your pro says something you don't understand. When communicating valuable information about the game, good coaches have a knack for doing it with memorable catchphrases or smart techniques. Instead of merely telling you that you're hitting a shot poorly, a good coach tells you what the problem is and then gives you clear, concrete ways to correct it.

TIP

In addition, keep these tips in mind to get the most out of your time with your pro:

>> **Show up on time, ready to play.** You don't want to be late, even if it does mean that your pro gets an extra ten minutes to cool their heels while the meter is running.

>> **Do your stretching beforehand.** And if you really want to impress your pro — and save your own time and money — warm up on another court before your lesson begins.

>> **Have all your stuff.** If you have only one racquet, make sure it's in good shape. Bring along your favorite beverage. If playing outdoors, bring a hat, sunblock, sweatbands, and anything else you may need to your lesson. Unless the pro tells you otherwise, they should supply at least one bucket of balls for your lesson.

>> **Be patient.** Give yourself time to loosen up and get in the flow of things. Don't be in a hurry to hit your best shots. The sound of the meter ticking in your ears won't help you play better, and it may make you play worse.

>> **Stay within your comfort zone.** Don't hit the ball too hard or try to hit winners to impress your pro unless doing so is part of the lesson.

>> **Enjoy yourself.** Remind yourself that a lesson is a great opportunity to hit balls with someone who is a terrific player and there to help you.

Mining Other Sources for Help with Your Game

Lessons with a pro are the surest way to make strides in your game. However, there are additional ways you can improve your game, often right in the palm of your hand. Websites, videos, and apps can provide useful, inexpensive ways to tap into the formidable body of knowledge about tennis.

YouTube videos

As it is with so many subjects, YouTube is a virtually bottomless resource of technical and tactical tennis advice. Whether they feature world-renowned coaches, tour players, unheralded teaching pros, or just crazed rec players, a wealth of instructional videos are available free of charge. If you're a visual learner — someone who finds it helpful to see proper technique in action — it can be particularly beneficial. Want a demonstration of a pro-grade stroke? Type "Roger Federer forehand" or "Serena Williams serve" in the search bar and watch dozens of slow-motion videos breaking down the mechanics of their swings. You don't need to emulate some of the greatest shots ever in the game, but seeing the finer points of fundamentals likes footwork, preparation, and racquet path can be very instructive.

REMEMBER

Because anyone can post a video, not everything is worthwhile or applicable to your stage of development. It may take some curating to find channels and instructors who appeal to you. But if you're looking for tips on just about every aspect of play — from hitting drop shots to beating pushers — there's a lot of gold to mine.

Online stroke analysis

Where YouTube is something of a free-for-all, there are other websites — Essential Tennis (www.essentialtennis.com), Kovacs Institute Academy (https://kovacsacademy.com), and Tennis Evolution (https://tennisevolution.com) to name just a few — dedicated specifically to tennis instruction. Many have free videos, tutorials, and newsletters, with deeper involvement such as membership and online courses available for an additional fee. Some even offer individual stroke analysis — upload yourself in action and get feedback on where you need to improve.

Most of these sites are run by tech-savvy coaches looking to expand their client roster beyond their local reach. And if you live in an area that doesn't have a wealth of good coaches it's a way to find one without any significant travel. It's also less expensive than paying for an on-court private lesson.

The downside: The coach won't actually be on the court with you when you practice. So, in a way, you're both coach and student. It's not unlike following a customized exercise plan from a trainer — you take the lessons and apply it on your own. And if you're self-motivated and you like figuring things out for yourself, it can be an effective way to see progress.

Instructional apps

Instructional apps are an emerging segment of instruction that could see rapid expansion over the next several years, especially as artificial intelligence (AI) becomes more refined and prevalent. As of this writing, a small number of smartphone apps allow users to record themselves on court and will analyze that video to provide detailed statistics and insights on technique. It's almost like having a coach sitting courtside, charting every ball you hit, and telling you where you need to improve.

For instance, SwingVision (`https://swing.tennis`) can record a match and relay such details as every forehand hit, the location and speeds of your serves, and compile some of your best shots into a highlight reel. It can even call whether shots are in or out fairly accurately. Pro players pay a hefty sum for this level of information, and all you need is a smartphone.

Apps like these offer a deep dive into your tennis. If you're a numbers person, or you appreciate real data to confirm whether a swing change is having an effect ("Hey, that new grip on my forehand is producing more pace"), then this type of training aid is right up your alley.

It helps to have established strokes and strategies to build upon — almost like putting icing on the cake. If you're just starting out, more basic how-to videos are probably better supplemental instruction for your needs. But after you develop a strong foundation, these apps can add another dimension to your development as you progress on your tennis journey.

4

Tennis Aficionados Only

Sometimes watching good players can give you ideas for improving your own game. And more important, watching the pros do what they do best can be some of the most fun you get out of tennis. Turn to this part for a guide to the pro game, the Grand Slam tournaments, and how to get the most out of watching the pros in action.

Chapter **19**

The Pro Game

A mong professional sports, pro tennis is the new kid on the block. Until 1968, you could play in the world's most important tennis tournaments only if you were willing to compete for trophies and glory, not prize money. That's fine for the ego, but it won't do much good for your bank account.

Before 1968, the best tennis players in the world usually became "touring professionals" after proving themselves at Wimbledon, the U.S. Nationals (the U.S. Open, after 1968), and the other great tournaments. They led the life of barnstormers, putting on exhibitions for anyone willing to watch, still shut out of the "official" game.

But after decades of pounding on the doors of tennis shrines like Wimbledon and the West Side Tennis Club (the ancestral home of the U.S. Open), the touring pros finally won acceptance. In 1968, the International Tennis Federation, spurred on by the biggest of all tournaments, Wimbledon, opened the gates of the great tournaments to players who earned their living from tennis.

Shortly after that, the popularity of tennis boomed, and the game became a new financial frontier for promoters, tournament directors, and a whole new breed of player.

In this chapter, you learn all about the different organizations and tournaments that make up the professional tours.

Alphabet Soup: The Governing Bodies in Pro Tennis

Unlike other professional sports, tennis doesn't have one centralized ruling organization. There's no commissioner (although my brother John has often publicly lobbied for the gig) who presides over the good of the sport or a group of franchise owners looking to chart its path. Instead, there are a select few groups and associations spanning the globe that have influence over the administration of the game. These bodies having their own turf to protect, so it's tough to get things done in the sport. New ideas are rarely universally accepted, so change often happens at glacial speed. In this cauldron of voices, the International Tennis Federation (ITF), Association of Tennis Professionals (ATP), and Women's Tennis Association (WTA) make the most noise.

ITF

The British-based ITF is the granddaddy of the powers that be, the governing body of world tennis since 1913. The ITF is an umbrella organization, with constituents, called *national associations,* in more than 100 countries. For example, the United States Tennis Association (USTA) is the national association in the United States and an ITF affiliate.

These national associations control tennis in their respective countries. Composed mostly of volunteers who serve because they play and love the game, the associations do the daily work of recruiting players to the game, staging tournaments (including the most prestigious ones of all, the four Grand Slam events, which you can read about in Chapter 20), and issuing official rankings for amateur players in various levels and age groups.

The ITF also owns and controls the most important international team competitions, the Davis Cup and the Billie Jean King Cup (formerly the Fed Cup, which I also discuss in Chapter 20). The ITF is also the official tennis affiliate of the International Olympic Committee (IOC); thus, it also presides over tennis in the Olympic Games.

However, since the advent of open pro tennis in 1968, the ATP and WTA tours have become the official promoters and rulers of the thriving international pro circuits for men and women. (You can read about both these organizations in the following sections.) This shift occurred because the ITF is dedicated to the amateur, grassroots, recreational game. When an entire new industry called pro tennis was born in 1968, the ITF was neither willing nor able to take control of it. The ITF and the ATP and WTA tours cooperate in the business of promoting the game, with different areas of responsibility.

THE BATTLE OF THE ACRONYMS: THE ITF AGAINST THE ATP

Controlling the Grand Slam events gives the ITF tremendous leverage in the pro game, which occasionally leads to conflict. One of the most famous of these quarrels occurred in 1973, the year that the budding men's players' union, the ATP, boycotted Wimbledon (an ITF ally).

The brouhaha started when the national association of the nation formerly known as Yugoslavia suspended a player named Niki Pilić for refusing to play on the Yugoslavian Davis Cup team. According to ITF rules, the national associations had to honor each other's disciplinary suspensions. Thus, the British Lawn Tennis Association (BLTA) asked Wimbledon to honor the suspension and prohibit Pilić from playing in the world's most important tournament.

Wimbledon complied, and tense, round-the-clock negotiations between the ITF and the ATP eventually came to an impasse. The ATP players called a boycott, and 79 of the 82 ATP members entered in the tournament withdrew.

Many great players lost the chance to play at Wimbledon that year. But in the long run, the boycott paid off, because it empowered the ATP and sent a signal to tournaments all over the world that the players were willing to present a unified front on issues that concerned them. (By the way, the president of the ATP at the time was none other than my frequent ESPN broadcast booth buddy, Cliff Drysdale.)

ATP

The ATP Tour began life as the union of male pro players. The ATP Tour organizes and runs the major men's international pro tour, which consists of more than 60 tournaments divided into four tiers held in 30 countries all over the world. The only important pro tournaments not controlled by the ATP Tour are the Grand Slam events and the Olympics.

The ATP sponsors its own player-ranking system. Entry into ATP Tour events (and the Grand Slam events) depends on this ranking. When you qualify to join the ATP Tour, which is also based on your ranking, you get a whole range of services. These benefits include administrative help for tournaments (in other words, you don't have to fill out a form, buy a stamp, and hope that your entry form arrives in a foreign country before the entry deadline), pension plans, and the services of on-site physical therapists and other personnel at many tournaments.

The ATP Tour is a lot like an employee-owned company that runs professional men's tennis. The players, the officials they elect, and the staff they hire make all the decisions in partnership with the tournament directors — their partners in the tennis business.

IT ALL STARTED IN A PARKING LOT . . .

The ATP was formed at the U.S. Open in 1972, four years after pros were allowed to compete in official ITF events. That year, 50 of the top players in the world forked over 400 bucks apiece to start a union. Things were so hectic that the players felt that if they didn't hang together, they'd hang separately.

In the sidebar "The battle of the acronyms: The ITF against the ATP," I describe one of the two defining moments in the history of the ATP, the Wimbledon boycott. The other fork in the road materialized in 1988, when the ATP rank and file got up in arms over the amount of control exerted over it by an entity called the Men's International Professional Tennis Council (MIPTC). This organism had three constituents: the ATP, the ITF, and the only non-acronym in the bunch, tournament directors from the everyday pro circuit.

The MIPTC ran the world men's tennis circuit and made all the critical decisions regarding pro tournaments at every level, from player conduct to prize money to ranking issues. Basically, the ATP players woke up one morning and decided, "Hey, we *are* the tournaments — what's going on here?" They felt that instead of having a third of the votes on the MIPTC, they could just cut to the chase and run the pro tour themselves, kind of like the employee ownership concept of companies like Avis and UPS.

The ATP players recruited a former White House chief of staff, Hamilton Jordan (he served under President Jimmy Carter), as executive director. Jordan was asked to come up with a workable plan that would allow the players to control their own destinies. At the 1988 U.S. Open, the ATP asked the USTA (the ITF affiliate that runs the U.S. Open) if it could use the official media room at the National Tennis Center (NTC) to make an important announcement. The USTA, figuring that the request was a little bold, considering the nature of the announcement, refused. The ATP then called the now-famous "parking lot press conference."

In the open air of the parking lot beside the looming Louis Armstrong Stadium, before a throng of curious reporters, ATP President Mats Wilander, an active player, made public the union's decision to take over the men's tour. Many of the members, include yours truly, stood by Wilander's side in that parking lot. Starting in 1990, the ATP would be known as the ATP Tour, and the ATP Tour board and the staff it hired would make all the key decisions regarding men's professional tournaments. The most basic and important of these decisions is determining who gets to put on tournaments and reap their rewards in partnership with the ATP Tour.

WTA

For all practical purposes, the WTA Tour is identical to the ATP Tour in its role and even in its basic structure — right down to the WTA Tour's relationship with the preeminent Grand Slam events.

The WTA Tour runs the entire women's international pro tour, issues the only rankings that matter in the women's pro game, and provides numerous services to its players, from its administrative offices to on-site services at tournaments. It holds more than 50 events each year on six different continents and has the same four-tier system of tournaments as the ATP, with the most well-known and lucrative events at the apex.

YOU'VE COME A LONG WAY, WTA

A seminal year in the history of women's tennis was 1970, two years into the Open Era. By then, it was clear to women tennis players that they were second-class citizens in a burgeoning pro tennis marketplace. Tennis has a great tradition of the two genders playing side by side at tournaments, as they still do at the Grand Slams and several other events. But in 1970, the women were consistently earning about one-quarter of the amount that the men received in prize money, week after week, at the same tournaments.

At the Italian Open in 1970, Ilie Năstase received $3,500 for beating Jan Kodeš in the men's final. The female winner, Billie Jean King, defeated Julie Heldman for the title and got a mere $600. The best woman player in the world that year was, by far, Margaret Court. She earned $50,000 for the year, while Rod Laver, who didn't have nearly as good a year, earned more than $200,000.

By late August 1970, a fiery women's rights activist and journalist named Gladys Heldman (Julie's mom) became the negotiator for the faction of discontented women led by King. They decided to do battle with the establishment at the Pacific Southwest Open in Los Angeles, where the prize money ratio favored the men by a whopping 8-to-1 ratio.

When tournament chairman Jack Kramer wouldn't give in to the demands of Heldman and her band of rebels, the women decided to bolt the establishment. Nine women, led by Billie Jean King, declared that they would boycott the Los Angeles event and play in a $7,500 event in Houston, sponsored by Virginia Slims cigarettes.

(continued)

(continued)

The establishment, still led by the ITF and its affiliated national associations, refused to sanction this upstart event. By withholding its official blessing, the establishment was saying that if the women went outside the system and still played in Houston, they might be ineligible to compete in future sanctioned tournaments, like the Grand Slam events.

The women took their chances and played anyway. The event was so successful that, by the next year, there was a full Virginia Slims circuit, featuring the top women stars. The establishment eventually backed off its threat to lock the women out of sanctioned tournaments, and it slowly began to offer them a better deal as the Slims circuit grew ever more popular and prestigious.

Eventually, popular antismoking sentiments and activists helped drive Virginia Slims sponsorship out of tennis. But history clearly shows that Virginia Slims was pivotal to the success of the women's tour. It did a terrific job at every level, from media relations to tournament administration. If they made the Slim Jim instead of Virginia Slims cigarettes, they may still be a part of tennis today.

Three years after the historic Houston event, the women officially formed the WTA. Naturally, the first president was Billie Jean King. The WTA eventually took the same path as the men, deciding to take over the pro game, with the exception of the Grand Slams, by becoming the WTA Tour. But like the men's ATP Tour, the WTA Tour works in partnership with the ITF and the Grand Slam events.

The Different Levels of Tournaments

Your success as a pro is measured by two yardsticks — your ATP or WTA rank, and your prize earnings. Your rank is actually more important than the money, because you need to rank high enough to be eligible to compete in the tournaments where you can earn good prize money.

MAC SAYS

The ATP Tour and the WTA Tour both have tournaments of greater and lesser value, based on prize money, computer points to be won, and the number of participants. They also share very similar naming and classification in terms of importance. Often, three or four tournaments occur during the same week, giving more players a chance to compete and earn prize money. It may seem complicated at first, but it becomes less so when you understand the basic hierarchy of the tournaments.

The following types of tournaments count toward a player's ranks:

» **Grand Slams:** These preeminent tournaments last for two weeks — the Australian Open and French Open actually stretch to 15 days — and involve 128 players. (You can read more about them in Chapter 20.) In addition to a whopping paycheck, the winner at a Grand Slam event gets more rankings points than the winner of any other tournament. These events are so important that there are no other high-level tournaments during the eight weeks when they're being played.

» **ATP and WTA Finals:** These events end the year by featuring the eight top-ranked players in the world vying for the season-ending championship. The prize money and potential rankings points gained are just beneath the slams. The tournaments are held at a host city for a few years before moving to a different site.

» **1000-level events:** Outside the slams, these are the events players covet. The *1000* moniker denotes the number of rankings points that go to the winner. They're held throughout the year in a variety of locations across the United States, Europe, and Asia. Most of the draws have 96 players (some have 56 players), and they can take nearly two weeks to complete. Unless a player is injured or has a valid excuse, it's mandatory for each ATP player ranked high enough to play eight of the nine 1000 events. The WTA Tour has four mandatory 1000 events, with five more falling just beneath with slightly lesser point value (the winner receives 900 rankings points). Some of these stops include the Canadian Open, Indian Wells, the Italian Open, and the Miami Open.

» **500-level events:** These tournaments — played on all three surfaces — have half the point value and often half the draw size of the 1000-level events. The smaller size generally means smaller venues in midsize cities, adding up to a more intimate fan experience. Typically, several top-ranked headliners will be in the draws, but there isn't the same level of depth as the 1000s. Some of these stops include Barcelona, Charleston, Seoul, and Washington, DC.

» **250-level events:** By now, you can probably guess how many rankings points these tournaments are worth. The lower point value and smaller purses often mean less star power in the draws. It's not uncommon to see players outside the top 20 competing in the finals. Even if the events lack some name recognition, the tennis is still top-notch and the settings are more up close and personal. Some of these stops include Budapest, Cleveland, Los Cabos, and Stockholm.

» **Challengers:** Offering modest prize money, these events net the winner between 50 and 125 computer points. Challengers are not very well promoted or covered by the media, and they generally take part in remote outposts of the game. However, you can see a lot of good tennis at Challenger events.

Over the last several decades, the depth of talent has considerably increased in pro tennis. Nowadays you often a see a player fresh off a successful stint in the Challengers making a deep run into the second week of a major.

>> **ITF Circuit:** These events typically cater to young players trying to work their way up to the big leagues. They usually offer small purses, with the winner earning 10 to 20 computer points.

In the following sections, I tell you about the rankings systems, how tournaments work, and some of the recent innovations in the pro game.

The points system

Players earn points based on their performance at the events described in "The Different Levels of Tournaments." The further a player goes in a tournament, and the higher level the tournament, the more points they accrue. That's why the top-ranked players are the ones who go deep at the bigger events like the Grand Slams.

For instance, if a man gets to the fourth round of a Grand Slam, he earns 180 points; getting to the same round at an ATP 500 tournament yields just 45 points. On the women's side, a trip to the fourth round of a slam results in 240 points. Why the difference? I'm sure there's a method to the madness, but you'll have to ask the statisticians who invented the systems for their reasoning.

Both the men's and women's tours generate their computer rankings in similar ways, on a year-round "rollover" basis. All the computer points earned by a player in the 52 weeks before any given ranking period are tabulated to create the rankings. The slate is never wiped clean, as it is in team sports where the records from the previous year are erased before each new season.

Instead, the rankings are computed and issued every week — except during Grand Slams — by the WTA Tour and by the ATP Tour. Each time the rankings come out, a player's points from the same ranking period in the previous year are dropped off the computer, replaced by the points earned since the last ranking was issued. For example, if a player got to the quarterfinals of Wimbledon one year, and the following year got to the finals, they would gain the difference (+900) in rankings points.

The ranking is not based on the sheer number of points accumulated, because then players who were out there playing week after week could hog up points little by little and attain artificially high rankings.

Among the men, the computer ranking is based on a player's best 19 tournament results. The women cap it at 16 tournaments. If you played in only the required number of tournaments, all your results count. But if you played in additional tournaments, you can throw your worst results out the window. So, if a man competes in 22 tournaments, his worst three still count on his overall match record, but they don't affect his ranking.

Of course, this system also favors players who compete frequently. It's also a great tactic for getting top players to enter a lot of tournaments, which is good for the tournament game. It's tempting and almost mandatory to play more than the required number, because even the best players get upset in tournaments now and then by lower-ranked players. If a woman plays more than 16 events, she can throw out the poor results, build her ranking on her 16 best performances of the year, and make loads of extra money to boot.

Rankings and seeds

The lifeblood of the pro tours is *draw tournaments,* and believe me, it can get pretty bloody out there! Most draw tournaments also use *single elimination* events, meaning that players get knocked out of play after losing one match — no second chances or best-of-three allowed.

A typical draw tournament starts out with between 32 and 128 players. The key question, of course, is: Who gets to play in the tournaments? That's determined by the ATP and WTA Tour computer rankings. If your ranking is high enough to get you in, you're in. Nobody can keep you out because they don't like your outfit, haircut, or Instagram feed. Of course, not all the players play all the events.

Some highly ranked players get injured, and others don't enter certain tournaments for any number of reasons, including the fact that they don't play well on the surface the tournament is played on. When these players decline to play, the tournament invites lower-ranking players to play in order to get the number of players needed to hold the tournament. (Some other "special cases" are also invited to play, which you can read about in the "Qualifiers, wild cards, and lucky losers" and "Bye-bye into the next round" sidebars.) This process creates a number called the *cutoff.*

The cutoff at an all important event like a Grand Slam, which most able-bodied players enter, can be as low as 104 — meaning that you have to be ranked 104 in the world or higher to win a place in the draw. At a 250-level tournament, when other events could be going on the same week, the cutoff could be as high as, say, 220.

Whatever the cutoff number, when you're in the tournament, you have the same chance as everyone else to cut your way through the field and seize the trophy.

After the tournament selects the players, the tournament's organizers pair the players to compete against each other by drawing their names from a hat. (Computer programs actually serve the role of the hat, but you get the idea). The only exception to this random pairing process is a number of privileged, *seeded* players.

Seedings assure against the (bad) luck of the draw, which could result in two top players meeting in the first or second round of a tournament. To ensure that doesn't happen, tournaments seed anywhere between 8 and 32 players. (The Grand Slams seed 32 because the draws are so large.) The tourneys place the seeds in predetermined positions in the drawsheet. The number-one seed goes to the very top of the draw, and the number-two seed goes to the very bottom. If no upsets occur in a tournament, the eight quarterfinalists are the top eight seeds, the semifinalists are the top four seeds, and so on. However, the eight top seeds rarely all make the quarterfinals. Upsets happen at all tournaments.

After the players are paired for competition, play proceeds in the following way. (I use a typical 128-player Grand Slam tournament as an example.)

>> **Round 1:** In this round, 128 players play, and the field is cut in half by the end of the round, as it will be all the way until a champion emerges. The winners advance; the first round losers hightail it to the airport. Actually, many of them stick around to play in the doubles or mixed-doubles tournaments that are held in conjunction with the singles.

>> **Round 2:** Of the 64 players who start this round, only 32 survive the second round. It's still too early to tell if a star is about to be born at the tournament, but by the end of this round, at least five or six seeds have usually bitten the dust.

>> **Round 3:** By the time the field of 32 is cut in half, at least a few interesting stories are in the making. Getting through three rounds of a Grand Slam is a real accomplishment.

>> **Round 4:** On paper, the players in this round are supposed to be the top 16 seeded players. Ha! As few as six or seven of them may be left by this round, in which 16 players fight it out for the privilege of making the quarterfinals. If you make the quarterfinals at a Grand Slam event, you get to join the elite

"last eight" club, meaning that you get good tickets and a special, private lounge to visit, free, for the rest of your life. Final-eight club tickets are how I get my friends tickets.

» **Round 5 (the quarterfinals):** The big boys and girls come out to play, and the serious head-knocking begins. Eight players who can sniff the title prepare to fight it out. Fasten your seat belts, folks, it's going to be a tense, rough ride from here on. Everybody in this round is entitled to feel that the title is within reach, which can do funny things to their minds — and games.

» **Round 6 (the semifinals):** This is the stage at which players who wondered whether they really could win the whole shooting match start to believe they can. Many unknown players reach this round at one time or another, but only the strong survive. That's what happened to me when I played Boris Becker in the 1991 Australian Open semis. I won the first set and had a chance to go up a break of serve in the second set. I thought to myself: "I've got a chance to reach the Australian Open finals." I lost focus, reality set in, and Becker beat me in four sets.

» **Round 7 (the finals):** The gravity of the occasion is awesome. It's down to one last match. History, fame, money, celebrity — they're all on the line. Which is why, traditionally, you may have unexpected finalists at many Grand Slam events, but you don't often have surprise winners.

SHOWING IT ALL OFF AT EXHIBITIONS

Promoters outside the system also stage exhibitions, which are usually one-night stands featuring two top players in action. Exhibitions never count in the official record of the game, and they don't offer ranking points. They're kind of like lucrative freelance jobs that the top players accept to bolster their incomes.

The way tennis works, there's nothing stopping a Carlos Alcaraz or Coco Gauff from deciding that during a week away from tournament play, they'll pick up a little "spending money" from playing an exhibition against another top player, usually in a city with a prestigious venue that can stage such a match. They can earn more than seven figures for such an appearance, although they may have to attend a cocktail party before or after the match as part of the deal. Oh, demands, demands. . . .

ROUND-ROBIN TOURNAMENTS

Traditionally, the pros in the Open Era have used the round-robin format at some of their biggest, year-ending "playoff" style competitions, like the season-ending tour finals.

In a round-robin format, an even number of players or teams are divided into groups. The players in each group all play each other, in a predetermined order usually based on seedings. The players or teams who post the best records in group play advance to the knockout-style, single-elimination semifinals.

You don't have nine lives like a cat in round-robin tournaments, but you may have two or three. You can lose one or even two matches and still advance out of group play. It all depends on how the others in your group fare.

QUALIFIERS, WILD CARDS, AND LUCKY LOSERS

Every tournament makes provisions for players whose rankings are higher (worse) than the cutoff.

At Grand Slam events, 16 places in the draw of 128 are reserved for players who advance far enough through a "qualifying event" that takes place right before the tournament.

Grand Slam draws also hold eight places open for wild cards. Tournament directors can give wild cards to anyone they choose, including you and me. Fat chance! Usually, wild cards are reserved for marquee names and former champions who may no longer play often enough to hold sufficiently high rankings, players coming off injuries that caused their rankings to plummet or disappear, or promising youngsters. For instance, the U.S. Open traditionally awards a wild card to the winner of its boys' and girls' national junior championships.

"Lucky loser" may sound like an oxymoron, but it's the perfect description for certain players who get into most tournaments. Lucky losers don't take reserved places in the draw. Instead, they're the players who just missed qualifying but wait around just in case a main-draw player gets sick or pulls out of a tournament at the last minute. If a spot opens up after the qualifying rounds are completed, the highest-ranking player who lost in the last round of qualifying gets to take it.

BYE-BYE INTO THE NEXT ROUND

When there aren't enough players to fill up a draw, the top seeds often get *byes*. They get to sit out the first round of play, and begin playing only in the second round.

You may wonder how a tournament ends up having to give out byes, with all the pro tennis players running around the globe just dying to compete in big tournaments. Well, the bye has become a technique for playing a big draw in a relatively short time. If you give eight byes in a tournament with a draw of 64, you allow your top eight players to sit out the first round. For them, it becomes a 32-draw event, with the finalists playing a total of five matches — a pretty heavy workload for a one-week tournament.

Unseeded players who don't get byes have to win six matches to win the event, which may not seem fair. But those players would rather face the challenge that poses, because a field of 64 with eight byes has room for 24 more lower-ranked players in it than a full draw in a typical draw-of-32 tournament. Byes create more jobs while giving top players, who carry the heavier workload, a much-deserved advantage.

Recent Innovations

As I mention earlier in this chapter, pro tennis is traditionally slow to implement changes. When something takes hold, such as the quirky game scoring (see Chapter 1 to learn how to keep score), it's tough to unstick. But over the years, a few modifications and additions have been implemented to improve life on the tours. The three I cover in this section are some of the latest and most impactful.

Automated line-calling

Unlike other sports, the officiating in tennis is pretty black and white. There are no penalties or fouls to call, just whether the ball is in or out. Yet, even though the scope is fairly limited, it's still incredibly difficult. The ball speed can exceed triple digits and land within millimeters of the lines, giving the linesperson a split second to make a decision. Everyone is trying their best, but human error is inevitable.

My brother John became somewhat infamous for his spats with line judges and chair umpires. Although he was probably the most demonstrative, he was hardly alone. Plenty of players had issues with line calls. These arguments added a theatrical element to matches, but at what cost? The game is dramatic enough without the need for potential controversy.

The concept for *automated* line calls — in which computers and cameras call balls in and out — dates back to the 1970s. When I played on tour, we had something called Cyclops. Serves had gotten so fast and so hard to judge, that infrared lights were used to call the service lines. Cyclops was introduced at Wimbledon in 1980 and soon after adopted by the U.S. Open and Australian Open. However, it was limited in its availability and never used for the entire court.

Cyclops eventually gave way to Hawk-Eye, a system of high-speed video cameras placed around the court that could call all the lines. In 2006, Hawk-Eye was approved for official use during tournaments. Due to the expense, it was primarily used only on show courts of major tournaments. Players were permitted to challenge calls they deemed incorrect. Only a few challenges were granted per set, so players had to be choosy — but if they were right, they got to keep the challenge.

MAC SAYS

The challenge system is fun for fans — it adds a game-show element to matches — but ultimately it should really be about getting the calls correct.

One of the unintended consequences of the COVID-19 pandemic in 2020 was the fact that we got to see the value of automated line-calling firsthand. To limit the number of people on court, the Australian Open and U.S. Open removed all line judges and used Electronic Line Calling Live (ELC Live) to make all the in and out calls. From a player and fan perspective, I don't think anyone missed a beat. I'm not one to advocate putting people out of jobs, but I believe automated line-calling is clearly the future.

The serve clock

According to the rules, players have up to 25 seconds between points. So, once a point ends, you've got less than a short commercial break to catch your breath and pull some strategy together before the next point. Some players like to play at a brisk pace and never come close to the allotted time. Others employ a series of rituals — toweling off, adjusting their clothing, bouncing the ball — that can make time stand still. It's up to the chair umpire to keep track of the seconds and play time cop when a player goes afoul of the law.

In 2018, in an effort to speed up matches and hold players more accountable to the 25 seconds, tournaments started instituting a serve clock. It's placed at the back of the court and often on the scoreboard, and it counts down the time left between points. It's similar to a shot clock in basketball or a play clock in football. The chair umpire is responsible for starting the serve clock when a point ends. If there's an exhausting point, the crowd is in a frenzy, or it's late in the match, the chair may use some discretion and not start the clock immediately. However, if the server isn't into their service motion before the clock hits zero, they're issued a warning. Every time after, it's a fault and they lose their first serve.

It's debatable whether the serve clock actually does anything to quicken matches. The players seemed to have mixed feelings about it as well. At the very least, it does give fans something else to look at between points.

On-court coaching

One of the aspects I feel separates tennis from other sports is you're all alone on the court. Even though you may work on your game with a coach, when you step between the lines, it's up to you. Unless you're playing doubles, you have to figure everything out on your own. Can't seem to find the range on your shots? Your opponent can't miss? Better think of something quick or you'll be taking the L. It is the ultimate do-it-yourself sport.

But at the pro level, a player's coach is almost always sitting courtside. And not idly, mind you. Whether using hand signals or uttering advice, they do what they can to help their charge out. It's technically outside the rules, but if done discreetly, it's viewed more as a victimless crime. If the chair umpire does spy obvious courtside coaching, they can slap the coach's player with an unsportsmanlike conduct warning. A second offense draws a point penalty.

Over the years, tournaments have experimented with allowing on-court coaching. For a brief time, the WTA Tour allowed coaches to come onto the court to speak directly with their players. One of the reasons given for adopting coaching is that many coaches were already giving cues to their players. So, why not end the charade and make it legal? Another reason is that it may help players perform better and produce more competitive, exciting matches.

The current setup allows coaches to converse briefly with players when they're on the same side of the court. It has to be in the flow of the match — essentially in the brief periods between points — and not during lengthier moments like bathroom breaks. Coaches are also permitted to use nonverbal cues like hand signals at any time. All of this coaching has to be done in a fashion that doesn't bother the opposing player.

MAC SAYS

Has on-court coaching had a major impact? I can see why traditionalists don't care for it, but I don't think it has significantly changed the fortunes of any players or major tournaments. There's really no harm if the players are for it, and it has the potential of enhancing the broadcast. The interactions between coaches and players can be enlightening and entertaining to at-home viewers — squabbles within the camp can play out like reality TV. Anything that adds to the fan experience without being a detriment to the players is a win for the game.

SO, YOU WANT YOUR KID TO BE A PRO . . .

If you'd like your child to have a career in pro tennis, my first words of advice are: Forget about pro tennis; take the game one step at a time. The rewards of tennis aren't an all-or-nothing proposition. If your child fails to make it as a pro player, it doesn't mean that playing the game seriously has been a big, fat waste of your and your child's time — not by any means.

Here are four great things about tennis that have nothing to do with becoming a pro:

- **Family bonding:** Tennis can bring and keep your family close together, because people of every age and gender can play together.

- **Discipline:** It takes work, training, and dedication to get really good in tennis. Those qualities will positively influence every other aspect of your child's life.

- **Scholarships:** The vast majority of gifted junior players never make it on the pro tour. But a lot of them get free or partial rides at college and have all kinds of valuable experiences along the way.

- **Longevity:** In becoming a good tennis player, your child develops a skill that will be useful, not to mention fun, throughout life. Tennis helps players form contacts and friendships that last a lifetime. My best friends to this day are four guys I met playing 10 and Under junior tennis. Nearly 50 years and many children later, we're still all regularly in touch.

If you get seriously involved in tennis because those benefits are attractive to you for your child, the road ahead is wide open.

Chapter **20**

The Four Grand Slam Events and Cup Competitions

We all have an ingrained interest and curiosity about the biggest and the best. When we're interested in mountain climbing, we're fascinated by Mount Everest. When we follow football, we want to see who wins the Super Bowl. If we like cycling, we want to know all about the Tour de France. If you're a tennis nut, the tournaments described in this chapter are Everest, the Super Bowl, and the Tour de France all rolled into one.

The Grand Slam: The Sport's Crown Jewels

Achieving a Grand Slam remains the greatest single triumph in tennis. As the great Pete Sampras once put it after winning a title in a big pro event in Philadelphia, "I'm glad to win this title. But in the long run, nobody remembers who won Philadelphia. If you want a place in tennis history, you have to win the Grand Slam events."

To win a Grand Slam, a player must win each of the following four major tournaments in the same year:

>> Australian Open

>> French Open

>> Wimbledon

>> U.S. Open

Each of the preceding major championships are called *Grand Slam events.* Sometimes, people refer to each of the tournaments as a *Grand Slam*, as in "Carlos Alcaraz won his second Grand Slam of the year at Wimbledon. . . ." That's a little misleading, because the Grand Slam is an accomplishment involving all four events, not a synonym for any of the tournaments. Sometimes Grand Slam events are also called *majors.*

But you aren't just playing for history at the Grand Slam events. In addition to earning loads of rankings points by doing well in the biggest tournaments, and thereby boosting your world ranking, you also get a hefty check. (Turn to Chapter 19 for more on computer points.) Try several million dollars on for size, because that's about what the champions get. So, stop buying lottery tickets and run out and win a Grand Slam event (although your odds of winning either are nearly the same).

The winners (and the contenders)

Many great players over the years have won three a majors in a calendar year but failed to accomplish a Grand Slam. They include Novak Djokovic, Roger Federer, Rafael Nadal, Martina Navratilova, and Serena Williams. Only two men and three women have ever completed a Grand Slam successfully: Don Budge (1937), Maureen Connolly (1953), Rod Laver (1962, 1969), Margaret Court (1970), and Steffi Graf (1988). It's closing in on nearly 40 years since a player has managed the feat. That should tell you how difficult it is to accomplish.

Over the past decade, the sport saw two near misses at a Grand Slam. In 2015, Serena Willliams won the first three majors and found herself two wins away in the U.S. Open semifinals, but she was upset by unseeded Roberta Vinci of Italy.

In 2021, Novak Djokovic got even one match closer than Serena. After capturing the first three majors, Djokovic made it all the way to the U.S. Open finals. He was literally on the doorstep of history, but he lost to second-ranked Daniil Medvedev, who Djokovic had beaten in straight sets earlier that year in the Australian Open final.

Why the slams are grand

The Grand Slam events are played on the same three court surfaces — hard, clay, and grass — as other tournaments. They're open to all players who are ranked high enough to qualify for entry, and they use the same draw system that other tournaments use (see Chapter 19 for more on the draw system). But the Grand Slam events are special for the following reasons:

>> **Size of the draw:** The Grand Slam events are the only tournaments with 128-player draws. Most tournaments have a 32- to 64-player draw so they can be played in one week. At a Grand Slam event, a player needs to win seven consecutive matches to take the title; no other tournament is as demanding.

>> **Duration:** Each Grand Slam event happens over a two-week period. They're designed to be outdoor events, but all have installed retractable roofs over stadium courts so matches can be played indoors during inclement weather. This creates a host of variable conditions for the players to deal with and overcome.

>> **Strength of the field:** All the top players on both the men's and women's tours enter the Grand Slam events. In fact, the rest of the tennis world essentially shuts down when these events occur. Occasionally, a top player may skip the event if they're injured or not feeling capable of putting forth the effort needed to win the tournament. The Grand Slam events also feature singles, doubles, mixed doubles, juniors, *legends* (retired pros), and wheelchair draws, unlike most other tournaments.

>> **Length of matches:** Grand Slam events are the only tournaments in which the men play best-of-five-set matches in every round. (The women play best of three.) This makes for longer, and often more thrilling, men's matches, but it can also play havoc with the tournament scheduling.

>> **Spectators:** The world media focuses on Grand Slam events. They're extensively covered by various sports networks, websites, and other news outlets. Television broadcasts from Grand Slam events are live, despite the time differences. The live telecasts explain why you end up watching the Australian Open in the wee hours of the morning in the eastern United States, and why the "Breakfast at Wimbledon" broadcast begins before many viewers are close to brewing their morning cup of coffee.

>> **Tradition:** The major tournaments work very hard to maintain continuity and tradition in every area, from the rules of the game to decisions about landscaping. Recent years have seen stadium renovations and expansions, and even moves into larger grounds to accommodate the growing crowds — but by and large, tradition is cultivated, giving each event a distinctive flavor.

>> **Atmosphere:** The Grand Slam events have an incomparable, electric atmosphere. When you attend a Grand Slam event, you know that you're at a shrine in tennis. When you play in a Grand Slam event, you know that all the marbles are on the table.

The Australian Open: Summer Down Under

The Australian Open, played in Melbourne, is the first Grand Slam event of the season. It begins in mid-January, when it's the middle of summer Down Under. Before 1987, the tournament started in late December, overlapping with the holiday season. Because of the inconvenient timing, many top players opted not to make the trip. The spotty attendance put it in lower regard than the other majors, but that isn't the case anymore.

The courts

Melbourne Park, where the Australian Open is played, was the first Grand Slam site that could turn itself into an indoor stadium. The state-of-the-art stadium, which you can see in Figure 20-1, is called Rod Laver Arena. Two additional smaller stadiums named after John Cain (an Australian politician and tennis patron) and Margaret Court (one of the country's greatest players; see Chapter 24) were subsequently built. All have retractable roofs that can be closed to allow play to continue in the case of rain or extreme heat. (It easily gets up into the 100-degree Fahrenheit range courtside at the worst of times.)

Up until 1987, the Australian Open was played on grass courts. Since then, it has been played for periods of time on three different types of hard courts (Chapter 2 has all the details on the different court surfaces). The current surface is called GreenSet, which is also used at other important events throughout the season. It provides a nice medium pace that gives players of all styles an equal chance.

On extra-hot days the surface heats up and it's common for players to sling towels full of ice over their shoulders to endure the conditions. You must be in great shape and have tremendous perseverance to survive grueling battles under the blazing sun in Melbourne.

FIGURE 20-1:
Melbourne Park,
site of the
Australian Open.

In addition to three arenas, there are three "mini stadiums" sunk into the ground. Each of these secondary or "show" courts holds about 3,000 people, making them small enough to allow spectators to get up close and personal with the action.

If you're interested in going, know that the Australian Open is the most-attended Grand Slam — more than 1.1 million people in 2024 — so tickets are at a premium. Like most Grand Slam events, the Australian Open also issues *grounds passes,* which are tickets that entitle you to watch tennis anywhere on the grounds with limited stadium access.

The atmosphere

The Australian Open is the most fan-friendly of all the majors. The Australians are a casual, space-loving people, and Melbourne Park reflects it. There's reason it's been nicknamed the "Happy Slam." It has the same atmosphere that you might find in the United States at a Fourth of July barbecue — it's party time! Most of the fans, young and old, are dressed in shorts, tank tops or T-shirts, and flip-flops.

The tournament takes place during the summer school vacation, so you see plenty of young people running around the grounds. The Aussies also love their little pies, except that theirs aren't apple, lemon, or cherry — the pies are made with various meats and vegetables, as in steak and kidney pie.

The Australian Open also features some of the zaniest fan antics anywhere. Many Swedes and other people from Europe go on holiday to Australia in the winter. They turn up in large groups at the tennis center, their faces painted in their national colors. So, when a Greek player is playing in Australia, you usually see a whole section of the stadium filled with fans whose faces are painted to look like the Greek flag. They also rock the house with orchestrated cheers and chants.

The spectator gets the best of both worlds at the Australian Open — a prestigious Grand Slam event featuring the top players in the world, along with the laid-back atmosphere of a U.S.-style county fair.

MAC SAYS

I turned in my best Grand Slam singles performance at the Australian Open in 1991, getting to the semifinals. Getting there got me *Tennis* magazine's quote of the year award. After I won my quarterfinal match against Cristiano Caratti of Italy, I was asked in a press conference if I was surprised to be in the semifinals. I said, "Hey, guys, you got what everybody expected in the semifinals: Lendl, Becker, Edberg, and McEnroe."

The French Open: Terre Battue

The French Open, played in Paris, is the second Grand Slam event of the year, spanning the last week in May and the first week in June.

The French Open is the only Grand Slam event played on clay, often referred to as *terre battue*. It's harder to put the ball away with a clean winner on slow clay, so points that would end sooner on hard courts or grass are prolonged, making for longer points. It's more difficult for aggressive players to take control of the point, but creativity, point construction, and perhaps, most of all, consistency are rewarded. *Dirtballers*, the players who are willing to get down and dirty and grind out matches, often do well in Paris.

The courts

Roland-Garros, home of the French Open, is located in the 16th arrondissement of Paris. Named after a famous French aviator from World War I, Roland-Garros is easily accessible by subway from anywhere in or near Paris.

If you want to become a tennis aficionado without any of those painful *faux pas* (that's French for "embarrassing mistake") along the way, remember this: Roland-Garros is not a person, at least not any longer. People often use *Roland-Garros* as an alternative name for the French Open. In fact, in 1997 the officials of the French tennis federation sent news desks around the globe a memo specifically requesting that their tournament be identified as Roland-Garros, not the French Open. But *French Open* is easier to remember and pronounce, so feel free to use it.

The main stadium, Court Philippe-Chatrier, which has been renovated over the years, now holds more than 15,000 spectators. It's named after the former long-time president of the French Tennis Federation (FFT). A retractable roof and lights were added in 2020 to keep play going during weather delays and night matches.

Another smaller stadium, Court Suzanne-Lenglen is named after one of the country's all-time great players and one of the game's first global stars. The women's singles champion receives the Coupe Suzanne Lenglen. The stadium (shown in Figure 20-2) was completed in 1995 and seats 10,000 spectators. A retractable roof was installed on the court just ahead of the 2024 Roland-Garros tournament and the 2024 Paris Olympics.

FIGURE 20-2: Suzanne Lenglen court at Roland-Garros.

Flickr/Benh LIEU SONG/CC BY SA 2.0

A third even smaller venue, Court Simonne-Mathieu, was built in 2019 and seats 5,000. Mathieu was a two-time Roland-Garros singles champion in the 1930s and went on to serve in World War II. The women's doubles trophy is called the Coupe Simonne Mathieu in her honor. The court was built to replace the old Court 1, a fan and player favorite known as the "bullring," thanks to its circular shape. Its replacement sits below ground with greenhouses surrounding it on all four sides. It's something to see.

Even with the expanded seating capacities at Roland-Garros, French officials can't keep up with the demand for tickets. It's all but impossible to walk up and buy a ticket for the stadium, although in the early rounds, grounds passes are available. The passes won't get you into Chatrier or Lenglen, but you can walk around anywhere else, see plenty of tennis, and soak up the flavor of this sophisticated, elegant event.

The atmosphere

About four months pass between the end of the Australian Open and the start of the French Open. The long gap between the two tournaments tends to wipe clean the mental slates of players and fans. When Grand Slam competition resumes in earnest in Paris, the environment is drastically different. Instead of Australian 100-plus-degree days, fans in shorts and flip-flops, and blue hard courts, Roland-Garros offers cool-to-comfortable spring temperatures, chic clothing, and clay courts the color of dried blood. The color of the court is kind of symbolic — major tennis wars are about to get underway.

The French are known for their cuisine and style, both of which are evident at and around Roland-Garros. I still don't know why one thin piece of cured ham on a long, heavily buttered roll tastes so good, but trust me, it does. It's a staple at the concession stands of Roland-Garros. And there's nothing like a blast of French espresso coffee to give you that midafternoon boost of energy that will see you through a few more hours of fascinating tennis.

In Paris, you see men and women dressed as though they're going to a Hollywood premiere. And in some ways there are — it's showtime, and tennis is the main attraction. They're knowledgeable and serious fans, and getting dressed for the occasion shows their respect.

Beau gestes at the French Open

In 1989, my longtime doubles partner, Jim Grabb, and I "grabbed" the French Open doubles title. We won in a real squeaker over Mansour Bahrami and Éric Winogradsky in a fourth-set tiebreaker! But what I most remember about that great event was going out to have our customary pre-match warm-up. As soon as we took up our positions to hit, the *groundskeepers* (the crew that takes care of the court) rushed out and tried to stop us. They said the court was too wet. I trotted out my pidgin and basically said, "I understand, but we're in the finals later today.

We have to hit to warm up." I finally convinced them to let us hit for ten minutes. That's how the groundskeepers who sweep and water the courts in Paris are. They consider the courts their private garden and protect them like watchdogs — even from finalists in the event.

Wimbledon: The Hallowed Grounds

Wimbledon, the third leg of the Grand Slam, is the preeminent tennis tournament in the world. It has managed to hold that position for nearly 150 years by building on its own traditions and mystique, instead of making any sweeping changes. Wimbledon usually starts on the last Monday in June and ends in the second week of July.

The courts

Wimbledon, the oldest continuing tournament of them all, has been played at what's now commonly called the All England Club since 1877. Remarkably, it has never left the village from which the tournament takes its name. The biggest change in the tournament's history was the club's move, in 1922, from Worple Road to its present location on Church Road. Figure 20-3 shows the grounds of the All England Club.

FIGURE 20-3: The grounds at the All England Lawn Tennis & Croquet Club, home of Wimbledon.

THOMAS LOVELOCK/Getty Images

Wimbledon is famous for its ivy-covered Centre Court, an octagonal edifice with a roof over the stands. The roof helps give Centre Court an intimate, theatrical atmosphere. In 1997, Wimbledon opened its secondary stadium, No. 1 Court, which has seen upgrades since. In addition, courts No. 2 and No. 3 have recently been rebuilt and are wonderful and more intimate spaces to watch the matches. In 2009, a retractable roof was installed over Centre Court in order to maintain play during wet weather. In 2019, No. 1 Court got the same treatment. If there's one drawback about Wimbledon, it's the rain.

There is no conspicuous sponsor signage at Wimbledon, as you find at other Grand Slam events. Companies like Slazenger and Rolex have had long-standing relationships with Wimbledon, but their presence is discreet. You may not even notice it, but the companies obviously feel that the investment is worthwhile.

But the truly singular thing about Wimbledon is the grass courts. Back when I played, critics said that tennis on grass had gotten too fast and power-oriented, and was mostly just a boring serving contest, especially among the men. Points were lightning quick, with lots of net play and limited rallies.

Steps were taken to grow the grass differently to help slow the ball down and give it a higher bounce. Today, the courts at Wimbledon play more like hard courts. Points are much longer, and the matches are more interesting to watch. In the past, the grass around the net would be torn up by the end of the tournament because of all the volleying, but today it's the baseline that suffers the most damage.

Ultimately, though, it's the very best players, not the hardest servers, who almost always take the title. Because the points can be short and power is still rewarded, Wimbledon is a remarkable test of nerves, not merely serves. When two players serve well, the outcome of an entire set can be determined by a single break-point opportunity or even a lucky bounce. The pressure to win those rare, key points is intense, and it brings out the very best — or worst — in many players.

The atmosphere

You can't help but love Wimbledon. London seems to shut down for two weeks while the tournament takes place. Fans who visit the grounds feel like they've arrived at a shrine, like the Baseball Hall of Fame in Cooperstown, New York, or the Sistine Chapel. Wimbledon works hard to keep it that way. It's still the only Grand Slam that actually has a curfew.

Wimbledon is a 30- to 40-minute Tube ride from central London. First-time visitors usually make the mistake of getting off at the Wimbledon stop. For the tournament, you get off one stop earlier, at the station called Southfields.

When you arrive at the grounds, the fans are in a long line that sometimes stretches for half a mile in front of the entrance. They wait for 48 hours or longer to get one of the few tickets available on a walk-up basis. When I played, it always made me feel humble, like I was privileged to be a tennis player, and I felt a heavy responsibility to make all those tennis fans happy. That undoubtedly adds to the desire to do well at Wimbledon and the pressure that accompanies it.

After you get inside the grounds, you feel like you're in a cross between a park and museum. The grass courts look and smell lovely. The players still compete in all-white attire. The concession stands feature outdoor tables, where fans eat strawberries and cream or *dutchees,* which are like a cross between a hot dog and an Italian sausage. Champagne and Pimm's — a fruity, gin-based spirit — are popular adult beverages. College kids picking up pocket money hawk *choc ice* (what the British call an ice cream bar) and other ice-cream treats. Various stands offer spicy Thai dishes and fish and chips, wrapped in the pages of yesterday's newspaper.

Wimbledon means so much to the Brits, but they haven't had a lot of hometown success at the tournament, especially on the men's side. Fred Perry won the title in 1936, but then came an epic drought. Roger Taylor made three semifinals in the 1960s and '70s, and Tim Henman made four semifinals in five years in the late '90s and early 2000s. Year after year, the British press, hungry for a champion, bemoaned its players' defeats. In 2012, Andy Murray — a Scot — broke through to the Wimbledon final but lost a heartbreaker to Roger Federer. The following year, under tremendous scrutiny and pressure, Murray ended the 77-year curse. In 2016, he repeated the feat for good measure. The British tennis faithful are still on a honeymoon.

Wimbledon fans range from little old ladies in sensible shoes carrying *brollies* (umbrellas), to bankers and debutantes chattering away on cell phones. The fans like to line up on either side of the barriers leading to the entrance to Centre Court to catch a glimpse of the royalty as they're driven right up to the entrance in chauffeured Rolls-Royces and Bentleys.

The players used to observe special protocols if royals were present for the matches. An attendant would tell you just before you walked out on Centre Court whether royalty was present in the Royal Box. If the royals were there, you had to pause on your way to your courtside chair, turn, and bow at the waist. The women players had to curtsy! However, in 2003, the All England Club and the Royal Family agreed it was time to end the tradition. It had grown a bit too stuffy, even for Wimbledon. Some players still opt to do it from time to time, but it's completely up to them.

It's fitting that the rain was just as much a part of my biggest match at Wimbledon as I was. There's always a threat of rain at Wimbledon because the weather is fickle. And when a grass court gets wet, it's almost impossible to play on until it dries out completely. For that reason, Wimbledon has a crack crew of groundskeepers who are ready at a moment's notice to pull tarps over the court as soon as the first raindrops fall — even if it's just a sprinkle.

Each court at Wimbledon has a little box by the umpire's chair with three different-colored lights. They correspond to the logic of the traffic lights we're used to in the United States. The green light means continue playing because rain is not a threat, yellow means rain is on the way, so get ready to cover the court, and red means cover the court immediately. When the umpire and groundskeepers see the lights changing, they go on alert.

One year I was playing the Dutchman Jacco Eltingh in a tight, third-round match. It was the fifth set of a real nip-and-tuck match on an outside court. The fans were packed 12 deep on either side of the court, totally jamming the walkways on either side. I was ahead, 6-5, and the score was deuce. Two more points and it was my match!

Then the light changed from yellow to red. All of a sudden, half a dozen guys barreled onto the court and began to drag a tarp across it. Jacco and I looked at each other, and we both threw up our hands, as if to say, "Hey, what's going on here?" Then we had to dash for the sidelines to grab our tennis bags before they too were covered by the tarps. It turned out to be just a sprinkle, and soon we were back on court, with the proverbial green light to finish the match. I won the next point, bringing me to match point. But Jacco fought it off, and he finally beat me, 12-10, in the fifth set. That was back when the tournament played out a final set until one player won by two games. (Chapter 4 has all the details on match scoring.)

STANDING ON CEREMONY IN CENTRE COURT

Centre Court at the All England Lawn Tennis & Croquet Club features a special area called the Royal Box, behind the baseline at the north end of the stadium. When certain members of British royalty are present, strict rules of conduct apply.

The Duke and Duchess of Kent are the official patrons of Wimbledon. When the Duke is present in the Royal Box on a hot day, none of the other male guests remove their suit jackets until the Duke does so. It's a very Wimbledon thing. So are the strawberries and Devonshire cream for which the event is famous, and the hydrangeas sprouting from flower boxes all over the place, and queuing overnight for tickets. The British love tradition, and nobody does tradition better than Wimbledon.

The U.S. Open: Under the Lights in NYC

The U.S. Open concludes the Grand Slam season. It's held in the New York City borough of Queens, in the last week of August and the first week of September. The tournament takes place at the United States Tennis Association (USTA) Billie Jean King National Tennis Center (BJKNTC), a facility built in 1978. For 49 weeks of the year, the BJKNTC is a public tennis facility serving the people of New York. But for the increasingly popular and expansive *Fan Week* (the week before the tournament that holds the qualifying round, exhibition matches, and other fan experiences) and the following two weeks of the tournament, it's the home of the U.S. Open.

The courts

The National Tennis Center was built in a great big hurry in 1977 and 1978, in order to get it ready in time to host the U.S. Open. The result was a bare-bones facility, featuring hard courts, a lot of asphalt, and a lack of any sense of tradition.

In 1997, the USTA completed a spectacular two-year renovation and opened Arthur Ashe Stadium (shown in Figure 20-4). Overnight, this least appealing of Grand Slam sites became a fitting home for the U.S. Open. The facilities and services were upgraded in a zillion little ways for fans and players alike. In 2006, the complex was renamed to the Billie Jean King National Tennis Center in honor of all the things Billie Jean did for the sport, both on and off the court.

The renovations haven't stopped — the grounds are constantly getting updated. Ashe Stadium now has a retractable roof, as does Louis Armstrong Stadium, keeping play going during rain delays. The Grandstand and Court 17 provide show-court settings for smaller audiences. Fans pack the side courts to get an up-close look at the top players in the world, or take a break from the action at one of the many upscale ethnic food concessions or memorabilia shops.

As far as the courts themselves, the Laykold hard courts offer a true and medium-fast bounce, suitable for both baseliners and attacking players. You can see great play from every type of player at the U.S. Open.

The atmosphere

At the end of the long, hot tennis summer, players arrive in New York hoping to catch one last second wind to power them through the tournament. During the last week of August, New York can produce debilitating heat and humidity. By the second week, just after Labor Day, the temperatures often drop, and the night matches can even have a chill in the air.

Besides the heat, the other distinguishing feature of the tournament is the New York thing. You know — it's all about energy. It's a place to see and be seen snapping a few selfies for your Instagram feed. The grounds are overflowing with people, and the luxury suites in Ashe are littered with the rich and famous. Plus, the U.S. Open puts on night matches, under the lights, which provide additional atmosphere for both players and spectators, especially as the patrons start to enjoy themselves with a few adult beverages. In fact, all the courts are lit, so in the early part of the tournament, many of the day-session matches extend well into the night.

If you want to have a great time at the U.S. Open, walk around, checking out the field courts, instead of feeling that you have to be in the stadium, watching Taylor Swift watching Janik Sinner. You'll see great tennis, and you'll get a good dose of New York madness at its best without even trying.

Experienced U.S. Open attendees know all about the Honey Deuce, the tournament's signature cocktail, made of vodka, lemonade, and raspberry liqueur, and served with a skewer of melon balls. Opinions vary on its taste, but there's no denying its popularity. In 2024, more than 500,000 of the drinks — at $23 a pop — were sold during the tournament. Night matches just wouldn't have the same level of "entertainment" without it.

Moments of glory at the U.S. Open

Some of the most memorable matches at the U.S. Open are the "twilight specials" — the matches that begin in the late afternoon but, because of the five-set format, end up stretching into the New York night. These matches give you a great sense of the New York crowd. The people inside the grounds jam into the seats surrounding the epic battle. The fans who have tickets for the night session are allowed into the grounds but held out of entry into the stadium. The confusion, impatience, and crowding all add to the tension created by the match.

MAC SAYS

Some of my favorite Open moments happened during these twilight matches. Like the time I lost the first two sets to the Russian player Alexander Volkov in the third round and came back to win in five sets, under the lights, on the old Grandstand court that used to be part of the Louis Armstrong Stadium structure. That year, 1995, I reached the quarterfinals, where I lost a real shoot-out with Boris Becker.

In 1996, Pete Sampras defeated Álex Corretja of Spain in a most memorable twilight special. Pete got so disoriented and exhausted in the fifth set on the Louis Armstrong Stadium court that he actually vomited between two points late in the match. Between points, Pete was leaning on his racquet like it was a cane, but he won the epic, five-set quarterfinal match and went on to take the title over Michael Chang.

JOHN MCENROE SHINES ON SUPER SATURDAY

One of the great traditions established at the U.S. Open when it moved to Flushing Meadows was "Super Saturday." Because of the needs of television, the two men's semifinals and the women's final all happened on the last Saturday of the event. Sometimes a doubles final or exhibition was also sandwiched in there, to give the crowd a little break from the intensity of the singles.

In 1984, "Super Saturday" started at 11 a.m. and didn't end until 11:14 p.m. That's over 12 hours of top-quality tennis, the best deal that die-hard tennis fans ever got.

The first men's semifinal, between Ivan Lendl and 19-year-old Australian Pat Cash, ended with a fifth-set tiebreaker. The women's final, between Chris Evert and Martina Navratilova, ended with Navratilova winning 6-4 in the third. My brother John and his opponent, Jimmy Connors, didn't even get on the court until 7:28 that night.

(continued)

(continued)

John ultimately beat Jimmy on the longest, and perhaps greatest, day in tennis history, 6-4, 4-6, 7-5, 4-6, 6-3. Luckily for him, John was able to bounce back just 18 hours later to beat Lendl for the title.

In 2001, the women's final between Venus and Serena Williams was moved to prime time on Saturday night, requiring a separate ticket, thus ending the "Super Saturday" tradition. And eventually the men lobbied to have the semifinals moved to Friday, squeezing in a day of rest before the finals. So, Saturday is currently just the women's finals in the afternoon. But for a brief time, it was one of the best tickets in all of pro sports.

International Team Competitions: The Davis, Billie Jean King, Laver and United Cups

International team tournaments are terrific, unique events for several reasons:

>> **The pressure:** The players play for their teams or nations rather than for themselves. In fact, their names often aren't even mentioned when the score is announced; the umpire just says, "Game, USA." Competing for your nation, and your team, is a lot more of a responsibility than doing it for yourself, so most players feel a lot more pressure to perform. Very strange things can happen in the heat of international team competition. Players can go to pieces from the pressure, or they can really rise to the occasion, defeating much higher-ranked opponents.

>> **The pageantry and color:** The events are much more lively and colorful than typical tennis tournaments. The atmosphere is often closer to the kind you have at a soccer match or big-time college football game, with fans cheering madly, waving flags, and banging drums. The chaotic atmosphere often gives players, even the heavy favorites, conniptions.

>> **The strategy:** At team events, the captain is allowed to sit courtside in a chair alongside the players. They can confer as much or as little as they like during changeovers. It's just one of the ways that strategy plays a key role. The doubles match often takes on major strategic importance in close ties. Deciding who will play your doubles matches, including whether to use your top singles player and risk wearing them out, is a crucial decision.

- >> **The team experience:** Playing on a team in an individual, sometimes lonely sport like tennis really makes you appreciate the benefits of the team experience — the communication, camaraderie, company, and mutual support.

- >> **The uniforms:** You get to wear really cool track suits and uniforms, often with the name of your nation emblazoned on the back. I cherish my USA Davis Cup team track suit and keep it under wraps in my closet because I'm so proud to have had the chance to represent my country in the Davis Cup. One day, my grandchildren will see the jacket, and I'll tell them all about what an honor it was to have played in the Davis Cup.

In the following sections, I walk you through the four major international team competitions.

The Davis Cup

In 1900, a Harvard student named Dwight Filley Davis invited some British players to visit Boston and compete for a silver cup that Davis himself purchased. They had so much fun (the host American team won) that they decided to have the competition every year, with the winner holding possession of the cup until beaten. Gradually, more and more nations were invited to compete. The International Tennis Federation and its national affiliates, like the USTA, run the Davis Cup. (You can read more about these two organizations in Chapter 19.)

I represented the United States in Davis Cup on four occasions as a player, and after retiring, I captained the U.S. team for ten years. Back then, the top 16 countries based on performance got to vie for the cup in the elite World Group. These were the teams that fought their way up through international, regional competition to claim their places. The competition was spread throughout the entire season, with each round pitting one nation against another in a single-elimination format. Home-court advantage was determined in an alternating fashion between the two countries. The winner of the team match, called a *tie*, moved on to the next round to face the winner of another tie. Eventually two nations battled it out at the end of the year for the cup.

MAC SAYS

My tenure as Davis Cup captain is currently the longest in U.S. team history. Without a doubt, it's one of the highlights of my professional career. I was lucky to coach great players and special teams, two of which made the Davis Cup finals. The first time, in 2004, we faced Spain in a soccer stadium in Seville on red clay. After we lost the first singles match, Spain threw us a curveball by subbing in an unknown lefty teenager in his first Davis Cup match ever against our top player, Andy Roddick. I thought: "We may actually have a shot to win this thing." Suffice it to say, after Rafael Nadal won the match in four sets, the rest was history.

We ended up losing that tie, but in 2007, our fortunes turned in Portland when we beat Russia to win the cup. It's the last time the U.S. team has held the title.

However, since my association with the Davis Cup, the format has gone through some changes. The length and demands of the tour schedule caused many top players to frequently skip their country's ties. Many supporters of the event felt the end product lost some of its significance without the biggest names involved. So, in 2019, the format was streamlined to culminate in a weeklong round-robin event held in one location for the top countries. It's still a bit confusing figuring out which teams qualify and when those ties take place, but the new system has been effective at drawing back some of the game's top talent to the finals.

The United States has been the most successful Davis Cup nation, winning the competition a record 32 times. Unfortunately, the Davis Cup doesn't have quite the same popularity and importance in the United States that it has in some other countries, despite our fabulous record. Not winning it since 2007 also hurts its relevance where the sporting public is concerned.

The Billie Jean King Cup

The women have their own version of the Davis Cup, called the Billie Jean King Cup. It was formerly called the Fed Cup because it's contested between teams representing their respective national tennis federations.

The Fed Cup — originally called the Federation Cup — began in 1963 with the entire competition held during one week in one location that changed from year to year. In 1995, the Fed Cup adopted its shorter name, as well as a Davis Cup home-and-away formula played throughout the year.

Since that time, the Fed Cup has undergone various formats. The current setup was instituted in 2020 — the same year the name was changed to the Billie Jean King Cup — in which the top 12 teams play over six days in one location for the cup.

The Laver Cup

Named in honor of Rod Laver (see Chapter 23), the Laver Cup is a three-day men's team hard-court competition held indoors in September. It was conceived by Roger Federer and his management company, pitting Team Europe versus Team World to mirror golf's Ryder Cup format. The location rotates yearly between venues in Europe and the rest of the world. It started as more of an exhibition in 2017, but by 2019 it had become an official Association of Tennis Professionals (ATP) event.

Each team is composed of six players — the three top-ranked players for each region are guaranteed a spot, along with three captain's picks. The competition uses both singles and doubles formats, with the point value of the matches increasing with each day. Each player must participate in at least one singles match during the first two days, and four of the players must play a minimum of one doubles match. The first team to reach 13 points wins the cup.

I was fortunate enough to be the vice-captain for Team World — my brother John was team captain — for the opening seven Laver Cups. It's a fantastic event featuring many of the best players all competing on one court. That said, it doesn't exactly push the needle in terms of media coverage and the more casual sports fan. Only time will tell if interest in the event ever rises to that of the Ryder Cup.

The United Cup

First contested in 2023, the United Cup is the latest entry to the international team event. It's held from the end of December through the beginning of January in multiple Australian cities ahead of the Australian Open. What makes the 18-team, round-robin format appealing is the fact that it's a dual-gender event. Each team match consists of three matches: men's singles, women's singles, and mixed-doubles. That's a setup rarely found on the tours, which the players themselves really appreciate and embrace. And with the Australian Open just around the corner, and several tough matches guaranteed, turnout is usually high-caliber.

Chapter **21**

Tennis from the Stands and On-Screen

You may wonder whether I can write a whole chapter about being a spectator. After all, watching tennis is pretty simple — you just sit yourself down and watch, right?

Watching tennis can be just that simple, if you want it to be. But if you put a little effort into *how* you watch tennis, you may be surprised by how many nuances to the game you can discover and how much you can really improve your own game by watching someone else (especially a pro).

Making the Most of Your Day at a Tournament

Nothing equals the thrill of really being there. Use this section as your guide to experiencing a tournament to its fullest.

Don't leave home without . . .

Bringing along the right gear can enhance your enjoyment of tennis by ensuring that you remain comfortable at all times. For example, getting caught in a sudden, brief rain shower and getting wet before you can find shelter can dampen your whole day.

TIP

For your big day at the tournament, have the following items handy:

>> **A light rain slicker:** If even a slight chance of rain exists, take a light raincoat. In addition to protecting you if you get caught in a shower, a raincoat can come in handy if you have to wipe down wet seats.

>> **A hat:** A hat or a visor provides protection against glare or a strong sun.

>> **Light-colored clothing:** White and other light colors reflect sun, helping to keep you cool. Dark colors soak up that sun, leaving you feeling like a baked potato. Wear a light-colored shirt to the tournament, and take a change of shirt if it's really hot.

They don't think they're actually going to play, but it has become something of a tradition for tennis fans to show up at tournaments wearing their tennis garb. Tennis fans wear tennis clothes to matches for probably the same reason that a Los Angeles Lakers fan wears a Lebron James jersey to a basketball game: to show support. Also, most tennis apparel tends to be lightweight and light-colored, which you'll appreciate as things at the match heat up.

>> **Sunblock:** You can get a painfully sunburned nose under a hot sun in less time than it takes for the players to complete a three-set match.

>> **Earbuds:** If the tournament you attend has streaming audio coverage (the Grand Slam events often do), listening to it can be very useful, even if you don't want to hear commentary. Sometimes a tournament sponsor such as American Express will offer card members headphones that carry the broadcast. Otherwise. you typically have to stream it from your smartphone off the tournament's app.

The broadcast often gives you up-to-the-minute updates from other courts, saving you the trouble of making a trip to the main scoreboard or around the grounds to find out what else is happening. That way, when a great match develops on a field court, you can get over there before the rest of the known universe arrives.

REMEMBER

You could technically use your phone like a radio, but having earbuds or headphones avoids the possibility of disturbing players or spectators.

>> **Money:** Tennis tournaments are typically full of concession stands and souvenir shops. Forewarned is forearmed. Many tournaments now use only

contactless pay, meaning they don't accept cash and take only debit cards, credit cards, or mobile payment services like Apple Pay. So, make sure you have some plastic on hand.

>> **A felt-tip pen or permanent marker:** You never know when you could run into a pro player. Feel free to ask for an autograph if you do! You can even buy balls for a small donation for that purpose at some events, or find them in the grass outside the practice courts.

WARNING

For safety reasons, most tournaments don't allow you to bring a backpack or larger bag into the venue. A small purse or handbag for personal items is usually acceptable. And in many cases, the stadium prohibits certain items, such as outside beverages. If you do happen to be carrying something too large or disallowed, bigger tournaments often have daily lockers where you can store them for a small charge. To avoid any nasty surprises, check the tournament website if your ticket doesn't explicitly state what's permissible to carry inside the tournament grounds.

Who to watch — and where

Buy your ticket well in advance to be sure that you can get into the tournament you want to attend. Usually, the ticket gives you an assigned seat number in the main stadium, which is where the top players play. You can go to your seat and watch the match in the stadium at any time or wander around checking out different matches that take place on the outside, or *field*, courts all the way up to the very last days of an event. Those seats are typically first come, first served.

TIP

If a marquee name plays on a field court, stake out a seat as soon as the previous match ends. Many savvy tennis fans attend tournaments, so matches involving big-name players get crowded quickly.

These days, more and more tournaments offer different ticket options. One of them is the ubiquitous *grounds pass,* which gets you into the tournament grounds but doesn't guarantee you a seat anywhere. This means that you don't have a seat in the stadium (but some ushers may allow you to slip in and watch for a little while unless the stadium fills up). A grounds pass is a great deal because you can see a lot of action, on various courts, during a typical tournament.

At many stadiums, the seats closest to the court are marked off in separate, four- to eight-seat sections called *courtside boxes.* These are the most expensive seats in the house, and they sell out in advance of the tournament, for the whole event, to private individuals and corporations who pay many thousands of dollars to reserve all the seats in the box for the entire event.

TIP

Don't try to sneak into one of the private boxes. People coming and going and checking seat numbers causes a disturbance to the players and fans around you.

The first thing to do when you walk into a tournament is to look over the *draw-sheet* (which tells you who plays whom next in the tourney) and the schedule of play. These details are usually available on the tournament app, or on the Association of Tennis Professionals (ATP) or Women's Tennis Association (WTA) apps, but some smaller events may still use printed programs that generally cost you a little cash. Having this information is especially important in the early rounds because you can plan your day by picking out the players and matches that seem most intriguing.

You probably want to watch at least one match with a big-name player. No doubt about it — people love to watch the top players, the "celebrities" of tennis. The top players have an aura about them, and there's no substitute for seeing them in person.

Most of the time, you find those big names hunkered down in the larger courts, like stadium court. However, you may get lucky and find a popular player on one of the smaller courts. You just need to check your schedule to see where the big names are slated to play that particular day.

TIP

Keep in mind, however, that if you limit your tournament experience to watching only the most popular players, you miss out on some of the best action. Day in and day out, until the last few days of a tournament, the best matches usually involve less well-known names playing on the field courts. By all means, hit the stadium court to see how the top seeds look and play in a live setting, but arrange your day so that you aren't missing a great match on an outside court.

TIP

You can find out who those good (but lesser-known) players are in any of the following ways:

>> Follow the game regularly by reading sports and tennis news websites, or by following journalists or broadcasters like me on social media.

>> Search online for previews of the event before you attend the tournament.

>> Ask a knowledgeable friend.

TIP

Keep your eyes peeled for good doubles matches. Although some doubles matches lack the drama of one-on-one competition, the points are often faster, more diverse, and more exciting. Many top singles players don't play doubles these days, but when they do, you're in for a real treat. In a doubles situation, many top singles players let their personalities — and strokes — really flow.

Don't feel committed to stay and watch a match to conclusion just because someone told you that the match would be good or because you've heard of one or both players. You can never tell beforehand whether a match will be a gigantic battle or a boring blowout.

If you're merely curious about some players, watch a few games early in the match, when you can sit nice and close. But keep moving and try to find the match that's turning into a real doozy, no matter who's playing.

In general, watch the beginnings of matches to satisfy your curiosity, and watch the later stages of close matches to see the nuances of the game and the personalities of the players. Let the scores, not the players' names, determine where you're going to spend your time. Close matches are the best matches.

The best vantage point

Sitting very close to the court, where you can actually hear the players talking to themselves and where you can really study their strokes and observe their reactions, is great fun.

Although sitting close to the court is great, you'll understand the game better if you sit up above court level and back a few rows. From that vantage point, you have a much better view of how points develop and which strategies work, without sacrificing intimacy.

Spectator etiquette

Tennis has a strong tradition of spectator etiquette, and you're expected to follow it at most tournaments. (If you don't, you'll hear from the umpire or the ushers — as well as the players.) The great thing about spectator etiquette isn't that you get to feel hoity-toity by observing it, but that it makes the fan experience richer and better.

Even if you forget everything else I tell you about watching live play, please remember this, the all-important, first rule of spectatorship: *Don't talk or cry out during a point.* You have lots of other opportunities to shout like a madman, if that's what you want to do — like when your favorite player successfully converts an important break point or when they win an important game or set with a winner. Wait until the point ends before you cheer, and calm down as the server gets set to serve again.

TIP

The following key suggestions also make watching tennis at a tournament more enjoyable for you — and for your neighbors:

>> **Mind the changeover protocol.** If you want to enter or leave a court, most tournaments require you to wait until the changeover. You may not have to do this when entering the upper-level portals of a stadium because fan movement and noise don't distract the players when they occur well above their line of vision. But at court level, movement is distracting — especially to the player serving. In 2024, both the Australian Open and U.S. Open tournaments did allow fans to enter and exit courts at the end of any game. The added freedom seemed to be welcomed by spectators, although it can cause small delays in play until everyone is out of the players' sight lines.

>> **Don't play linesperson.** During a long rally at a key time in a close match, people *ooh, aah,* and even scream while the ball is in play. It's a natural human reaction, no matter how hard you try to stop it. But occasionally, someone yells "Out" loudly enough to make a player think that it's an official call from the linesperson. That's a terrible thing to do. A spectator should never directly influence play.

MAC SAYS

In the past few years, fans got into the habit of whistling after they thought one of the players got a bad call. It's okay to do that, I guess. But it's funny how often the loudest whistles emanate from the section of the seats with the worst view of the line in question. And with many tournaments now changing over to automated line-calling, it's really just a waste of breath. (Turn to Chapter 19 to learn more about other recent innovations in the pro game).

>> **Respect your neighbors.** The people sitting in front of you don't care how that personal injury lawsuit is going or why your friend is getting divorced. Keep your comments at an intimate volume, even after a point has ended.

>> **Turn off your ringer.** The ringing of a phone is a real distraction to the players, not to mention your fellow spectators. Turn on the Do Not Disturb or vibrate setting on your smartphone so you remain a spectator, not a participant.

>> **No flash, please.** Make sure when you take that courtside selfie, the flash on your smartphone isn't set. Some phones have an automatic flash when lighting is dim, which can really distract the players.

>> **Get a babysitter.** It's a long, exhausting day at a tennis tournament. The sun can get very hot. It's no place for young children, no matter how proud you are of your 18-month-old's ability to wave their hand in a perfect forehand fashion.

Watching Tennis on Television and Streaming Services

Televised tennis allows people who can't go to a real tournament to watch the pros in action. People in Pittsburgh, Pennsylvania, and Bonn, Germany, and all those other cities that currently don't have big pro events can watch them on TV, computer, or smartphone.

The electronic advantage: ESPN, Tennis Channel, and the apps

Televised coverage of tennis allows you access to information that the spectator in the stadium can't get. In the United States, ESPN and the Tennis Channel are the networks that provide pretty much all the television coverage. Each of these networks also has an app that provides additional coverage, as well as stands in for viewers who have "cut the cord" and don't subscribe to traditional cable. Tennis Channel also has a second network, called T2, with original programming and extended coverage of ATP and WTA tournaments; it's available through various streamers, such as Amazon Prime Video.

When you watch a tennis match on TV or streaming platform, you get not only commentary on the play from experts (such as myself) but also a bucketload of statistics and other interesting bits of information. In fact, we broadcasters work with people whose specific job is to put together interesting statistics and lists to add an extra dimension to our audience's experience. As camera and computer technologies continue to advance, these tidbits get even more sophisticated.

TV tennis also gains you access to many more matches than you could follow if you were at the venue. Because most networks cover several matches at once, if one battle experiences a lull, the network can switch to a match that's just starting to heat up. When ESPN covers a Grand Slam event (it has broadcast rights for the Australian Open, Wimbledon, and U.S. Open), it has cameras on just about every court. Subscribers to the network's app, ESPN+, can watch play on the outer courts, even if there are no broadcasters providing commentary. Even though I'm paid to be a talking head, it can be fun to watch a match with just the sounds of the ball hitting the racquet, the players' effort, and the crowd reaction.

In addition to all that, you also get the technical benefits of the mediums, including slow-motion instant replay, which can help you analyze the play, and candid glimpses of important folks in the crowd.

What you can't see on your screens

For all its splendors, viewing tennis at home remains a two-dimensional endeavor. Some subtle things just don't come across clearly on a screen, so pay attention to the commentators, who are usually on top of the nuances, including the following:

>> **Spin and slice:** You can't see spin, one of the most common tactics used in tennis today. Broadcasts can give stats on how much topspin a player puts on the ball — usually given in revolutions per minute (RPMs) — but the numbers can't convey the impact it has on the shot. Viewers also have a hard time seeing a slice that really bites into the court and stays low. (Chapter 7 tells you all about slice and spin.)

>> **Height of the bounce:** Because the camera that shows most rallies resides well above court level, you can't tell how high the ball bounces. High- and low-bouncing balls, which are often unbeknownst to the viewers, always create problems for players.

>> **Pace:** Television doesn't give you a good idea of how fast and hard the ball travels. Statistics give you an inkling of the speed, but to really appreciate the power of a 145-mph serve or a powerful forehand, you have to see it firsthand.

Viewing the Pros — like a Pro

TIP

Regardless of whether you watch a match live from the stadium or from the comfort of your living room, you can improve your own game by watching the pros closely. Specifically, focus on how pros deal with the following:

>> **General strategy:** Watching the pros shows you that players who can do anything with the ball don't do just anything with the ball. They plan their work and work their plans. Watch the pros to see the strategies they adopt and the tactics they use to implement them.

>> **Shot selection:** Watch which shots the pros hit at key times in a match. That's usually the difference between a top-10 and a top-100 player.

>> **The attacking mindset:** Most beginners don't like to play *attacking tennis,* in which players move forward to end points at the net. But even if you don't want to attack, consistently failing to come to the net when it's a clear advantage to do so is a wasted opportunity. The pros have no such fears. Even though baseline play dominates the game, coming forward is still a worthwhile strategy when given a good opportunity.

In the following sections, I tell you about the key moments and stats to be aware of when watching a pro match.

The first two service games

Players usually make opening statements in the first games they serve. In the first few games, the player in effect declares, "This is who I am, and this is what I'm going to do."

For example, when players serve to set up an aggressive forehand on the next shot, you can bet that they'll continue with that strategy until it proves futile. You can pretty much count on big hitting and a fast-paced match. But if the server favors spin and location over pace, and backs it up with a barrage of steady groundstrokes, their plan is probably one of consistency, which leads to slower-paced matches with longer points.

REMEMBER

Don't read too much into an early service break. Often it's just a sign that a player is a little jittery or not fully warmed up rather than a sign of a poor strategy.

Always watch where returners line up to receive serve. This position tells you a lot about how the returner wants to play and about the effectiveness of the server. Players who line up more than a foot behind the baseline are either counting on their ability to prevail in baseline rallies, with good defense, or worrying about getting aced. Players who line up near the baseline or even inside the court are usually intent on playing aggressively, dictating the pace and tone of rallies, even in baseline rallies. They also show that they aren't afraid of the server.

Key games

All the games in tennis are worth the same amount, but they don't all have the same value. For example, the game that a player serves when it's 2-2 isn't as important as the one that they serve with a 5-4 lead, for the set.

The tiebreaker is the only game that decides the outcome of a set all by itself, so naturally it deserves your full attention. Other games can significantly impact the outcome of the match, including the following games:

>> **The all-important seventh game:** Players sometimes crank it up a notch in the seventh game. If it's 3-all, scoring a break in the seventh game creates a great advantage. Holding serve focuses pressure on the opponent to hold serve from 3-4. If either player has scored one break or more, the seventh game usually determines whether the set will be won easily or salvaged by the player who's behind.

IT AIN'T OVER UNTIL JIMMY SINGS

During the U.S. Open of 1991, I had the misfortune to meet Mr. Jimmy Connors, when he was 38. Jimmy had been my older brother's rival, but it seemed that he just wouldn't vanish from the scene, even though everybody kept writing him off.

I won the first two sets in that match, and I had a break in the third. At that point, just about everyone watching the match went home or turned off the TV. Jimmy ultimately kicked and clawed his way back into the match. Worse yet, he beat me. He went on to become *the* story of the tournament, getting worldwide attention for his unlikely and remarkable run to the semifinals.

It was bad enough that I lost. But over the following years, an incredible number of people came up to me and said, "Gee, I can't believe I missed that great match between you and Connors. I went home during the third set."

I'd reply, "Thanks for reminding me." Believe it or not, people still talk about this match — and what they missed. For years after the match, CBS had it on steady rotation anytime the U.S. Open was in a rain delay. One of the many great benefits of having a roof on Arthur Ashe Stadium is I never have to turn on the TV and relive blowing that two-set lead ever again.

» **Games after breaks:** The player who scores a break really needs to consolidate the advantage by serving a solid game. The broken player can't mope with a crucial return game coming up. The way players handle games after breaks tells you a lot about how they cope with the twin perils of success and failure.

» **Set games:** The way that the pros serve and return during set games is telling. An unsure player often plays it too safe or takes too many chances. Both mistakes are born from lack of confidence. A confident player takes the game to an opponent but doesn't take stupid or unnecessary chances and trusts their own will and skill.

Statistics

In competitive tennis, patterns of play emerge from all matches because players try to use their strengths to attack their opponents' weaknesses.

For example, Jannik Sinner likes to hit his serves off to the side of the service box to open up the court for his aggressive groundstrokes. He feels comfortable engaging in rallies with the court open because he's fast enough to run down an opponent's shots, and he's precise and consistent enough to run other players ragged. Watch three or four of Jannik's matches, and you can see this pattern as plain as day.

All-out attacking players — serve and volleyers in my day — are in very short supply these days. Players have gotten so good at returning serve and hitting passing shots that it has become an extremely difficult style to win with consistently. But creative players still serve the ball and rush to the net, or approach net after hitting a ball from the midcourt to keep their opponents off-balance.

Not all patterns are obvious to the naked eye. That's why people keep *statistics*, the black-and-white numbers that quantify trends in a match.

TIP

The following statistics can help make patterns of play emerge for you:

>> **Second-serve points won:** This is a seriously significant statistic because, as the old adage goes, "You're only as good as your second serve." This is one of those age-old words-of-wisdom sayings that's actually true!

Top servers often win as many as 80 percent of the points played with their first serves. But even at their best, pro players can't expect to get much more than 70 percent of their first serves into play. And on a bad day, their first-serve percentage may be as low as 40 percent. That makes the second serve crucially important, especially in pressure situations, like when they're behind 15-30 or down break point.

Even the top-ranked players in the world usually only win slightly over 50 percent of their second-serve points on a good day. A player who wins only 25 percent or 30 percent of their second serves is usually in trouble in the match.

>> **Break points converted:** The returner's most significant statistic. When the returning player can break serve by winning the next point, that's a *break point*. Those are the biggest points in tennis because breaking serve puts you in position to win the set if you just manage to hold your own serve until the end of the set. The serve is such an advantage in tennis that break points can be hard to come by, especially on fast surfaces.

This is also why even the best returners rarely convert even 50 percent of their break points. And conversion rate isn't nearly as important as the amount of break points converted. Would you rather be 2-for-3 or 3-for-10 on break points in a match? The more breaks, the better.

>> **Break points saved:** This important statistic shows how well servers perform under pressure. Players with powerful serves tend to rank among the best in this category because they're capable of serving aces or unreturnable serves in threatening situations.

>> **Aces:** Players who hit a lot of aces and unreturned serves have a huge advantage. Getting one or two free points in a game in which you need to win only four points is a real asset.

>> **Unforced errors:** Players who make a lot of unforced errors don't win many matches, period. An average of two unforced errors per game really reduces your chances of winning.

5

The Part of Tens

IN THIS PART . . .

You get some tasty treats in this last part of the book. I give you ten fundamental tips to jump-start your game. Then, to finish things off, I tell you about my personal tennis favorites — the men and women tennis greats and the best Grand Slam matches of the Open Era.

Chapter **22**

Ten Tennis Tips

The great thing about a good tennis tip is that it cuts right to the chase. It's a little bit of advice that goes a long way. It's a teaspoon full of medicine that can cure a game that seems to be stuck in a terminal stage of going nowhere. In this chapter, you get not just one tip, but ten really great tips.

Watching the Ball

Keeping your eye on the ball doesn't sound like a tall order, but the truth is, tennis players find all kinds of excuses to break the focus they need to play well. Your concentration and attention could wander while you play, either because of something actually going around within view, or because you start thinking about other things. The result: You forget to watch the ball.

TIP

Follow these tips to help yourself watch the ball:

» **Move your head.** Don't focus on your opponent. Move your head to track the ball, right up to the moment of contact.

» **Look for the writing on the ball.** Doing so naturally makes you watch the ball more closely as it comes closer to you.

» **Watch the point of contact.** Keep your head still as you hit, which is just as important as moving your head as the ball approaches.

Moving Your Feet

When you plant your feet, you slow your reaction time to the next shot. You automatically curb your ability to get to the ball in time, making it hard to get in position to make a good, smooth, controlled stroke.

Good tennis players have happy feet. They dance around as they wait to return serve or start for the next ball. If your heels hit the court during a point, they shouldn't be there for very long. Hurry back to the middle of the court after you hit a groundstroke. Take longer strides to cover big chunks of the court; then use short, quick steps to find the perfect hitting position.

Getting the Racquet Back Early

Late swings account for the majority of poor shots. Except when balls whiz around at warp speed, you always have time to get the racquet back early enough to make a good shot. As soon as you see where the ball goes, forehand or backhand, get the racquet back. And remember to turn those shoulders and hips as you do so instead of just whipping your arm back.

Turning Your Shoulders

When you hit groundstrokes, volleys, and overheads, your opposite shoulder should turn toward the net before you hit the shot. In other words, if you're a righty and your opponent hits the ball to your forehand, you turn your left shoulder toward the net. This helps get your racquet back into the proper position without having to think about making a big backswing.

Keeping Your Head Up When You Serve

Keeping your head up helps you watch the ball all the way to the point of contact. You'll have a better chance of hitting the ball solidly, as well as avoid pulling your upper body down and the ball into the net with it.

The best way to get into the habit of keeping your head up is to make a conscious effort to look up at the sky or ceiling when you serve. Try not to move your head until the racquet passes through contact. You'll be in great shape if you do that.

Following Through

Many players have trouble mastering a nice, smooth, full, low-to-high swing and resort to flat, short strokes. Such a swing may get the ball back over the net in the short term, but it lowers the ceiling on your potential to produce steady, deep, powerful shots.

Practice your follow-through on the forehand side by catching the racquet in your other hand, up around your shoulder, as you finish your shot. Doing so encourages you to take a nice, long swing with an appropriate follow-through. If this exercise feels strange or uncomfortable, you aren't hitting with an effective, low-to-high swing.

Using Your Hips with the Two-Handed Backhand

Many beginners have trouble controlling their two-handed backhands, and even advanced players often struggle with hard shots hit to their backhands.

Concentrate on turning your shoulders and hips away from the court as the ball approaches, keeping your arm at a relaxed, comfortable distance to your body. You automatically give yourself a nice, compact backswing. Then use your hips and shoulders in unison, turning toward the court as you make your swing. Using your hips gives you a compact but solid backhand.

Stamping Out Bad Volleys

Stamping your foot on the volley is a great way to make sure that you get a little bit of shoulder turn and a lot more oomph into your volleys. If you're a righty, you stamp your left foot on your forehand volley and your right foot on the backhand side. (Lefties use their opposite feet.)

Don't just lift your foot and stamp it, step forward and stamp. This helps you on two critical fronts: It promotes a slight shoulder turn, and you step into the shot.

Pointing at the Overhead

No matter how tricky or easy the overhead, you can take out a great insurance policy by making sure that you point at the ball as you prepare to hit it. If you hit the ball while it's in the air, point at it with your free hand as soon as you see where it's going. If the overhead is up in the ozone layer and you have the time and position to let it bounce before you hit it, wait until the ball bounces and then point. Pointing creates a target and also tells your brain when it's the right time to swing.

Loosening Up Your Competitive Game

Tennis players quickly find out that there is a big difference between hitting good shots during practice and repeating those shots in a match. You can tell yourself to relax and that it's just a silly game, but it doesn't always help.

To loosen yourself up during competition, create a practice situation at the match. Take a deep breath and blow it out to release some tension from your body. When the next shot is hit to you, let it bounce and then simply focus on taking a smooth, fluid swing, the kind you routinely make during practice. Just try to meet the ball in the sweet spot. Turning the stroke into a practice swing loosens you up and allows you to hit with more racquet speed and spin, both of which are critical to control.

If you can play as well in a match as you do in a typical practice session, you're really on the road to tennis success.

Chapter **23**

The Ten Best Men Players of the Open Era

B oy, was this rough! I didn't realize how many great players the game has produced until I started closely examining the stats. Some guys are going to @ me for not making the list, but I have my reasons — and they have their titles for comfort. My biggest criteria for making the list is performance in Grand Slam events. They're the heart and soul of this game. The guys who win the most Grand Slam titles are the best players, end of story.

I also decided that I would stick to players who won at least one Grand Slam singles title in the Open Era, which began in 1968, when pros were finally allowed to compete at the biggest tournaments. For that reason, players like Australia's Roy Emerson didn't make the list, even though he won more Grand Slam singles titles (12) than several of the players on this list.

I considered listing the ten in order of merit, but then everybody except the number-one guy would want to kill me. So, I decided to make things easy on myself by listing the guys alphabetically. One of the nice things about picking players from only the Open Era is that I watched them play, took my lumps against them on court, or called their matches from the booth.

Andre Agassi

Straight out of Las Vegas, Andre Agassi was a tennis rock star. Sporting bleached blond, feathered hair and clad in denim shorts and neon colors, Agassi burst onto the tour in late '80s like a supernova. He flew in a private jet, had a tabloid love life, and was the biggest box-office attraction in the sport. To be honest, I can't do Andre's colorful life justice in this short write-up (I'd recommend his extraordinary autobiography, *Open*, for the full picture). Let's just say his career was something of a roller-coaster ride, and it was never boring.

Although he didn't possess the physical gifts of some, Agassi may be the best pure ball-striker ever. (When Ivan Lendl played him for the first time, he quipped that Agassi was nothing more than a "haircut and a forehand.") He had incredible timing and stood right on top of the baseline to bully opponents around the court with his punishing groundstrokes. His two-handed backhand down the line and aggressive return of serve were particularly devastating.

Agassi's look and brashness fit well with Madison Avenue. In 1989, he took part in a Canon Rebel camera ad campaign with the slogan "Image Is Everything." Many felt that basically summed up Agassi's attitude for the early part of his career, and the tagline dogged him. Even though he quickly rose into the top five, the belief was he'd rather be a flashy showman blistering winners than grinding out tough wins — the proof being losses in the finals of the 1990 U.S. Open and 1990 and '91 French Open, each in which he was the heavy favorite.

It wasn't until the 1992 Wimbledon that Agassi finally broke through at a major. Ironically, he had skipped Wimbledon for three straight years (1988–1990) because he didn't like grass courts or being forced to wear all white. That kind of paradox was a through line of Agassi and his career. He didn't play the Australian Open until 1995 because the tournament was held in January, and he didn't want to interrupt his holidays. Not only would he win that tournament, but he'd be champion Down Under three more times, making it his most successful slam.

Agassi's game evolved when he took Brad Gilbert on as coach in 1994. Gilbert convinced Andre to employ higher-percentage tactics. Instead of always wanting to outhit opponents, he would try to outwork them. He would eventually cut off his signature locks — it was actually a wig — and his shaved head added to his more workmanlike persona. Getting into tiptop shape gave Agassi the confidence he could thrive with the strategy. That year he won his first of two U.S. Open titles.

In April 1995, Agassi reached number one in the rankings for the first time. By the fall of 1997, a wrist injury and off-court struggles caused his ranking to plummet to 141. In one of the more remarkable comebacks, Andre rediscovered his passion for the game and in 1999 won both the French Open and the U.S. Open, and for the only time in his career ended the year as world number one. The French Open title gave him a career Grand Slam, becoming the first man to win all the majors on three different surfaces. In a tennis fairy tale, Agassi married fellow all-time great Steffi Graf in 2001 (see Chapter 24 for more on Graf). In 2003, at 33, he become the oldest player at that time to hold the number-one ranking. Agassi was also a U.S. Davis Cup stalwart, playing on three winning teams, and won an Olympic gold medal.

A troublesome back forced Agassi to retire from tennis at the 2006 U.S. Open. He finished with eight Grand Slam titles and was runner-up seven times. Since leaving the tour, he has been no stranger to playing exhibition matches for charities or to support his own Andre Agassi Foundation for Education. He has also helped coach several touring pros, although he refrains from full-time travel.

Björn Borg

Björn Borg stole the hearts of teenyboppers around the world with his flowing blond locks, and he destroyed opponents with his impregnable game, steely concentration, and incredible speed and fitness. He also amassed one of the most unique and puzzling records in modern tennis.

Björn was barely 18 years old when he won his first Grand Slam title on the clay at the French Open. He would win five more titles in Paris, establishing the male record at that tournament. Borg performed well on clay because he was a remarkable athlete — fleet, powerful, and amazingly consistent from the baseline. Nobody could out-rally or outrun him.

But this quintessential baseline player confounded experts by winning at Wimbledon, the domain of attacking (not baseline) players, five consecutive times, from 1976 to 1980. The feat is simply mind-boggling. Björn was legendary for his ability to play without showing any emotion or anxiety, and many believed that temperament allowed him to thrive under the intense pressure at Wimbledon.

Yet Borg was consistently frustrated and anxiety-prone at the U.S. Open, even during the three years that it was held on his beloved clay courts. And he bothered to make the trip Down Under to compete in Australia only once. So Borg ended up winning all of his Grand Slam titles in Paris and London, on the slowest and fastest of surfaces. (Turn to Chapter 2 for more information on court speeds.)

Björn shocked the tennis world when he walked away from the competitive game at just 25 years old. He still had lots of great tennis left in him, but he felt too burnt out. He had won 11 Grand Slam single titles, tying at the time for second place on the all-time list with Rod Laver. Björn made two half-hearted comeback attempts, but he couldn't make his game click after he left the tour. Borg would show up occasionally at the European Slams, but he really got introduced to a new generation of tennis fans when he served as captain for Team Europe for the first seven years of the Laver Cup. (You can read more about the Laver Cup in Chapter 20.)

Jimmy Connors

Let me tell you about Jimmy Connors. He was just a few days short of his 39th birthday, and seemingly way over the hill, when I played him in the first round of the U.S. Open. I won the first two sets and led 3-0 in the third set. Then Jimmy stormed back and beat me and a bunch of other people to reach the semifinals. It was an astonishing run that nobody would have predicted. But that's Jimmy for you. He had the longest career of any great player ever, competing in Grand Slam events for 22 years, starting in 1970.

Jimmy "Jimbo" Connors quickly became the poster child for the new Open Era in tennis when he stormed the international scene in 1972, two years after competing in his first Grand Slam event. He was brash, cocky, outspoken, and always at odds with the establishment. He often got into verbal sparring matches with opponents, officials, and even fans. His on-court behavior was often offensive to many fans. People either loved or hated Jimmy; there was no middle ground. And he didn't seem to want any.

Connors's grandmother and his teaching pro mother, Gloria Connors, designed his game. This slender mama's boy played like a badger, ripping apart opponents with devastating groundstrokes and laserlike backhands that he threw himself into with abandon. Jimmy also had impeccable footwork and an iron will.

Jimmy built his résumé at his beloved U.S. Open, winning the tournament five times, at least once on each of the three surfaces used for the tournament in his time — grass, clay, and hard court — proving his talents on all three surfaces. He said he always loved to play for the New York crowds because "They like to see you spill your blood and guts out there, and I'm willing to do that. That's my kind of tennis."

Eventually, Jimmy collected eight Grand Slam singles titles (five at the U.S. Open, two at Wimbledon, and one in Australia). He held the number-one world ranking for a total of 268 weeks. Connors also holds the record for most titles on the pro tour, with 109.

Novak Djokovic

The most Grand Slam singles titles (24), weeks ranked number one (428), Masters titles (40), and year-end championships (7). When it comes to the most important titles and achievements, Novak Djokovic's résumé is tops in the men's game. Relying on a steady, almost technically flawless ground attack, unparalleled defensive skills, and an insatiable will to win, the man from Serbia has rewritten the record books.

The numbers and consistency are almost inconceivable. Four times in his career, the Djoker won three of the four slams in a season (2011, 2015, 2021, and 2023). In one of those seasons (2021,) he was just one match shy of completing the Calendar Slam, losing in the U.S. Open finals. Over a span of 24 Grand Slam tournaments from 2010 to 2016, Djokovic made it to at least the semifinals 23 times, winning 11 of the titles. From 2021 to 2023, he won seven of ten majors entered and lost in the finals twice. As Rafael Nadal came to rule in Paris, so does Djokovic Down Under, winning the Australian Open a tournament-record ten times.

Early in his career, though, Djokovic's level of fitness and toughness were actually considered shortcomings. He retired from several high-profile matches, which drew the ire of fans and even fellow players. But Djokovic just used that as fuel to become one of the game's greatest big match players and fiercest competitors. He searched for ways to bolster his stamina, including adopting a gluten-free, vegan diet that he credits with improving his health and endurance. He trains his flexibility more than most players work on their groundstrokes and will experiment with all forms of training modalities — even famously relaxing inside a pressurized pod to speed recovery — if there's a chance it will enhance his tennis.

All that work has paid off in giving Djokovic tremendous inner belief. When he needs a point, he has an uncanny ability to go into "lockdown" mode and simply not miss. Like his remarkable ankle-breaking slides, when a match is in doubt, Djokovic will bend, but he rarely breaks. On three enormous occasions against Roger Federer — 2010 and 2011 U.S. Open semifinals, and 2019 Wimbledon finals — Djokovic saved two match points and went on to win the match. In his matches that have gone to a fifth set, he has a sparkling 40-11 record. He also currently holds the best tiebreak winning percentage (65.5 percent) in the Open Era. When everything matters most, Djokovic is at his best.

THE GOAT DEBATE

The incredible accomplishments and rivalry between Novak Djokovic, Roger Federer, and Rafael Nadal (the "Big Three") spurred what became known as the GOAT debate. That's shorthand for *greatest of all time*. The discussion over which of the three deserves the title sparks lots of passionate back-and-forth among their loyal and very vocal fan bases — it has become sport on social media. The lines are drawn and there's no crossing them. If you're going strictly by records and accomplishments it's tough to argue against Djokovic. If the ultimate measure is dominance, there's no topping Nadal's work at the French Open. But if the criteria is sheer brilliance, peak Federer is second to none. Just remember: Whichever player you side with, fans of the other two will think you're nuts.

For all his success, Djokovic has had a complicated relationship with fans. He certainly has his supporters, but playing against the immensely popular Federer and Nadal put Djokovic in more of the villain role. It doesn't help that he's not afraid to be controversial and can be confrontational on court, even egging on spectators in the stands. But that combativeness has been a great source of motivation for him; I don't think he'd be nearly as successful without it.

As of this writing, Djokovic is still active. At 37, most of his chief contemporaries have already retired and there's no telling how many more years he will play. But it wouldn't surprise me at all if he grabs a few major titles before he's through.

Roger Federer

Roger Federer is tennis royalty. Blessed with jaw-dropping racquet skills, the Swiss Maestro played with flair and artistry that seemed almost effortless. He floated across the court like a dancer, and then struck like a viper, carving up opponents with a varied assault of power, precision, and finesse. When he would take off into full flight, it was a joy for fans to watch — and a horror show for his opponents. Federer amassed an astonishing playing record, all while carrying himself with the grace and style of an old Hollywood star. This combination of otherworldly shot-making and suave demeanor made him admired in the locker room, adored in the hearts of tennis fans, and an endorsement machine.

Federer rose to the top of the ranks right on the heels of Pete Sampras, who was retiring from the game. In fact, the first time the tennis public really took notice of Federer is when he beat Sampras — one of his idols — in a five-set classic in the fourth round at the 2001 Wimbledon. Federer had a potent serve and a beautiful, versatile one-handed backhand, but it was his lethal, quick-strike forehand that became his calling card.

Of the players in his immediate generation, such as Lleyton Hewitt, Andy Roddick, and Marat Safin, Federer had no equal. From the 2003 Wimbledon — the first of his record eight titles in London — through the 2010 Australian Open, he won 16 of the 27 major tournaments. Perhaps his greatest masterpiece was 2006; that year, Federer compiled a 92-5 match record, won 12 titles including three majors, and reached the finals in 16 of 17 tournaments he entered. His 15th major singles title at the 2009 Wimbledon pushed him ahead of Sampras into sole possession of first place on the men's all-time list.

But Federer had to contend with two rivals from the next generation — first Rafael Nadal, and then shortly thereafter, Novak Djokovic — whose ascension loosened Federer's stranglehold on the men's game. The "Big Three," as they were referred to, battled it out for major titles during the 2010s. Federer's Grand Slam successes dwindled — at one point enduring a streak of winning just 1 in 21 entered — and he suffered numerous heartbreaking defeats.

In 2017, after not having won a slam since the 2012 Wimbledon and missing chunks of time due to knee and back injuries, Federer enjoyed a late-career renaissance. He captured both the Australian Open and Wimbledon titles, and defended that win Down Under in 2018. That February, he moved back into the number-one ranking, becoming the oldest player at the time to do so, at 36 years old. Injury bug crept in again in 2020, and after surgeries and rehab proved ineffective, Federer officially retired in 2022.

All in all, Federer captured 20 Grand Slam titles (11 times the finalist) and 103 career titles, spent 310 weeks at number one, and finished year-end number one five times. He was and remains arguably the most popular and marketable player the game has ever seen.

Rod Laver

The legendary Australian Davis Cup coach, Harry Hopman, gave Rod Laver the nickname "Rocket" when Laver was just a teenager. Hopman called Laver "Rocket" sarcastically, because Laver was a scrawny, frail youth. Also, his shots rocketed all over the place back then, landing inside the boundary lines of the court only on select occasions. But Hopman recognized Laver's genius, even at that early age.

The freckle-faced southpaw stood just under 5-foot-9 and weighed a mere 145 pounds at the peak of his career, but Laver developed a massive left arm and wrist with which he pioneered the use of topspin in the modern game. (Read more about topspin in Chapter 7.)

Laver remains the only man to complete a Grand Slam in the Open Era, and the only player of either gender ever to win two. Laver won his first Grand Slam as an amateur in 1962, and another one as a pro in 1969. (You can read more about the Grand Slam in Chapter 20.) Granted, three of the four Grand Slam events were held on fast grass courts back then, favoring attacking players like Laver. But Laver won the French Open on clay twice, proving that he was a multifaceted player. In 1969, the year of his second Grand Slam, Laver amassed one of the greatest single-year records in history. He won 17 singles titles and put together a 106-16 record.

Laver also was a major force in popularizing tennis in the early 1970s. The only thing Laver missed out on during his career was the explosion of prize money that began shortly after he stopped playing. He finished his career with 11 Grand Slam titles. Today, you can often find "Rocket" in the stands at Grand Slam tournaments or attending the Laver Cup, which is named in his honor.

Ivan Lendl

You know the bad guy in the old-fashioned cowboy movies, the one in the black hat? That was Ivan Lendl, the bony, angular, self-made champion from the Czech Republic. Right from the start, the 6-foot-2, 175-pound Lendl made an effort to become tennis's version of the Terminator, and he came to take great pride in being compared to a machine.

Beneath that image, Lendl was a relentless worker who overcame a lot of youthful insecurity and a reputation for choking away big matches. He went on to set new standards for tennis players in training and fitness. He took special pleasure in outslugging opponents with his heavy, powerful groundstrokes, hit with one hand on either side, under conditions that demanded the most in stamina and perseverance.

Lendl won eight Grand Slam singles titles, three each at the French Open and U.S. Open and two in Australia. In the late stages of his career, Lendl made a Herculean effort to win Wimbledon. But he was never quite comfortable enough at net to accomplish the feat, even though he got to the finals twice (1986 and 1987) and posted an excellent lifetime winning percentage of 77.4 percent at Wimbledon.

Lendl claimed a seemingly permanent place in the U.S. Open finals, reaching the championship match an incredible eight times in a row, starting in 1982, and winning the title three times. His main rivals were two Americans, Jimmy Connors and my brother John, and Lendl's performances in New York gave them fits.

Building his résumé over a 17-year career, Lendl won 94 pro titles and was ranked number one for 270 weeks. A bad back sidelined Lendl for good in 1994. He initially stayed away from the pro game after retiring to help raise his four daughters, but he eventually returned to coach Andy Murray and was in the Brit's player's box for all three of his Grand Slam titles.

John McEnroe

John McEnroe burst on the tennis scene by reaching the Wimbledon semifinals of 1977 as an 18-year-old, after fighting his way through the qualifying tournament. (See Chapter 20 for more information on the qualifying tourney.) In 1977, punk-rock music was storming England, and rebellion and in-your-face honesty were in the air. It was the right time for John, and he quickly set the tennis world on its ear.

A left-hander, John just carved and diced opponents to pieces with his slice serve and razor-sharp volleys. He was also such a good doubles player that Peter Fleming, one of his regular doubles partners, once made the wisecrack, "The best doubles team in the world is John McEnroe and anybody." Unlike a lot of other artistic players, John was also a fiery, volatile, indomitable competitor who feared no one. He ended Björn Borg's streak of five consecutive Wimbledon titles in 1981, one year after Borg beat him in what many people still think is the greatest tennis match ever. (You can read more about that match in Chapter 25.)

All told, John won seven Grand Slam singles titles — four on his home court at the U.S. Open and three Wimbledon titles, all between 1979 and 1984. He also won ten Grand Slam doubles titles. He played the Australian Open only five times, getting to the semifinals once. John had a great chance to win the French Open in 1984, leading his rival Ivan Lendl by two sets to love, but he let the match get away. It was the most heartbreaking loss of his career.

In 1984, John posted the highest winning percentage of the Open Era with his 82-3 record. That year, he won 13 of the 15 tournaments he entered. John was also the greatest Davis Cup player in U.S. history. He helped the squad win the cup five times, and he established new records for singles wins (41), years played (12), and combined singles and doubles wins (59). When John was asked why he was such a stellar and reliable Davis Cup performer, he said, "My mother, Kay, made me promise to play Davis Cup with all my heart and soul whenever I was asked." Obviously, John was a good son. He also single-handedly reignited declining U.S. interest in the Davis Cup with his heroic performances.

John played his last Grand Slam event in 1992, the same year as one of his great rivals, Jimmy Connors. These days, John keeps a hectic schedule. He has six kids, owns an art gallery, oversees the John McEnroe Tennis Academy, and does TV commentary. Being able to share a booth with my brother is one of the highlights of my broadcasting career.

Rafael Nadal

More than anything Rafael Nadal loved a good fight. Simply known as Rafa, Nadal was a relentless baseline brawler. He had the speed to track down any shot, the consistency to endure 40-ball rallies, the power to crush a winner at any moment, and the doggedness to do it point after point, hour after hour. If you were going to beat Nadal, you were going to have to earn it. And very few could.

Hailing from the Spanish island town of Mallorca, Nadal was taught to play and coached early on by his Uncle Toni. When he picked up the sport, Nadal played with two hands on both his forehand and backhand. As he got older, his uncle encouraged him to pick a side for his forehand, and even though Nadal does many things right-handed — writing, basketball, golf — swinging a racquet left-handed felt more natural. It was a genius decision.

Nadal's trademark lasso-whip forehand developed into one of the game's all-time great shots. He hit his topspin forehand with such a ferocious vertical swing that he often followed through over his head, with the racquet finishing above his dominant shoulder instead of across his body. As a lefty, he could pound his forehand crosscourt to pick on most of his opponent's backhands and wear them out — a tactic he used to repeated brilliance on his beloved red clay, where he won 63 of his 92 ATP Tour singles titles. At one point, he won an Open Era record 81 consecutive matches on the surface.

Indeed, there was no surer bet in tennis — all of professional sports, really — than the "King of Clay" winning the French Open. Just after turning 19, Nadal won his first title in Paris in 2005. Another 13 (!) more would follow, including one streak of five, and two streaks of four titles in a row. His overall career record at the French Open was an eye-popping 112-4. In 2021, the tournament paid tribute to Nadal by erecting a statue in his honor.

But Nadal was clearly more than a one-surface wonder. Early in his career, people questioned things like the reliability of his backhand, the quality of his net game, and his lack of touch. He was full of tics and quirks like constantly fiddling with his shorts before serving and lining up his water bottles just so after a changeover. None of it mattered because he simply loved to compete. He quickly proved he could win any tournament on any surface. At 24, Nadal was the youngest player in the Open Era to win each major, and he would eventually win them all multiple times.

Beyond his extraordinary abilities, it was Nadal's tenacity and exuberance on court, punctuated by his leaping fist pumps and roars of *"Vamos!"* that endeared him to fans. He rarely, if ever, took a point off. Playing such a physically taxing style exacts a toll, and Nadal battled knee and foot problems throughout his career. He still managed more than 20 years on tour before announcing his retirement in 2024. Rafa finished with 22 major singles titles, second all-time among men, just ahead of his great friend and rival, Roger Federer.

Pete Sampras

"Pistol" Pete Sampras was a mild-mannered, even-tempered, great sport, who also has one of the deadliest and smoothest games that tennis has ever spawned. The California kid played in his first Grand Slam event in 1988 at just 17 years old, and went on to compile a remarkable record that made him one of the greatest and most well-liked players in tennis history. If he had a flaw, it may be that he made the game look so easy, and appeared so laid-back, that people tended to take his genius for granted.

Pete had tremendous power, and he liked to play an attacking, serve-and-volley game on fast surfaces. He delivered his serve with one of the cleanest and smoothest service motions ever. Pete also felt comfortable playing in the backcourt, using his groundstrokes to set up his patented, lethal, running forehand winner.

Sampras's game and athleticism translated particularly well to the grass courts of Wimbledon. He won the title in London seven times in eight years (1993-1995 and 1997-2000). His 2000 win was his 13th major title, which moved him ahead of Roy Emerson into first place all-time. Pete also won five U.S. Open and two Australian Open championships.

When describing Pete's record, it's really more telling what he never managed to accomplish. He made one semifinal at the French Open but never played for the title. That's the glaring hole in his résumé. Everything else is there. Pete even had many glorious Davis Cup moments, none better than the 1995 final played on a clay court specifically made to slow the game down to Pete's disadvantage. But Pete won both his singles matches and partnered with Todd Martin for the doubles win, as the United States prevailed, 3-2. It was one of the greatest performances in Davis Cup history.

Pete also had a career walk-off for the ages. In 2002, his game appeared to be sliding. He came into the U.S. Open that year seeded 17th, coming off a shocking second-round loss at Wimbledon, and not given much of a chance. But he found the old magic in Flushing Meadows and made it to the final for a third straight year, where he faced a familiar foe: Andre Agassi. The two had contested the 1990 and 1995 U.S. Open finals, both Sampras wins. This time was no different. Sampras raised the trophy, soaked in the ovation, and never played another match again. Talk about a mic drop.

When Pete retired, he held the records for most Grand Slam singles titles (14), weeks at number one (286), and consecutive seasons finishing as the year-end number one (6), which he still owns. Many fans once considered him the best of the best. That sentiment may have changed because of the accomplishments of Djokovic, Federer, and Nadal, but there's little doubt that Pete was tops of his generation.

Chapter **24**

The Ten Best Women Players of the Open Era

The women I mention in this chapter changed the face of tennis forever. They all helped turn the sport into an art form, and they provided inspiration for both men and women players all over the world. Facing the difficult task of selecting only ten such players, I picked this group of players, listed alphabetically, from those women who play (or played) in the Open Era, which started in 1968.

Margaret Court

This shy, gangly Australian was not a leader off the court like her contemporary, Billie Jean King. All she did was personify the words of Al Davis, the iconic owner of the Oakland Raiders football team, whose team motto was "Just win, baby." Court did that in spades, rolling up a mind-boggling combination of 62 titles in Grand Slam events, including the most singles titles of any woman ever, 24.

Margaret was an introvert who shunned the limelight. She sprouted to nearly 6 feet tall in her youth and worked very hard to improve her coordination, fitness, and strength. Her hard work paid off as she matured and began to bludgeon opponents into submission with an attacking game that was almost impossible to thwart. Her wingspan, endurance, and consistency were formidable assets.

Margaret won her native singles title a record 11 times. She also won three Wimbledon, five French, and five U.S. singles titles, bringing her Grand Slam total to an unmatched 24 titles. In 1970, Court became the second woman in history to win a Grand Slam. She won 21 of 27 tournaments that year and compiled a 104-6 match record. She's also one of three players to have completed a career Grand Slam in singles, doubles, and mixed doubles, often called a *Boxed Set*.

Court retired in 1976 to a married life of semi-seclusion in Australia. She became a lay Christian minister and subsequently founded Margaret Court Ministries. Some of her hardline conversative views on social issues, such as same-sex marriage, have not been well-received in an open-minded sport like tennis. As a result, in recent years, there have been calls to change the name of Margaret Court Arena — named in her honor in 2003 — at the Australian Open. But Tennis Australia hasn't budged, believing that the naming first and foremost recognizes Court's outstanding playing record.

Chris Evert

Chris Evert established a new, er, baseline for baseliners, taking the defensive, consistent game to the highest realm.

Chrissie didn't have the obvious athletic gifts of players like Martina Navratilova or Steffi Graf. She wasn't powerful, but she hit the ball cleanly and crisply, with the balance of a ballet dancer. She also had wonderful anticipation and a great innate strategic sense. But more than anything, she could place the ball with pinpoint accuracy. Her groundstrokes were so steady that nobody could outlast her in a rally. When her opponents attacked to avoid getting into rallies with her, Chris would fire passing shots by them.

Over the years, Chrissie had great rivalries with a succession of players, starting with Evonne Goolagong and extending through Tracy Austin and, eventually, Steffi Graf. But the woman who brought the best and most out of her was Martina Navratilova.

Chris had a rich 20-year career ending in 1989. By that time, she had compiled the highest winning percentage in pro history, winning 1,309 matches to a paltry 146 losses for an .899 percentage. She reached the finals in 76 percent of the 303 tournaments she entered. Chrissie won at least 1 Grand Slam singles title for 13 consecutive years, gathering a grand total of 18. She won seven titles at the French Open alone. She may have won even more, but she skipped the event for a few years in favor of team tennis.

Today Chrissie helps run her family's tennis academy in Boca Raton, Florida, and remains a steady presence in the broadcast booth. In 2022, she revealed that she is fighting ovarian cancer and has become a staunch advocate for early detection.

Steffi Graf

A superbly athletic player, Steffi Graf was a prodigy from the small town of Brühl in Germany. She won her first important title at age 16, beating Chris Evert on clay to claim it. Graf didn't have perfect textbook strokes — but she covered the court like a blanket and developed a monster forehand and vicious slice backhand that helped her win 22 Grand Slam singles titles.

Steffi was blessed with Olympic-caliber speed. Her opponents desperately tried to find Graf's backhand, but she used her flawless footwork to stalk the baseline and set up her atomic forehand. She had a powerful, dominant style of play that often resulted in lopsided scorelines in her favor.

Above and beyond those qualities, Steffi was an utterly focused, dedicated, and consistent champion. She won each of the Grand Slam titles at least four times and held the number-one ranking for a record 377 weeks. Over a three-year span (1987–1990), she reached 13 consecutive Grand Slam finals, winning 9. In 1988, Graf became the third woman in tennis to win a Grand Slam, adding a unique twist: That year, she also won the gold medal at the Olympic Games in Seoul, South Korea, completing a Golden Slam.

In the early '90s, Graf was overtaken in the rankings by Monica Seles. Clearly through no fault of Graf's, one of her crazed fans stabbed Seles during a match between the two, sidelining Seles for several years. With no comparable rival, Graf won 10 of the next 13 Grand Slams she entered.

By 1997, Graf was struggling with a host of recurring injuries. Her results and participation were both inconsistent over the next few years. In the spring of 1999, Graf found her form again and made Open Era history by beating the top three seeds on her way to winning a memorable French Open final over Martina Hingis. Steffi followed that up with a run to the Wimbledon finals. That summer she announced her retirement at age 30.

In 2001, Steffi married fellow all-time great, Andre Agassi (see Chapter 23). She occasionally plays exhibition matches and still cracks a mean forehand.

Justine Henin

Playing in the era of *big-babe tennis* (a term coined by tennis commentator Mary Carillo to describe an era dominated by powerful women players), diminutive Justine Henin still managed to stand out. Standing just shy of 5-foot-6 put the Belgian at a competitive disadvantage to many of her peers. However, Henin used exemplary technique and an aggressive mindset to punch well above her size. When almost all the top players preferred a two-handed backhand, Justine's signature shot was a deadly one-handed backhand that set up the rest of her well-rounded, all-court game.

Henin forged her reputation on the red clay at Roland-Garros. Her heavy topspin groundstrokes and superb court coverage translated perfectly to the surface. Henin captured the championship four times in five years (2003, 2005–2007). She won all four finals and the entire 2006 and 2007 editions without dropping a set.

But Henin was no one-surface wonder. She had a sneaky fast first serve and textbook volleys that made her a threat at any tournament. Of her 43 career titles, 30 came away from clay. She was particularly good on hard courts, picking up a couple of U.S. Open titles (2003, 2007) and one Australian Open (2004). Even though a Wimbledon crown eluded her throughout her career, Henin still made two finals and three semifinals appearances in London. She also won the 2004 Olympic gold medal in Athens.

Playing a determined style, not to mention battling several injuries, took a toll on Henin. In 2008, ranked number one and just before heading to the French Open, where she was the three-time defending champ, Henin abruptly retired at just 25 years old. It turned out to be more of a long hiatus. She returned to competitive play in 2010 and won Women's Tennis Association (WTA) Comeback Player of the Year, but she sustained an elbow injury that proved too difficult to overcome. Henin retired for good after the 2011 Australian Open.

In addition to the seven Grand Slam singles titles, Henin won back-to-back season-ending tour championships (2006–2007), helped Belgium win its first Fed Cup (2001), spent 117 weeks at number one (ninth all-time), and finished as the top-ranked player in 2003, 2006, and 2007.

Martina Hingis

Pert, confident, and mischievous, the "Swiss Miss" burst on the tennis scene in 1995, turning conventional tennis wisdom right on its ear. At the time, few people thought that the game still had room for a lightweight counterpunching type of player. But for several years between the end of Steffi Graf's reign and the rise of the Williams sisters, Hingis's clever and cunning style ruled the women's game.

When Hingis turned pro at just 14 years old after a stellar junior career, she had a fully formed game that belied her age. Her strokes were all very solid, but it was her smarts and crafty shot selection — mixing up pace, spin, and location — that separated her from her competition. Where most players that young played checkers, Hingis played 3-D chess.

The beginning of Hingis's career was strewn with records and firsts. She won her first Grand Slam title in Australia in January 1997, becoming the youngest-ever Grand Slam event champion at 16 years, 3 months, and 26 days of age. She replaced Tracy Austin as the youngest player ever to hold the number-one ranking when she reached the top in late March 1997.

When Martina won at Wimbledon the same year, she became the youngest Open Era champion there, too. By adding the U.S. Open title to her collection as well, in 1997, Martina joined Steffi Graf and Monica Seles as the only teenagers in the Open Era to win three of the four Grand Slam titles in one year. She fell a single match short of the Calendar Grand Slam when she was upset in the finals of the French Open.

Hingis won two more Australian Open singles titles and two tour championships over the next few years and finished as year-end number one three times (1997, 1999, 2000). She held the number-one ranking for a total of 209 weeks, putting her fifth all-time. Her unique skill set also made her an instinctive and, arguably, even better doubles player. All told, Hingis won 13 doubles and seven mixed-doubles major titles. However, although she was remarkably steady in singles, her successes on the biggest stages were relatively brief. Hingis started 5-1 in her first six Grand Slam finals appearances, but finished 1-6 in her final seven.

In 2003, citing injuries and constant foot pain, Hingis retired at the age of 22. She mounted a successful comeback in 2006, winning two tournaments and finishing the season ranked number seven. However, in 2007, she tested positive for a banned substance and, facing a two-year ban from the sport, chose to retire again. In 2013, Hingis returned again, just on the doubles tour. In 2017, she won nine tournaments, including three majors (two doubles and one mixed doubles) and finished the year ranked number one in doubles at age 37. She retired for good at that season's WTA finals.

Billie Jean King

Pop star Elton John wrote a Top 40 hit about her entitled "Philadelphia Freedom." *Life* magazine (ask your parents) named her one of the 100 most important Americans of the 20th century. Billie Jean King's reputation as a professional player and her strength as a leader also earned her a place in tennis history.

Billie Jean King did more than any other person to establish an entire sport, women's professional tennis. She encouraged women players worldwide when she beat male player Bobby Riggs (a retired former number-one player in the 1940s) in 1973 in a televised "Battle of the Sexes" extravaganza that was watched by more people than any other tennis match in history. (Check out the 2017 movie *Battle of the Sexes*, starring Emma Stone and Steve Carell, to see the match dramatized on film.)

The daughter of a fireman, Billie Jean began her career during the amateur era. She was once kept from sitting in a group picture with other junior tennis players because she was wearing shorts instead of pants. That helped fuel her determination to see the old establishment swept from the game in favor of an open, pro game. (You can read more about how she helped bring about equality for women in the Open Era in Chapter 19.)

Billie Jean played a daring, athletic game. She served and volleyed and had a great appetite for playing close, pressure-packed matches. She had a love-hate relationship with Wimbledon because of her lifelong aversion to things that she perceived as elitist and conservative. But she also played her best there, winning more combined (singles, doubles, and mixed doubles) titles (20) than any other player.

Billie Jean amassed 39 combined singles and doubles Grand Slam titles. She was the fifth woman in tennis to win all four Grand Slam singles titles. She won 12 in all: 1 at the French Open, 1 at the Australian Open, 4 at the U.S. Open, and 6 at Wimbledon. She scored three Grand Slam triples, sweeping singles, doubles, and mixed doubles twice at Wimbledon and once at the U.S. Open. All told, Billie Jean won 71 singles titles as a pro and 37 as an amateur.

These days, BJK has made her peace with the establishment. The U.S. Tennis Association (USTA) even renamed its National Tennis Center in Queens, New York — home of the U.S. Open — in King's honor. The Fed Cup is now similarly called the Billie Jean King Cup (which you can read more about in Chapter 19). And wherever she goes, Billie Jean remains one of the sport's great ambassadors.

Martina Navratilova

Martina Navratilova's life story is almost as exciting and intriguing as her tennis record. She was born near Prague, in the nation formerly known as Czechoslovakia, and defected to the United States in cloak-and-dagger fashion in 1975. Early in her career, she was an underachiever and an overeater, but she went on to become a disciplined, fit competitor who put together some of the greatest winning streaks of all time.

Although she developed her game on slow red clay courts, Navratilova became the quintessential attacking player. The serve-and-volley style, with its emphasis on acrobatic shots and flashy volley winners, suited Martina's mercurial temperament. Although she was nicknamed "the Brat" early in her career (at one point she even wore a gold chain bearing the moniker), Navratilova matured superbly under the guidance of two successive coaches, Renée Richards and Mike Estep. Her work with these coaches enabled her to embark on what may be the greatest rivalry ever in pro sports, her battles with Chris Evert.

The two players were as different as night and day. Evert was an ice-cool, impeccably mannered baseliner. Navratilova was a temperamental, attacking player who freely vented her feelings. This odd couple became great friends — they even partnered up to win two Grand Slam doubles titles together — and battled each other for 16 years, with Navratilova coming out on top, 43-37, in their career rivalry.

Navratilova collected 59 combined major titles (18 singles, 31 doubles, 10 mixed doubles), the most in the Open Era. She holds the record for most tournaments won (167) and most matches won (1,442), and her 332 weeks at number one is second all-time to Steffi Graf. Navratilova's nine Wimbledon singles titles is the most ever.

In 1983, Navratilova won 16 of 17 tournaments and posted an 86-1 record. In 1984, she broke Evert's record of 55 straight wins with a whopping 74-match winning streak. After Helena Suková interrupted that streak, Navratilova took off on a 54-match tear. She also had a 58-match winning streak that was snapped early in 1987.

At 37, Martina made her 12th Wimbledon final in 1994. Later that year, she retired from full-time singles competition. In 2000, she returned to the tour, playing primarily doubles. However, in 2004, she received a wild card into Wimbledon and won her first match, making her, at 47 years old, the oldest player to win a singles match in the Open Era. She also collected three mixed-doubles majors, the last a month before her 50th birthday, making her the oldest Grand Slam champion ever.

Monica Seles

The only woman who ever won the French Open three times with her hair a different color on each occasion was Monica Seles. How's that for a record? I mention it to highlight (no pun intended) the sense of whimsy and style that Seles brought to tennis.

Seles was known for the high-pitched shriek ("Ahhh-heee!") with which she punctuated the awesome, accurate, two-handed groundstrokes with which she simply blew rivals off the court. She had a minimalist's game, showing that if you hit your groundstrokes savagely, close to the lines, you would win, period.

A left-handed Hungarian born in the former Yugoslavia, Seles became the youngest-ever champion at the French Open in 1990, when she was 16. For almost three years after that, she was unbeatable. Then, in April 1993, she was stabbed in the back during a tournament in Germany by an insane fan of Graf's. A full 28 months passed before Monica, suffering mostly from psychological wounds, returned to tennis.

Before she was stabbed, Seles won eight Grand Slam titles, three each in Paris and Melbourne and two in New York. No woman had ever accumulated Grand Slam titles at such a startling pace. She added another Australian title during her comeback in early 1996.

Unfortunately, Seles was never able to recapture her level from before her stabbing. What she could've accomplished had it not been for that attack is one of the great "what if" questions of the Open Era, because when she was at the height of her powers, Monica was the best in the game.

Serena Williams

As a fellow younger sibling to an all-time great player, I related to Serena Williams. However, where I couldn't match my brother John's Hall of Fame credentials, Serena blew right past her big sister Venus. Behind her massive strokes and incredible physicality, Serena captured the most Grand Slam singles titles (23) by any woman in the Open Era and spent 319 weeks ranked number one in the world.

At 18, Williams upended the natural order by winning the 1999 U.S. Open before her sister, Venus, won her first. She became the second Black woman to win a

Grand Slam after Althea Gibson. Serena then won the four Grand Slam tournaments from the 2002 French Open through the 2003 Australian Open — beating her sister in each final — to become the fifth woman to simultaneously hold all the majors. She duplicated the feat, dubbed the "Serena Slam," again over parts of 2014 and 2015.

At the height of her powers, Serena simply overwhelmed her competition with her serve, athleticism, and intensity. Her aura alone was often enough to win her matches. At one point, she held the number-one ranking for 186 consecutive weeks, tying Steffi Graf for the all-time record. Her last Grand Slam win, the 2017 Australian Open, was more than 17 years after her first — and, unbeknownst to anyone watching, she did it while pregnant.

Beyond the victories, Serena was a larger-than-life personality, a global icon known just by her first name. Growing up in Compton, California, she brought a toughness and swagger to the court that was unusual for the traditionally buttoned-up sport. She wore head-turning outfits and spoke her mind in press conferences. She would lose her temper if she felt wronged by a linesperson or umpire, sometimes drawing negative attention to herself and the match. It made Serena one of those polarizing players that, no matter how you felt about her, you still had to watch.

Serena retired after the 2022 U.S. Open. She finished with seven Australian and Wimbledon titles, six U.S. Opens, and three French Opens. She also won 14 Grand Slam doubles titles — all paired with Venus — 2 mixed-doubles majors, and four Olympic gold medals (one singles, three doubles).

Venus Williams

If the circumstances of Venus Williams's life weren't real, no one would believe her story. After watching the winner of a women's event receive a large paycheck on television, her father, Richard Williams, decided that he and his wife, Oracene, would have a daughter, Venus, and make her a tennis champion. To increase his odds — and potential earning power — they would double down on the bet and have another daughter, Serena. Richard had zero coaching experience, and the family lived in Compton, California, an area known for gang violence, not country clubs. Yet his vision and their dedication made it a reality.

Regardless of whether all the details are true, Black girls from impoverished inner cities don't often pick up tennis racquets, let alone become two of the all-time greats. But it was obvious when Venus turned pro in 1994 at just 14 years old that she was special. Her combination of size — she would eventually stand 6-foot-1 — and athleticism was unlike anything in the women's game. She covered the court like a gazelle and used long, windmill strokes to pummel the ball. Her first serve routinely reached more than 120 miles per hour, a huge asset in the women's game.

In 1997, in just her third Grand Slam tournament, Venus reached the U.S. Open finals. She broke through a few years later in 2000, winning both Wimbledon and the U.S. Open back-to-back. She repeated the double the following year before reaching number one in 2002, becoming the first Black woman to do so in the Open Era. Three more Wimbledon titles in the ensuing few years (2005, 2007, 2008) completed her Grand Slam singles haul. She also won 14 major doubles titles (all with Serena), two mixed-doubles Slams, and four Olympic gold medals (one singles, three doubles).

Venus spent a total of just 11 weeks ranked number one, and never won an Australian or French title. The biggest detriment to her success was probably her younger sister. Venus was a nine-time runner-up at slams; seven of those losses were to Serena.

However, Venus's impact on the women's game looms larger than mere titles. Her physical gifts and aggressive style raised the level of play to new heights. She was also instrumental in helping women achieve equal prize money at the slams. And she was a trailblazer and inspiration for a generation of young Black players to follow.

Chapter **25**

The Ten Greatest Matches of the Open Era

isting ten of my favorite matches of all time is like picking my favorite ten movies — there's just too much to choose from. So, I had to limit myself by only picking Open Era Grand Slam matches. Even further, I tried to choose matches that exemplified a classic rivalry or significant moment in the sport. Besides being some of my personal favorites, these matches all share a common trait: They're examples of tennis taken to the genius level. Don't just take my word for it — they're all available to stream on YouTube. Be warned: Watching these matches can become habit-forming.

Björn Borg Defeats John McEnroe, 1980 Wimbledon

John really lobbied hard for me to put his 1981 Wimbledon final in here instead, but that may have had something to do with the fact that he beat Björn Borg in that one.

What can I say? The 1980 Wimbledon final, which ended 1-6, 7-5, 6-3, 6-7 (16-18), 8-6, is one of the greatest tennis matches of the Open Era — perhaps any era — and the fourth-set tiebreaker was one of the most riveting, brilliant, extended moments in all of tennis history.

At the time, Björn was shooting for a historic fifth consecutive Wimbledon title, and John, just 21, had only one Grand Slam title to his name, the U.S. Open of 1979. John had Björn in his sights, and everybody — including Björn — sensed it.

Forgive me for dispensing with the preliminaries and cutting right to the chase, er, tiebreaker. Björn had the match on his racquet at 5-4 in the fourth set. He quickly went up 40-15 — that's double match point. But John battled back to break serve. At 6-6, they began a tiebreaker that lasted 22 minutes. Björn had another five match points in the 'breaker. John reached set point seven times, but each time Borg had an answer. Finally, Björn missed a drop volley that gave John the tiebreaker, 18-16.

As was his steely nature, Björn bounced back from losing the tiebreaker. He lost the first two points in the first game of the fifth set, but then he dug down into his incredible, competitive spirit. He held serve from then on and broke John in the 14th and final game of the match with three great shots — a down-the-line service return winner, a volley winner, and a backhand passing shot. The match lasted 3 hours and 53 minutes.

In a funny way, that match was a turning point in the careers of both men. John finally tagged Björn a few months later at the U.S. Open, winning his second Grand Slam title. Björn won just one Grand Slam title after, at Paris in 1981. After that, John stopped Björn's streak in the next Wimbledon final and beat Björn again at the U.S. Open. Björn walked away from tennis after that last loss, never to return despite two brief, aborted comeback attempts.

Martina Navratilova Defeats Chris Evert, 1984 U.S. Open

The women's 1984 U.S. Open final, which ended 4-6, 6-4, 6-4, was sandwiched between the two men's semifinals in the traditional "Super Saturday" format. Chris Evert and Martina Navratilova whiled away the time waiting to play by sharing bagels in the locker room while the first men's match was underway.

Their friendly pre-match behavior bespoke their great relationship. These two rivals had become best of friends, and even the high stakes in this match couldn't threaten that. Their career rivalry stood at 30 wins each before the final, and Navratilova was riding a 54-match winning streak, one shy of Evert's Open Era record. No big deal. Hey, Martina, pass the cream cheese and chives, please.

The match fit the classic mold of Evert–Navratilova clashes. When the two played, it was always a battle between Martina's firepower and volleys, and Chris's consistency and passing shots.

After the first set, it seemed that a combination of the mental pressure and Chris's relentless accuracy and pinpoint passing shots might carry the day. Everyone expected Martina to grow tentative and back off her attacking game to regroup. But Martina stuck to her guns; she continued to press the attack, conceding Chris her share of passing shots. The third set was tight, but Martina clung to a single service break and won the set.

The match was a courageous performance by Martina, and it marked the high point in her evolution from a mercurial but not entirely confident champion into a woman who could do whatever it took to fight her way into the record books.

Monica Seles Defeats Steffi Graf, 1992 French Open

Steffi Graf had a clear mission in the French Open final of 1992: Stop the juggernaut called Monica Seles. No longer an upstart, Seles had zoomed to the top of the game, winning the last four Grand Slam events she had entered. Because of an injury to Graf, and the luck of the draw, the two women had not met in over a year, despite their flourishing careers. All of Paris, not to mention tennis fans worldwide, was fired up about the meeting. No one walked away disappointed by the level of play in the match, which ended, 6-2, 3-6, 10-8.

The matchup between Seles and Graf was an intriguing, subtle one. Manic Monica pounded the ball hard with her groundstrokes, but Fraulein Forehand had the speed to run down even the hardest of shots on the slow red clay of the French Open.

That was how the match played out, with Steffi using her speed to stay in and win her share of points. In the third set, with Steffi already down a break at 3-5, Monica reached match point four times.

Steffi erased them all with courageous, bold shots. After holding serve, Steffi broke Monica's serve when Monica committed four unforced errors in a row. It looked like the match was there for Steffi's taking.

But Monica roared back. She held her ground and caught her second, or third, or fifth, wind. Serving in the 18th game, Graf saved another match point. But she eventually netted a forehand to give Monica her sixth Grand Slam title — and the keys to the kingdom Steffi once ruled.

Although Graf got her revenge against Seles in the Wimbledon final a month later, Seles was the dominant force in the game until she was stabbed in April 1993 by a deranged fan of Graf's.

Pete Sampras Defeats Andre Agassi, 2001 U.S. Open

Pete Sampras and Andre Agassi had met twice before at the U.S. Open; both were finals (1990 and 1995) and both were straight-set victories by Sampras. However, Agassi came into this U.S. Open quarterfinal enjoying a four-match win streak over Sampras, not to mention better recent form. Their seeds bore that out: Agassi was number two; Sampras number ten.

From the first ball, the contrasting styles of the familiar foes were apparent. Sampras used his massive serve to set up his smothering net game, and Agassi fended him off with blistering returns and pinpoint passing shots. Nothing separated them as Agassi survived three set points to take the first set in a tiebreaker. Sampras returned the favor by winning the following two sets, both in tiebreakers.

The match was a true tug-of-war, with neither player relinquishing an inch of rope. Over 24 service games apiece, there was not a single break of serve. Anytime Agassi had the slightest of openings, Sampras had the answer, most often thanks to his fantastic serve. He finished the match with 26 aces and seemingly as many unreturned serves.

The match started on a Wednesday night and finished early Thursday morning. The Arthur Ashe Stadium crowd ate it up, giving the players a boisterous, standing ovation before the start of the fourth-set tiebreaker. In the end, Sampras played the big points better, and closed it out 6-7(7), 7-6 (2), 7-6 (2), 7-6 (5). The only disappointment: The match lacked a fifth set, which would've made a fitting final.

Serena Williams Defeats Venus Williams, 2003 Australian Open

Playing against your sibling isn't easy. Believe me, I know from experience. But only two sisters in the Open Era know what it's like to do it in the pressure cooker of a Grand Slam final. Serena and Venus Williams squared off 31 times in their careers, 10 of the matches in major finals. Their play often didn't measure up to their abilities or the occasion, yet the significance of the match was always undeniable.

The 2003 Australian Open finals was such an encounter. It marked the fourth consecutive Grand Slam in which they had faced each other in the final, the first players ever — male or female — to do so. Serena won the first three, and Venus took the court in Melbourne determined to stop the trend.

In the first set, the two showed off their superb power and athleticism, engaging in several fierce baseline exchanges. Venus proved a bit steadier and earned a late service break to serve for the set at 5-4. But she couldn't close it out, and Serena managed to steal the set in a tiebreaker.

Venus was undeterred in the second set. The crowd got behind her, pulling for the underdog and hoping for a third set. The sixth game with Serena serving at 2-3 proved to be the tipping point for Venus. She needed four break points, but she secured the break and served out the set 6-3.

Serena jumped out in front in the third set with an early break, but showing her championship mettle, Venus stormed back to level the set. The two hit numerous hard and penetrating shots that would've been winners against just about any other opponent, only to see the ball returned time after time until one committed an error. The tension kept building, and you could see it on the players. Serving at 4-5, Venus lost the rhythm on her first serve, and her second serve — a weakness in her game — buckled under the increasing strain. She hit a few floaters that Serena punished, and she tossed in a double fault that helped put Serena in the winner's circle.

Rafael Nadal Defeats Roger Federer, 2008 Wimbledon

Is this the greatest match ever played? Many people think so. I'd certainly put it at the pinnacle of this seminal 40-match rivalry. A seesaw battle filled with glorious shot-making and perseverance between two all-time greats at the height of their powers.

The stakes of the match couldn't have been higher. For the third consecutive year, Roger Federer faced Rafael Nadal in the Wimbledon final after losing to Nadal a few months earlier in the French Open final. Federer had won the previous two, with Nadal inching closer each time. If Rafa, the "King of Clay," could finally unseat the five-time defending champ on his best surface, he would assert himself as the top player in the world.

When the points started, the players did what they do best. Rafa prowled the baseline, directing his heavy lefty forehand into Roger's one-handed backhand until it cracked or drew a short ball he could bludgeon. Federer used his serve, forehand, and creativity to open up the court and attack Nadal. Both players took turns making incredible gets and circus shots.

For the first half of the match, Nadal's execution was superior. He won the first set 6-4, and repeated that scoreline in the second set, coming back from a 1-4 deficit. And when Federer served at 3-3, 0-40 in the third set, it looked for all the world that it would be the Spaniard's day. But Federer dug himself out of that hole and, with the score 5-4 in his favor, had to wait out an 80-minute relay before winning the set, 7-6 (5) in a tiebreaker.

The fourth set saw no breaks of serve, setting up a dramatic tiebreaker for the ages. The momentum swung back and forth: Federer saved a championship point with a service winner, Nadal set up another with a remarkable forehand passing shot up the line, and then Federer returned the favor with a miraculous backhand pass to keep the match alive. Two points later, the Swiss had the breaker 10-8, and forced a fifth set.

Even after squandering a two-set lead, and two championship points, Nadal remained steadfast. At 2-2 in the final set, there was another 30-minute rain delay. With darkness approaching, some people thought the match may have to be completed the next day. At 7-7, Nadal finally broke Federer's serve. Just past 9 p.m., after a finals record 4 hours and 48 minutes of match play, Nadal won the set 9-7 on his fourth match point to capture his first Wimbledon title. Two months later, after spending a record 160 consecutive weeks at number two, Nadal overtook Federer at the top of the rankings.

John Isner Defeats Nicolas Mahut, 2010 Wimbledon

70-68. A score that would be fitting for a college basketball game was the astounding fifth set of this Wimbledon first-round match. Not an all-timer in terms of quality, John Isner and Nicolas Mahut's Groundhog Day match made history for its sheer spectacle and the doggedness of its combatants.

Played on side-court 18, the match started as a ho-hum encounter between the 23rd seed (Isner) and a qualifier (Mahut). Both players possessed big serves and a preference for quick points. The players split the first two sets, each with a single break of serve. Then they split the next two sets, both in tiebreakers. After the fourth set, the match was suspended due to darkness with the score leveled at two sets apiece.

That's when things went bonkers. At that time, Wimbledon had no tiebreaker in the fifth set. Players had to keep playing until one player secured a two-game lead. There had been numerous extended fifth sets in the past, but what was about to happen was inconceivable.

Resuming the match the following day, Isner and Mahut traded service holds until sunset. Most were of the routine variety, creating long periods of play with limited drama. As the game count kept creeping higher, the fascination with the match swelled. People just couldn't comprehend the scoreline or the players' resolve. They even outlasted the scoreboard, which was programmed to stop at 47-47. Nothing was settled by 59-59, and play was suspended a second day due to darkness.

Day 3 started out with much of the same. The servers had their way until Isner got a chance at a break and match point with Mahut serving at 68-69. The big American threaded a backhand passing shot down the line to win the match and then collapsed to the court. The match needed 183 games and took 11 hours and 5 minutes stretched over three days. The fifth set alone lasted 8 hours and 11 minutes, longer than any previous match. The players combined for 215 aces (Isner 112, Mahut 103). Having little fight left, Isner lost his second-round match in straight sets.

Novak Djokovic Defeats Rafael Nadal, 2012 Australian Open

These two titans of the game locked horns with each other 60 times over their careers, a men's Open Era record. Nine of those matches occurred in major finals, and none was closer or more hard-fought than this barn burner Down Under.

Nadal took a tense opening set 7-5, only to see his lead erased as Djokovic won the second set 6-4. Both players were supreme movers with rock-solid groundstrokes, making for lengthy, grueling baseline exchanges and deuce-filled games that tested their psyches and lungs. That pattern continued as Djokovic won the third set 6-2.

Things tightened up again in the fourth set. After a brief rain delay — and subsequent roof closure — with the score at 4-4, it would take a tiebreaker to settle it. When Djokovic took a 5-3 lead, it appeared he'd soon be lifting the champion's trophy. Hower, Nadal, always the fighter, willed his way to four straight points and the set, dropping to his knees in celebration.

With momentum on his side, Nadal jumped out to 4-2 in the fifth set. Serving at 30-15, Nadal had an easy backhand passing shot into a wide-open court that he steered wide. That costly miss kept Djokovic in it; he broke back and evened the score. The drama continued with numerous gut-busting points. When the final ball was struck, it was Djokovic ahead on the scoreboard, 7-5.

With a match time of 5 hours and 53 minutes, it's the longest in Grand Slam finals history. Both players were so weary, they needed chairs to make it through the trophy presentation. It's an indelible image from an epic battle.

Novak Djokovic Defeats Roger Federer, 2019 Wimbledon

No one should pity Roger Federer. He has a beautiful family, tons of money, and legions of adoring fans. His career was filled with the highest accomplishments and unforgettable moments. But the guy did suffer some of the toughest defeats in history. And the cause of many of these heartbreakers was Novak Djokovic.

When the two rivals took Centre Court, it marked the third time they would contest a Wimbledon final, the previous two going Djokovic's way. With Federer at 37, there was a sense this could be his last shot at a major, and it did turn out to be his last slam final.

The first set was controlled by the servers and had to be settled in a tiebreaker. Federer pushed the action and went up 5-3. But four straight errors allowed Djokovic to win the set 7-6 (5).

Federer took advantage of a Djokovic lapse in concentration to rush out to a 4-0 lead in the second set. Federer closed it out 6-1 and carried over his fine form to the third set. Djokovic, one of the game's great returners, struggled mightily all day to do anything on the Federer serve. But he managed to protect his own serve — fighting off a set point along the way — to force another tiebreaker.

In vintage Djokovic fashion, he buckled down and waited for Federer to make mistakes as he did in the first-set tiebreaker. Once again, the Swiss obliged, and Djokovic took the breaker 7-4. Without ever earning a break point, he was still somehow leading two sets to one.

It was then Federer's turn in this back-and-forth battle. He upped his aggression even further, moving forward on the grass court whenever possible to make use of his superb net play. Leaning on his tremendous serving — he finished with 25 aces — Federer won the fourth set 6-4, leveling the match at two sets apiece.

The fifth set would be unlike any in finals history. That year Wimbledon had instituted a rule change to its deciding set format: Instead of playing the set out until one player had a two-game lead, a tiebreaker would be played if the score reached 12-12. The two players exchanged breaks early on in the set, and then traded games until Federer broke Djokovic to go up 8-7 and serve for the match. Two aces by Federer set up two championship points. Djokovic erased both, the second with a clutch crosscourt forehand passing shot. A couple of points later, the score was tied at 8-8.

After missing such a glorious opportunity, Federer did well to remained focused and push on. The players held serve until the score hit 12-12. It would be the first tiebreak finish at Wimbledon, and it would play out like the earlier two in the match. After 4 hours and 57 minutes, the longest final in the tournament's history, Djokovic prevailed 13-12 (3).

"I will try to forget," said Federer after the match. "I had my chances, so did he. We played some great tennis."

Carlos Alcaraz Defeats Novak Djokovic, 2023 Wimbledon

I know what you're thinking: Not another Novak Djokovic match. Hey, the guy has played some jaw-dropping matches. Plus, this gives me the chance to tell you about Carlos Alcaraz, one of the most exciting current players (as I write this) and one of the most talented I've ever seen.

Entering this Wimbledon final, Alcaraz, 20, had one major title to his credit (the 2022 U.S. Open), to Djokovic's 23 Grand Slams, including seven Wimbledon titles. Even though the Spaniard was the top seed, given the disparity in experience, the Serb was the betting favorite.

The first set — a 6-1 rout to Djokovic — didn't diminish that sentiment. But Alcaraz rose to the occasion in the second set, as did the level of play; at times, the brilliant shot-making and athletic court coverage looked out of a video game. It came down to a tiebreaker that Alcaraz eked out, 8-6, saving a set point to even the match.

Alcaraz used that momentum to win a commanding 6-1 third set. Carlitos is a grinning assassin — brave and creative with a rare combination of explosive power, jackrabbit speed, and feathery touch. But in this set, he demonstrated his determination, highlighted by winning a marathon 32-point, 27-minute fifth game.

To the surprise of no one, Djokovic regrouped. He took a bathroom break after the third set and, resilient as always, took advantage of some careless Alcaraz errors to win the set, 6-3, and force a fifth set.

It appeared that Djokovic, one of the game's great closers, had the youngster right where he wanted him. But Alcaraz, seemingly unfazed by the pressure, kept his wits in the crucial moments and seized the day. With Djokovic serving at 1-1, 30-40, Alcaraz played sensational defense to stay in the point before breaking Djokovic's serve with a bullet backhand passing shot down the line. Djokovic splintered his racquet against the net post in disgust. Alcaraz would continue to hold his nerve and his serve — and eventually his first Wimbledon trophy — winning the final set 6-4. The 4 hour, 47 minute match time made it the third-longest final in tournament history.

Index

About the Authors

Patrick McEnroe: Patrick enjoyed a very successful junior career before going on to play at Stanford University where he graduated in 1988 after earning All-American honors for four years and leading his team to two NCAA Championships. He turned professional later in 1988 and played on the ATP Tour until retiring in 1998. He reached a career-high number 28 (1995) in singles, won one ATP Tour singles title (Sydney 1995), and reached one Grand Slam semifinal (Australian Open 1991) and quarterfinal (U.S. Open 1995). In addition to his singles accomplishments, Patrick won 16 ATP Tour doubles titles, including two with his brother, John McEnroe. Patrick won the 1989 French Open doubles and 1989 year-ending ATP Tour Masters doubles titles, both with his Stanford teammate Jim Grabb. Patrick was an Australian Open doubles finalist with David Wheaton in 1991. He achieved a career-high ATP Tour doubles ranking of number 3 in the world in 1993. Patrick also had a strong relationship with U.S. Davis Cup, first playing on teams in 1993, 1994, and 1996, and then serving as team captain from 2000 to 2010. He was captain for the 2007 Cup-winning team, and he is still the longest-serving captain in team history. He also served as the general manager of the U.S. Tennis Association's player development program from 2008 to 2014. Since 1995, Patrick has enjoyed a successful broadcasting career. He is currently a tennis commentator for ESPN and performed the same role at CBS from 1996 to 2008. When he is away from the broadcast booth, he serves as president of the International Tennis Hall of Fame and is executive director of the John McEnroe Tennis Academy and its five New York–area locations. Patrick lives in Bronxville, New York, with his wife and three daughters.

Jon Levey: Jon has been working in tennis media since 2000. In various roles at *Tennis* magazine and Tennis.com, he has covered every facet of the game, from the pro tours to the recreational level. He has coauthored two other books: *Championship Tennis* (Human Kinetics) and *The 3D Body Revolution* (Harmony Books). A lifelong player, he continues to compete regularly, still trying to iron out his backhand. Jon lives in Pound Ridge, New York, with his wife and two daughters.

Dedication

To all you tennis players out in continuous search for that perfect stroke, we are in this together. Thank you for your passion for this greatest of games!

—Patrick McEnroe

To all the hackers and hopefuls addicted to hitting a fuzzy yellow ball over a 3-foot-high net. Tennis is life.

—Jon Levey

Authors' Acknowledgments

Patrick McEnroe: As someone smarter than me once said: The more things change, the more they stay the same. I wrote the first edition of *Tennis For Dummies* more than 25 years ago. When I look back over that book, I see that so much of the core of this great game really has remained true. However, a lot has changed in the world of tennis. A few new rules, tweaks to technique, better equipment, and a bunch of new stars who took the pro game to a whole new level. This was the impetus for creating a new edition.

In putting this book together, Jon Levey, my coauthor this time around, has been an absolute joy to work with, never getting too stressed about us missing a deadline . . . or two. And thanks to everyone at Wiley for their patience and skill in shepherding this book to completion.

As I get closer to my 60th birthday, I still love this game and am incredibly appreciative of all that it has given me both personally and professionally. There are too many specific individuals to thank, but to all my tennis lifers — through broadcasting, Davis Cup, USTA, and my own family — your enduring support means the world to me. My parents moved on a number of years ago to that great tennis court up high, and hopefully they're still watching those yellow balls from up above. It has been awesome to work with both of my older brothers, Mark and John, at our tennis academy in NYC these past years, and of course, with John in the broadcast booth at ESPN.

Biggest thanks and appreciation to my incredible wife, Melissa, and our three daughters for always putting up with me — and tennis, because they go hand and hand. As Melissa says: Our family calendar still revolves somewhat on the tennis tour. I love you ladies.

Lastly, always remember one thing: Tennis really does rule.

Jon Levey: Thanks to Patrick for letting me be his doubles partner in this project. It had been a long time since our first instruction article together, and it was a pleasure getting to work with you again. Hopefully, one day we can take it from the book to the courts.

Thanks to Jennifer Yee, Elizabeth Kuball, and everyone at Wiley; Jennifer has the patience of a saint and could not have been more supportive. Thanks to Peter Bodo, my old friend and *Tennis* magazine colleague, for laying such a solid foundation in the first edition of this book; thanks for all the advice and encouragement. Thanks to Joel Drucker for recommending me for this assignment; the check-ins and chats were most appreciated. Thanks to Mark Kovacs for coming aboard as technical editor and lending his expert eye. Thanks to all the great coaches and players I've collaborated with and learned from over the years; I hope some of that wisdom found its way into this book.

And finally, Allison, Mia, and Charlotte, thanks for putting up with all the racquets and the constant tennis soundtrack. You ladies make the game of life worth playing. I forgive you for picking swimming.

Publisher's Acknowledgments

Managing Editor: Ajith Kumar

Acquisitions Editor: Jennifer Yee

Editor: Elizabeth Kuball

Technical Editor: Mark Kovacs, PhD, FACSM, CSCS, CTPS, MTPS

Production Editor: Tamilmani Varadharaj

Cover Image: © DDurrich/Getty Images

Special Help: Carmen Krikorian, Kristie Pyles

PERSONAL ENRICHMENT

9781119187790
USA $26.00
CAN $31.99
UK £19.99

9781119179030
USA $21.99
CAN $25.99
UK £16.99

9781119293354
USA $24.99
CAN $29.99
UK £17.99

9781119293347
USA $22.99
CAN $27.99
UK £16.99

9781119310068
USA $22.99
CAN $27.99
UK £16.99

9781119235606
USA $24.99
CAN $29.99
UK £17.99

9781119251163
USA $24.99
CAN $29.99
UK £17.99

9781119235491
USA $26.99
CAN $31.99
UK £19.99

9781119279952
USA $24.99
CAN $29.99
UK £17.99

9781119283133
USA $24.99
CAN $29.99
UK £17.99

9781119287117
USA $24.99
CAN $29.99
UK £16.99

9781119130246
USA $22.99
CAN $27.99
UK £16.99

PROFESSIONAL DEVELOPMENT

9781119311041
USA $24.99
CAN $29.99
UK £17.99

9781119255796
USA $39.99
CAN $47.99
UK £27.99

9781119293439
USA $26.99
CAN $31.99
UK £19.99

9781119281467
USA $26.99
CAN $31.99
UK £19.99

9781119280651
USA $29.99
CAN $35.99
UK £21.99

9781119251132
USA $24.99
CAN $29.99
UK £17.99

9781119310563
USA $34.00
CAN $41.99
UK £24.99

9781119181705
USA $29.99
CAN $35.99
UK £21.99

9781119263593
USA $26.99
CAN $31.99
UK £19.99

9781119257769
USA $29.99
CAN $35.99
UK £21.99

9781119293477
USA $26.99
CAN $31.99
UK £19.99

9781119265313
USA $24.99
CAN $29.99
UK £17.99

9781119239314
USA $29.99
CAN $35.99
UK £21.99

9781119293323
USA $29.99
CAN $35.99
UK £21.99

dummies.com

dummies
A Wiley Brand